Blood
On Black

The Case Against
the West Memphis 3 Killers,
Volume I

By Gary Meece

Gary Meece

Copyright © 2017 Gary Meece
All rights reserved.

ISBN: 10: 0692802843
ISBN-13: 978-0692802847

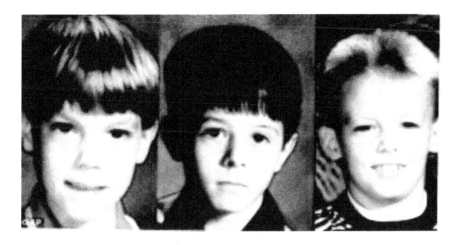

For Christopher, Michael, Stevie

and those who honor their memory

Gary Meece

BLOOD ON BLACK

TABLE OF CONTENTS

"I know I'm going to influence the world. People will remember me."

87

"I'll get you, I'm gonna kill you. You're gonna die."

99

"When I do get angry it is usually not a pretty site."

114

"I'm going to kill you, I'm going to rip your eyes out"

133

"Jessie took a knife out of his pocket and put a knife to my throat"

140

"He stated that the boys probably died of mutilation, some guy had cut the bodies up, heard that they were in the water, they may have drowned."

145

"We never walked on the service road. Ever."

"We've been wanting to get a bum from underneath one of the overpasses and torture them."

"We hurt a couple of boys, that Jason and Damien killed."

"Damien stated … that he killed the boys"

"He said, I was there when the three little kids got killed. ... That's what he told me."

"Stated he was a white witch who worshipped the devil"

Gary Meece

"For the highest spiritual working one must accordingly choose that victim which contains the greatest and purest force. A male child of perfect innocence and high intelligence is the most satisfactory and suitable victim."
— Aleister Crowley

PREFACE

They did it.

The West Memphis 3 are guilty. They are guilty not just because they were convicted, though they were convicted. They are guilty not just because they pleaded guilty, though they did plead guilty. They are guilty despite what the documentaries, books, television shows, newspaper and magazine stories have said over and over again.

Guilty beyond a reasonable doubt.

Damien Wayne "Icky" Echols aka Michael Wayne Hutchison, Charles Jason Baldwin and Jessie Lloyd Misskelley Jr. killed three 8-year-olds, Christopher Mark Byers, James Michael Moore and Steve Edward Branch, on May 5, 1993, in a wooded area in West Memphis, Ark.

The murders were thrill kills, according to Echols himself. But they were much more than that. Police were struck by the ritualistic aspects. Local dabblers in the occult immediately came under suspicion.

Under questioning, Echols, already acknowledged as a witch, flaunted his knowledge of the occult, his theories of how the killings could have "magickal" implications and his insights into how the killer would think and feel. He demonstrated special knowledge about the case beyond the little publicly known. He gave out signals that he was a prime suspect; a series of witnesses further implicated him.

A confession broke open the case.

The widely accepted WM3 storyline is that inept police and prosecutors, with a howling mob of religious fanatics to placate, somewhat arbitrarily picked out three innocent boys to blame for horrific murders because Damien and his best pal Jason wore black T-shirts, listened to heavy metal music and had funny haircuts and because the third boy, Little Jessie, was practically retarded and thus easily manipulated.

Almost every element in the standard storyline is a myth with little relation to reality.

Take the longhaired teens in black T-shirt myth, for instance. Longhaired teens had been wearing rock concert T-shirts in Crittenden County for several decades at the time of the arrests.

If rock and roll wasn't exactly born in West Memphis, the music arguably was conceived there at KWEM, which from 1947 to 1955 featured such blues artists as B.B. King, Howlin' Wolf, Ike Turner, Junior

Parker, Sonny Boy Williamson, James Cotton, Elmore James and Arthur "Big Boy" Crudup as well as live performances from Elvis Presley and Johnny Cash.

Pitchfork-wielding fundamentalists did not burn down the studio playing "the devil's music" in 1953. By 1993, rock music and a certain rebellious spirit had become endemic to the rough-edged little town across the river from Memphis, Tenn. The locals dug the beat.

The weirdness that drew the attention of authorities in 1993 stemmed from bad choices made by the suspects rather than clothing, haircuts or staying up late rocking out to Megadeth.

The West Memphis police, so often excoriated for misjudgments, missteps or worse, did their duty in a diligent if imperfect manner. The investigation, despite mistakes and oversights common to complex criminal investigations, was professional and painstaking. Detectives took many statements, followed all sorts of strange and unpromising leads and administered the polygraph dozens of times.

Other than a confession, most of the evidence was circumstantial.

Murderers have been convicted on less. Prosecutors and investigators, for example, were often hard-pressed to come up with more than highly circumstantial evidence in most of the 30 or so murders credited to Ted Bundy; despite multiple attackers bloodying up two homes while killing seven people in the Tate/LaBianca murders, police in Los Angeles, with vastly greater resources than West Memphis, were unable to come up with viable clues or significant suspects until long weeks later, while missing potential breaks in the case — Charles Manson's connections to the Tate murders were far more tenuous than Damien Echols' role in the killing of Michael, Stevie and Chris.

All three of the teens from the trailer parks were convicted. The convictions held up on appeal. The persistent claim that police, prosecutors, the juries and the judge were all ignorant, incompetent, and even corrupt says more about the lack of character of their critics than the good folks of Arkansas.

Eventually, thanks to Hollywood celebrities and misleading documentaries that left out crucial evidence, the killers who became the West Memphis 3 walked free.

No exonerating evidence, despite many years of investigation and a defense fund in the millions of dollars, has been produced. None of the three has offered a credible alibi.

Most "supporters" —- as proponents for the alleged innocence of the West Memphis 3 are styled — remain ignorant of the facts. The mainstream media, not just various authors and filmmakers with their own agendas but most of the true crime and interview television shows as well as magazines and newspapers, have bought into the premise that "those boys were innocent."

Some news accounts have even referred to the West Memphis 3 as "exonerated," despite their convictions and guilty pleas.

Even well-meaning, more responsible journalists can get the facts right and still be so very wrong. Often overworked and under constant deadlines, the average reporter tends to opt for the easy narrative, one that won't raise a red flag with editors or readers. Consider, for instance, the familiar narrative of the three boys: The oft-told story of the three victims as best friends, all members of the same Cub Scout pack, was the narrative served up largely by the perspective of one voluble parent, Mark Byers; the truth was that Chris Byers wasn't a member of that Cub Scout pack, and Michael and Chris weren't best friends. But, as a journalist in "The Man Who Shot Liberty Valance" sagely observed: "When the legend becomes fact, print the legend."

Other journalists have their own agendas, often tied into a commitment to "social justice" and its manifestations of anti-police bias, anti-religion prejudice and anti-Southerner bigotry. Progressive crusading goes far to explain the more egregious misrepresentations of the West Memphis case in movies, true-crime TV series or books that gloss over or ignore much of the evidence. Such attitudes are not confined to this case — witness such put-up jobs as the 2015 Netflix series "Making a Murderer," which disregarded key evidence and common sense in a style reminiscent of the "Paradise Lost" movies.

By putting the focus on mullet-headed rednecks, drawling overweight cops and righteously angry Christians, the media have been able to play upon the most egregious stereotypes of Southern whites, while positioning a murdering sociopath as a hip kid who was just too damn cool for the uptight hometown idiots. The West Memphis 3 myth was made to order for the familiar narrative of the perceptive young outsider that every hipster and modern-day aspiring artist imagines himself to have been. Among the sensitive souls who found a doppelgänger of their teenage selves in Echols were those on the list of professional outsiders — celebrities such as Johnny Depp and Henry Rollins.

Some of the critical commentary, particularly from the secular progressive wing of the "supporter" network, has expressed amazement that witchcraft, black magic and blood sacrifices would play any sort of role in a case of modern justice.

Many Americans believe in the reality and power of demons. Various polls have found that well upward of half of all Americans believe in angels, demons, the influence of spirits, the Devil and miracles.

Echols believed not only in demons but in the spiritual efficacy of blood sacrifice.

Tied into the idea of the blood sacrifice were elements of "sex magick." In Aleister Crowley's "magickal" system, which Echols claims to have embraced in his preteen years, orgasm and ecstasy are equated with death and sacrifice and the sexual fluids are often represented as blood or water. Crowley devoted a whole chapter of "Magick in Theory and Practice" to the "Bloody Sacrifice"; while Echols claimed not have read Crowley at the time of the murders, he also claimed a deep knowledge of the black arts.

Echols described the invocation of spirits in his own writings; back in 1993 and 1994, he felt he was in transition to a state of being a god, something other than human; he believed that drinking blood invested him with spiritual energy. Those were the deepest beliefs of a young witch, not imaginings of investigators and prosecutors.

The 1994 trials in Arkansas were like those in Salem three hundred years ago in that they all were courtroom proceedings and that witchcraft figured into the cases. That's about the extent of an apt comparison.

The "why" of the crime seemed incomprehensible because the horror of the act and the sick motivations driving the killers were so foreign to the healthy mind. To the sick mind, the slaughter made perfect sense. As Echols told police, it made the killer "happy."

Echols and his "blood brother" Jason had formed a pathological dyad, cultivating elaborate violent fantasies.

Via the ritual torture, killing and eating of dogs, cats and other animals, they educated themselves in the curriculum of occult murder.

The lurking allure of a "thrill kill" finally became irresistible when the killing time coincided with sunset, the rise of a full moon and the pagan holiday of Beltane.

In some respects they actually got away with the crime. Echols has profited nicely from the murders. Many books have been written about the case; there are still at least two stories largely untold worthy of a book treatment — one, how the victims' families were devastated first by the loss of the boys and then by a series of betrayals and accusations that still dog them over 20 years later, and two, how a network fueled by the news media, Hollywood, musicians, occultists and gullible HBO subscribers delivered upward of $10 million to WM3 advocates and how that money was spent.

This is not a book for fans of lurid fiction. Stevie Branch, Michael Moore, Christopher Byers and their families, friends and other mourners are owed an honest accounting, whether in horrific fact or drawn-out detail. Baldwin and Echols have been given an opportunity to respond to questions regarding the case but gave no comment, blocking contact via social media. Contact with the reclusive Jessie Misskelley was blocked. Questions posed via social media to Matt Baldwin, Stacy Sanders-Specht, Pamela Metcalf (Pam Echols/Hutchison), Angela Gail Grinnell, Constance Echols Mount (Michelle Echols), Garrett Schwarting, Kenneth "Lilbit" Watkins, Stephanie Dollar, Holly George Thorpe, Jennifer Bearden and John E. Douglas were not answered. The former Deanna Holcomb, who still lives in Arkansas under another name, gave no answer to a Facebook query on an account that otherwise appears active. Heather Dawn (Cliett) Hollis threatened legal action to prevent her name from being used and otherwise refused to explain the many discrepancies in her stories. Domini Ferris (Domini Teer) graciously and freely gave a phone interview. Susie Brewer responded with a forthright, honest update on her troubled relationship with Misskelley.

Much of the following was drawn from the official record in the words of actual witnesses, friends and neighbors of the killers and their victims.

Some misspellings, etc., in the transcripts have been corrected to facilitate comprehension; obvious transcription errors or lack of punctuation have been addressed, if not completely resolved. Excerpts from transcripts have been minimally edited for readability, sense and flow of narrative. Some information has been repeated to set forth as complete a record as feasible. Quotes represent evidence as recorded, as well as common usage in the Arkansas Delta.

At times, the investigation stepped into pathological quicksand, with seemingly no bottom to the sickness. As Deputy Prosecuting Attorney John Fogleman told the court: "… We ran across some very strange people, I mean very strange people. …"

This is not a tidy, by-the-numbers narrative typical of the true-crime genre.

Fogleman also once said that it would take a book of 1,000 pages to tell the story of the case. Would even that be enough? These two volumes by no means exhaust the topic. If the case was not so controversial, the story could be told in a standard true-crime format of some 300 pages or so. That would have been easier to write -- would have been a nice, quick read --- but would have left room for "supporters" of the West Memphis 3 to exploit every omission.

The field of investigation was full of unreliable narrators, with alternately fascinating and frustrating variations, changes and outright contradictions in stories, with plenty of dead end questions and unsolved puzzles.

Despite the detours, the trails of evidence inexorably lead time and again back to the guilt of the West Memphis 3 killers.

"I THOUGHT WE WERE SORT OF FRIENDS"

Damien Echols and Jason Baldwin were best friends, blood brothers, two boys from the trailer parks who had formed an inseparable bond.

In May of 1993, Echols was a high school dropout who received Social Security Disability checks due to various mental illnesses. He stayed some of the time at his parents' home at Broadway Trailer Park in West Memphis and some of the time at his 16-year-old pregnant girlfriend's home in Lakeshore Estates, a trailer park between West Memphis and Marion, Ark. Jason's trailer was just down the street from where Domini Teer and her mother lived.

Echols' parents had recently remarried after years of separation. His mother, who had lifelong troubles with mental illness, had divorced his stepfather the previous year over allegations of sexual abuse of Echols' younger sister, Michelle.

The sprawling, trash-strewn trailer parks were near where Interstate 55 came from the north to join east-west Interstate 40 for a brief stretch through West Memphis. While Baldwin, a skinny 16-year-old, lived in Lakeshore and attended Marion High School, much of his social life revolved around the video galleries, bowling alley and skating rink across the interstate in West Memphis.

Baldwin lived with two younger brothers and a mentally ill mother who had recently separated from his habitually drunken stepfather. His mother's new boyfriend, a chronic felon, had moved in a few weeks ago.

Echols told officers handling a juvenile offense in May 1992 that he and Baldwin were heavily involved in "gray magic."

One of their mutual friends, Jessie Misskelley Jr., 17, a school dropout and another trailer park teenager, was regarded as a bully and a troublemaker. Misskelley had been in repeated trouble for attacking younger children. He eventually would admit that he had been involved in satanic rituals with Echols and Baldwin.

One of the WM3 myths is that Misskelley was a distant acquaintance of the other two. Misskelley and Baldwin had been off and on as close friends for years, and Misskelley and Echols often spent time together. In a letter to girlfriend Heather Cliett written from the detention center, Baldwin, showing a sense of betrayal, wrote: "What gets me is why Jessie would make up such a lie as that, because I thought we were sort of friends except for the night at the skating rink when he tried to steal my necklace, and that made me pretty mad, but not as mad as all of this is making me."

Mara Leveritt's book "Dark Spell: Surviving the Sentence" tells of Baldwin's first encounter with

Misskelley on his first day in sixth grade at Marion Elementary School.

According to the book, Misskelley attacked Baldwin without provocation during recess, "hollering like he meant to kill him."

In eighth and ninth grades, the two boys lived on the same street in Lakeshore. They "got to be pretty good friends."

Around that time, Echols' grandmother moved to Lakeshore and Echols began hanging out, mowing lawns and using the money to fund his interest in skateboards.

In "Life After Death," Echols described first noticing Baldwin, "a skinny kid with a black eye and a long, blond mullet." Echols was struck by the number of music cassettes Baldwin carried in his backpack — "Metallica, Anthrax, Iron Maiden, Slayer, and every other hair band a young hoodlum could desire."

After his Nanny suffered her second heart attack and had her leg amputated, the Echols family moved to Lakeshore.

In "Life After Death," Echols described Lakeshore as full of "run-down and beat-up" mobile homes, filled with jobless drunks and addicts who earned their money through petty crime or scrounging up recyclables.

Echols more recently imagined that the dilapidated trailers somehow have improved with age along with the neighborhood: "I suppose it would now be considered lower middle class." Not so. While some of the homes are kept up nicely, many of the yards are littered, youths roam the streets aimlessly and trailers often catch fire, sometimes from meth labs.

Lakeshore residents routinely show up in Municipal Court hearings, often for petty crimes and drug offenses, for failing to appear at hearings, for not paying fines, for the sort of offenses committed by chronic small-timers everywhere.

The "lake" at Lakeshore is the same scummy, trashy stinkhole that Echols remembered.

Lakeshore is still populated by many carnies and other itinerant workers. It remains a hotbed of occultism, witchcraft and Satanism, with the West Memphis 3 having achieved the status of folk heroes.

Similarly, Echols in "Life After Death" described Marion High School as a sort of "rural" "Beverly Hills 90210," "a place where kids drove brand-new cars to school, wore Gucci clothing, and had enough jewelry to spark the envy of rap stars." Actually, the students of Marion High were and are the typical mix of modestly attired kids from a modestly middle-class community.

Marion is a small Arkansas town with a traditionally agriculture-based economy, with a number of residents who commute to jobs across the river in Memphis. As in many similar towns, a deeply entrenched elite holds sway over most municipal affairs. Their style is far from ostentatious. Marion is not an elite suburban community, though Marion residents do hold themselves aloof from the larger, predominately black and considerably rougher town of West Memphis to the immediate south.

Median income in Marion today is roughly twice that of West Memphis. By comparison, median income in the elite Memphis suburb of Germantown is roughly twice that of Marion.

Nonetheless, there was a class divide between the trailer park kids and the more affluent students. Local teen Jason Crosby described "high society people which would be the people who come to school in shirt and tie, don't want to get messed up, want to stay on the sidewalk all the time."

Among students with parents with steady jobs, a strong work ethic, no arrest record and solid social standing, kids from the trailer parks often didn't fit in.

As outsiders together at Marion Junior High, Damien and Jason became fast friends, sharing interests in music, skateboarding and video games.

In "Life After Death," Damien described how he met Misskelley through Jason. Knocking on the door of the Baldwin trailer, Damien was told that Jason was over at Misskelley's trailer, four or five trailers away. Damien described Misskelley was a short, greasy, manic figure prone to funny and slightly odd antics. The Misskelleys were pumping up the tires on the old trailer and moving it to Highland Trailer Park, just across the way, that very day.

Still, said Echols, "I never did see Jessie a great deal, but we became familiar enough to talk when we met. Jason and I would run into him at the bowling alley and spend an hour or two playing pool, or hang out for a little while at the Lakeshore store."

Echols former girlfriend Deanna Holcomb described a tighter relationship between Echols and Misskelley, naming Jason, Jessie and Joey Lancaster as particular friends of Echols.

When Damien moved up to high school, he left Jason a grade behind. Damien made no attempt to fit in and soon adopted his trademark all-black wardrobe, complete with black trench coat, partially inspired by the Johnny Depp character in "Edward Scissorhands."

All three hung around typical hangouts in West Memphis such as the bowling alley, the skating rink and video game booths. A surveillance video from the skating rink posted on William Ramsey's Occult Investigations YouTube account recently showed Echols and Misskelley as two of the older boys hanging out at the skating rink soon after the killings.

Jennifer Bearden was a 12-year-old Bartlett girl when she first encountered the three killers at the rink around February 1993. She struck up a romantic relationship with the 18-year-old Echols. Concerning Misskelley, "I knew him a little bit. ... I saw him at the skating rink several times."

Asked about the relationship of Misskelley to the other two, she testified in an August 2009 hearing: "....

Whenever we were at the skating rink, uh, Jessie was, he, he was a little bit louder, he was a little bit more —- I don't know — he liked to cause a little bit more trouble. … We kind of like stayed to ourselves and there was an incident that he stole the 8-ball from the pool table at the skating rink. … And uh, he showed (it) to us and actually, Damien and Jason got blamed for it. And they got kicked out of the skating rink for it. … They were pretty upset with him."

Joseph Samuel Dwyer, a younger playmate of Baldwin living two doors down at Lakeshore in 1993, described in a hearing on Aug. 14, 2009, what he knew of the relationships among Echols, Baldwin and Misskelley.

Dwyer said that he knew Misskelley quite well from the neighborhood, particularly since Misskelley's stepmother, Shelbia Misskelley, separated from "Big Jessie," lived on the same street as Dwyer and Baldwin.

Though Dwyer was in frequent contact with the Baldwin boys, he merely knew Echols but did not associate with him. Echols shared few interests with most boys and usually dressed in black. "I just never really hung out with him or even tried to get to know him," testified Dwyer.

He explained: "I really didn't have anything to do with him just because, uh, just the way he acted. … We'd get off the school bus and he'd be standing there, it's almost like craving attention in an all-black outfit so all of the kids on the bus would see him."

Dwyer pegged Echols as a poser who reveled in drawing negative attention to himself. "… He liked horror movies. He would talk about watching horror movies and stuff like that."

In an affidavit in 2006, Dwyer said of Echols: "I didn't like what I saw of him. He liked to call attention to himself. One day he painted a star over one of his eyes. Damien was a talker. He liked to say things to get peoples' attention."

Dwyer characterized Misskelley as a "trailer park redneck."

Dwyer recalled the relationship of Baldwin and Echols: "I did see Damien and Jason together after Jason started getting friendly with Damien, I was around him less than before because I didn't like Damien. I know that after Jason started hanging out with Damien, he got a trench coat just like Damien's. It was a long black trench coat. Damien had a certain way of talking and Jason picked up some of Damien's way of talking."

Another myth in the standard WM3 storyline is that the police pegged Damien as the killer partially because he wore a black trench coat .

In 2009, Dwyer explained "the trench coat thing, at the time that was sort of a fashion fad. I have one, uh, everybody, if they didn't have one they wanted one. That was kind of a fashion thing. … It was the rock shirt, rock T-shirts and the trench coat." So "everybody" had or wanted to have a black trench coat as part of a "fashion thing," along with rock T-shirts.

Baldwin and Echols tiresomely claim they were singled out, persecuted, arrested and convicted because they "didn't dress like everyone else." But "everybody" wanted to dress the way they dressed.

Dwyer added: "Everybody out there in the trailer park was terrified; everybody was profiled because of our rock T-shirts, the trench coat , the long hair. Everybody look at us like we were just part of this cult thing, and it was totally made up, if you ask me. Totally made up. And we all felt like we could just as easily have been, uh, picked as a suspect because we were in the the same trailer park, dressed the same. We were all scared about that. Channel 3 news, all the news station were riding through there every day trying to film us as we were walking down the street, you know."

Echols testified that after he began dressing in all-black, other students followed his example.

Consider, too, the myth that the boys were singled out for their interest in heavy metal.

In 2006, Dwyer said, "A lot of people in our age groups at the time were interested in rock and roll music, and in heavy metal music … I remember that after the three boys were found dead, and the news cameras came out to Lakeshore from time to time, anyone wearing a Metallica t-shirt, or some other heavy metal band t-shirt, was viewed as a devil worshipper, especially if the person had long hair."

Longhaired kids who were heavy metal fans were common, as were black T-shirts.

At trial, defense attorneys elicited police
testimony that Echols was wearing a Portland Trail
Blazers black T-shirt on the night of his arrest,
establishing to no clear end that black T-shirts were
mainstream enough to be worn by NBA fans. Or by
Reba McEntire fans, as demonstrated by a T-shirt from
the Misskelley home.

Juvenile Officer Jerry Driver testified about
Misskelley's links to Baldwin and Echols in Misskelley's
trial.

Driver, who died in August 2016, had seen the
three together for the first time around Nov. 15, 1992, at
Lakeshore. Damien, Jason and Jessie walked by while
he and a sheriff's deputy were dealing with a suspected
drunken driver. "It was nighttime ... They all had on
long black coats, and Damien had a slouch hat and they
all had staffs. ... Long sticks that they were walking
with."

Misskelley dismissed the story as ridiculous
during one of his many confessions, saying he did not
have a black coat. Driver's account has been widely
ridiculed, though never refuted.

Driver repeated the story at the Echols/Baldwin
trial. "We saw three gentlemen walking by ... Damien
Echols, Jessie Misskelley, and Jason Baldwin ... with
long coats" and "long sticks or staffs."

Driver had seen them together on a few other
occasions, "maybe two or three times," ... "Twice, I

think, at uh — at Walmart and once out in the trailer park."

Otherwise, he had seen Echols and Baldwin together dressed in black.

Echols girlfriend Domini Teer, in a Sept. 10, 1993, statement, surprised Deputy Prosecuting Attorney John Fogleman by volunteering that "Jessie came around after them kids was killed."

Fogleman: "OK, what do you mean by that? That he came around after the kids were murdered? What do you mean?"

Domini: "I mean, the boy shows up a week after them kids were killed …. Out of nowhere. I mean we hadn't seen Jessie for months. I mean he did that when Damien and me got back together, and Damien was living with his stepdad, Jack. All of a sudden, Jessie comes showing up, and the first time we've seen Jessie since the year before that. …"

Fogleman: "And … then Jessie was around quite a bit then?"

Domini: "Every once in a while, like once or twice, yeah, I saw him. … I mean, when all the cops were bringing everybody in and all and talking to everybody … It was like two days after the cops were coming around, um … Jessie came over to Jason's house one day while I was sitting there, and wanting Damien to take Blockbuster movies to Blockbuster … And they went, and I guess, took Blockbuster movies back and they wound up over at Jessie's house … because his mom had come over to get Damien … Damien's mom … cause he was supposed to be at Jason's house….

"And it made me mad, and I called over to Jessie's and said where's Damien. And he goes, Damien's on his way back. Matthew just come get him. I said I know, I sent Matthew over there to come get him, cause his parents are here. And then I hung up the phone."

Fogleman: "And about when did that happen after this Wednesday?"

Domini: "Um … it was about like that next week." That would have been when Damien's parents supposedly were temporarily separated, according to some contradictory accounts of Echols' mother, Pam, and after Damien had been interviewed by police several times and failed the polygraph.

Jessie was trying to get Damien and self-appointed detective Vicki Hutcheson together about that time. "Dark Spell" described Baldwin's version of the visit.

According to Baldwin, Misskelley showed up unexpectedly at the Baldwin trailer because a friend from Highland Trailer Park wanted to meet Echols.

Echols got into the truck and went to meet the 30-year-old Hutcheson.

Domini told Fogleman she had seen Misskelley a total of three times. "The first time, we had come up the street, and he was messing around with Matt, and we thought somebody was getting beat up, because they were all screaming and hollering out there, and when we walked out there was Jessie." "Messing around" with younger kids was routine for Jessie.

"And the second time I seen him, they had come over there and me and Damien was together, and they had just come knocking on the door with him and B.J. … And that was the last time I'd ever seen him until that time that he …. came over to Jason's to go get Damien."

Charlotte Bly Bolois, who lived at Lakeshore the summer of 1992 and visited there often, told police that Echols and Misskelley were close friends at that time, constantly seen together along with her cousin, Buddy Lucas.

She also described how Misskelley got into a fight in June 1992 with her husband, Dan Bolois: "My husband has two younger brothers, one is fixing to be 16 and other one is fixing to be 18, and he started a fight with my husband younger brothers and um, my husband went up there and ask him what was the deal and little Jessie Misskelley was going to pull a knife, but I got behind Jessie and took the knife from him."

The younger brothers were Johnny and Shane Perschke, and there have been various accounts of fights involving John Perschke.

Bolois recalled a fight "right there at my trailer" with Misskelley. "Him and my husband got into a fight later on down Fool Lake." That was the fight involving the knife. She requested that Misskelley give her the knife. "And he turned around and handed me the knife, I said if you're going to fight, fight fair. … He busted a hole in my husband's lip."

A recent account from a West Memphis resident who asked that her name be withheld painted a disturbing portrait of Damien, Jason and Jessie interacting with children from the neighborhood where their victims lived:

"In 1993 I used to live in Mayfair Apartments. I lived in the townhouses that are located in the back of the complex. I lived there for around a year and a half.

"One day I was coming home and parked in front of a park on the property close to my apartment. As I parked I noticed 3 teenage boys and 3 young boys. It caught me as strange cause one of the teenagers was dressed all in black with a long black coat the other 2 were standing a few steps back from the one in black. So I sat there in my car watching for a few minutes. The teen in black was coaching those 3 little boys (I guessed at the time were 8 or 9 years old) how to hold their bikes on their shoulders and climb a ladder of a slide and how to ride down. The other teen boys were just standing a little behind the one in black not doing much except watching and laughing from time to time. One was kinda stocky the other one skinny. It didn't seem to bother them that I was watching. They saw me.

"Any way one of the little boys was about to start up the ladder so I got out of my car and told him to get down. That's when the teen in black made a couple steps toward me and said I needed to shut the f--k up and take my ass into my apartment. This was none of my business. At that point I said if it didn't stop I was going to call the police. Then I was called a f--king bitch. So I got my kids out of my car as he stood there and watched. He watched me all the way to my apartment. It was kinda frightening. I go to call the police but looked back out to see if he or they were headed toward my apartment but instead they just left. So I decided to not call the police and never thought anything else of it.

…

"About 3 weeks to a month later three 8 year old boys were murdered in the woods right out the back door of the apartment I used to live in. I remember thinking I was so glad we had moved. Well then I was watching the news showing that 3 teenagers had been arrested. When I saw the pictures of the boys I told my husband that the one called Damien Echols was the one that cussed me out and was the one trying to make the kids carry their bikes up the slide. I also recognized the other 2 boys. They are Jessie Misskelley and Jason Baldwin.

"The three little boys I saw Echols, Misskelley and Baldwin with that day I can't swear was Michael, Stevie or Chris. I do remember 1 of the boys was blonde and 1 had a red bike. If I'm remembering correctly it was the blonde that had the red bike on his shoulder. I really wasn't watching the little boys. I was paying more attention to the 3 teen boys and what they were doing.

"I never told anyone what I saw but family and friends. I never thought it was very important at the time since they had caught them. I was in my early 20's, working, taking care of 2 young kids and my grandparents. My husband was working and going to school at night. I had my hands full. Looking back I wish I had told what I saw."

"DAMIEN ADMITS TO A HISTORY OF VIOLENCE."

The central figure in the investigation, prosecution, incarceration and release of the West Memphis 3 was the flamboyant and problematic Damien Echols, whose boyhood ambition to become a world-class occultist put him out of step with his peers in the Arkansas Delta.

Quickly pegged as a likely suspect in the murders from multiple sources, including his own all-too-knowing initial interviews with police, Echols seemed to have adopted his black-clad "figure of the night" persona as a defense against often-rough circumstances.

Becoming a self-proclaimed witch and part-time vampire made sense to a mentally ill misfit who could turn his outsider status into a means of drawing attention to himself.

Intrinsic to this dark image was the creation of the impression that he was capable of great and weird violence. For those who knew him, it was not surprising that he fulfilled his self-created legend as a dreaded monster.

He worked hard at becoming the terror of the town. On the road to infamy, he built up a history of violence that gave credence to an ability to torture and kill.

According to his discharge summary from Charter Hospital of Little Rock in June 1992: "Supposedly, Damien chased a younger child with an ax and attempted to set a house on fire. He denied this behavior. He reported that his girlfriend's family reported this so that they could get him in trouble. He was also accused of beating a peer up at school. Damien admits to a history of violence. He said prior to admission he did attempt to enucleate a peer's eye at school. He was suspended subsequently from school. He was suspended on seven different occasions during the school year. He related he was suspended on one occasion because he set a fire in his science classroom and also would walk off on campus on several occasions. He was disruptive to the school environment. He was also disrespectful to teachers. He has been accused of terroristic threatening." Echols had gotten into trouble in one instance for spitting on a teacher.

Much of this history of violence came from Echols himself.

His teenage acquaintances told grisly stories about Echols' casual cruelty.

Joe Houston Bartoush, Jason Baldwin's cousin, offered another insight into Echols' violent character; a portion of Baldwin's "alibi" centered on the fact that he had cut the lawn of his great-uncle Hubert Bartoush, Joe's father, on May 5.

On June 14, 1993, Detective Bryn Ridge was

interviewing Hubert when Joe Bartoush volunteered a
statement. Joe, in his early teens, said he and Echols
had been walking down the road west out of Lakeshore
into a field when they came upon a sick dog. Echols
grabbed a brick and began attacking the dog.

Joe told Ridge: "On 10-27-92 I was at Lakeshore
Trailer Park with Damien Echols when he killed a black
Great Dane. The dog was already sick and he hit the
dog in the back of the head. He pulled the intestines out
of the dog and started stomping the dog until blood
came out of his mouth. He was going to come back later
with battery acid so that he could burn the hair and skin
off of the dog's head. He had two cat skulls, a dog skull
and a rat skull that I already knew about. He kept these
skulls in his bedroom at Jack Echols house in Lakeshore.
He was trying to make the eyeballs of the dog he killed
pop out when he was stomping. Damien had a
camouflage survival knife to cut the gut out of the dog
with."

Joe was sure of the date of the dog killing because
he had skipped school that day and had been caught.

Joe said Echols had used the survival knife to
carve his name into his arm on another occasion. A
similar survival knife recovered behind the Baldwin
home, known as the "lake knife," was a highly
publicized piece of prosecutorial evidence. His former
girlfriend also described Echols having a similar knife,
and Echols testified that he had owned "a bunch" of
Rambo-style camouflage survival knives.

Heather Cliett, Baldwin's girlfriend, told investigators of similar animal cruelty: "States that one time at the skating rink Damien told her that he stuck a stick in a dog's eye and jumped on it and then burned it."

Timothy Blaine Hodge, a 14-year-old ninth-grader at Marion who lived in Lakeshore, had known Baldwin for some time but only knew Echols since his return from Oregon. "I've heard Jason say that Damien was in the crazy house in Oregon. Damien and Jason were always together. They spent a lot of time in West Memphis at Wal-Mart. They stole a lot of stuff. I always seen just Jason and Damien and Domini together walking around Lakeshore. There was a big black Great Dane dog at Lakeshore that I was on the trail over the bridge to the right as you go over the bridge. It was dead. Its intestines was strung out of his butt. A boy named Adam told me he heard Damien did it."

Chris Littrell, a neighbor of the Echols family and a Wiccan, told the police that Echols liked to stick sharpened sticks through frogs to see how long it took them to die.

He said Echols claimed that he had burned down his father's garage and then stood in the flames chanting.

Echols told Murray Farris, another teen who was a Wiccan, that he once poured gasoline over his own foot and set it aflame.

Reports of Echols planning to sacrifice his own child in a ritual were persistent. Littrell told police that Echols did not intend to kill the baby that Domini was expecting, as the child would entitle him to a larger government check.

The story surfaced after Echols was arrested with Deanna Holcomb as they attempted to run away.

Jerry Driver, the juvenile officer in charge of the Echols case, mentioned the baby sacrifice rumor on June 1, 1992, in a phone message to Charter Hospital, where Echols was taken for his first hospitalization for mental illness. The message read "Court-ordered to Mid South Hospital. Suicidal, self-mutilating -- made pact ... girlfriend & Devil to sacrifice 1st born."

A psychiatric evaluation at Charter dated June 2, 1992, stated: "There was a conversation that concerned staff at the detention center. Reportedly Damien and his girlfriend were going to have a baby and then sacrifice the child. Damien denies this type of behavior."

The discharge summary on June 25 repeated that information, as did the discharge summary on Sept. 28 after his second trip to Charter. The Sept. 28 discharge summary also noted that Echols had been on probation for threatening his girlfriend's parents and for a charge of second-degree sexual misconduct stemming from having sex with his underage girlfriend.

Driver's dealings with Echols dated from that arrest on May 19, 1992, when Damien and Deanna were found partially clothed in an abandoned trailer at Lakeshore.

In a series of contacts with law enforcement over the next year, Echols described a network of occultists active in Crittenden County. In turn, Echols consented to have his home searched and officials confiscated Echols' notebook, full of somber and morbid poetry, and artwork from his bedroom, full of demonic and occult images. Driver believed a drawing of four tombstones, with a baby's foot and a rattle, under a full moon, indicated Echols' plan to sacrifice his own child.

Deanna told West Memphis police on May 11, 1993, well before the arrests: "I found out that he planned to kill our first born if it was a girl. Damien would not do it. He is a coward and would have tried to get me to do it. That's when I knew he was nuts and I had nothing else to do with him."

Stories about Echols drinking blood were similarly persistent and pervasive.

The West Memphis Evening Times ran a story quoting an anonymous girl who said she had seen Echols drink the blood of Baldwin and Domini. The same story quoted a Lakeshore resident who said that dogs had come up missing in the trailer park. Schoolmates often asked Echols if he drank blood, and he didn't deny the practice.

The Sept. 28 discharge summary from Charter noted that, "While at the Detention Center, he reportedly grabbed a peer and began 'sucking blood from the peer's neck'. According to Damien, he relates that the peer was aware that he was going to do this. Staff reports that Damien was not remorseful for his behavior. Damien indicated that he sucked blood in order to get into a gang. He denies it was any type of ritual. ...

"Damien laughed when he was called a 'blood sucking vampire'. He relates that he does not know why people think this."

After an office visit on Jan. 25, 1993, his therapist noted that Echols believed he obtained power by drinking the blood of others, that the practice made him feel godlike.

At trial, John Fogleman asked Dr. James Moneypenny, a psychologist from Little Rock testifying for the defense, "In your business, is it not unusual to find people telling you about drinking blood, and that they do it to make them feel like a god?"

"It's highly unusual," said Dr. Moneypenny.

"It's what?"

"It's not usual at all," said the psychologist. "It is very atypical. I think that represents some of the extremes of his thinking and beliefs and what it has come to for him."

Driver found that Echols was not the only blood-drinker in his circle of friends. Driver had transported Domini to Charter Hospital after she broke probation on a shoplifting charge. "She discussed with me the blood-drinking and said 'Why should I not drink blood, because my mother drinks blood?' and I thought, now that's a strange thing to say." Domini, consistently dismissive of the most damaging evidence, denied making this statement.

While there is little else to suggest that Baldwin was an avid blood-drinker, testimony from a fellow detainee at Craighead County Juvenile Detention Facility centered on a gory confession made to Michael Carson.

Carson, a 16-year-old admitted drug user, testified, "I said, just between me and you, did you do it. I won't say a word. He said yes and he went into detail about it. .... He told me how he dismembered the kids, or I don't know exactly how many kids. He just said he dismembered them. He sucked the blood from the penis and scrotum and put the balls in his mouth."

Carson stood by his testimony when reports surfaced in 2000 that he had committed perjury. Carson said he didn't cut a deal in exchange for the testimony. He had passed the polygraph before testifying.

Christy Jones, a friend of Misskelley's who had attended school with Damien, told police on Oct. 1, 1993, about Damien "I saw him cut his arm with something and he then sucked the blood out of the wound. I had heard that Damien was weird and part of a satanic cult."

The evidence of his cruelty to animals continues to dog Echols. When such talk surfaced on Twitter in 2013, Echols referred to the many stories as "animal lies" and suggested that, if the stories were true, they would have showed up in the court record.

After all, Damien's dad, Joe Hutchison, had told the "Paradise Lost" documentary filmmakers: "This boy is not capable of the crime that he's been arrested for. I've seen him take a little kitten and love it just like you love a little baby." Considering that Echols intended to sacrifice his own little baby, Hutchison's statement held a certain ironic truth.

Documentary filmmakers have made no mention of Damien's history of torturing animals, drinking blood and planning human and animal sacrifices.

'AN ALIEN, FROM ANOTHER WORLD, NOT LIKE ANY HUMAN ON EARTH"

"I think at the time I probably suffered from what most teenagers suffer from, you know, just teenage angst, maybe depression, maybe sometimes even severe depression," Damien Echols explained to CNN's Larry King in 2007 about his adolescence, making it sound as if he was a typical moody teenager.

Echols painted a self-portrait of a fairly ordinary kid just a little out of the norm: "Things weren't exactly the same — especially in the South — as they are now. I believe that I probably stood out in the small town where we were living just because of the music I listened to, the clothes that I wore, things of that nature. They considered me an oddity. So I drew attention. For example, one of the things they used against us at trial was the fact that I listened to Metallica. You know, back then, 15 years ago, that was something that was considered strange. Now you hear it played on classic rock stations. It's no big deal at all."

The West Memphis police had more promising leads than who was listening to Metallica, which would have been a rich field for suspects. By 1993, Metallica was one of the top rock acts internationally, playing 77 shows worldwide on its "Nowhere Else to Roam" tour, including dates in such Southern towns as Johnson City, Tenn., Lexington, Ky., and Greenville, S.C. Five years earlier, Metallica had been one of the headliners for the Monsters of Rock Tour at Liberty Bowl Memorial Stadium, just across the river from West Memphis. Two years before that, Metallica had opened for Ozzy Osbourne at the Mid-South Coliseum at the Memphis Fairgrounds.

Then as now, being a Metallica fan was no big deal and not something that would single anyone out as a murder suspect.

Echols was known around Marion and West Memphis for his carefully cultivated persona as a sneering specter in black stalking along the side of the road, reveling in his bad reputation as a practitioner of the dark arts.

What troubled authorities was not an immature poseur with Gothic pretensions but the deeply troubled youth behind the cliched facade.

In 2001, Dr. George W. Woods, a Berkeley, Calif., psychiatrist, attempted to clarify what was wrong with Damien Echols in a lengthy statement with an encompassing survey of Echols' mental troubles and background, based greatly on suspect self-reporting.

Dr. Woods' evaluation was requested by the Echols defense to determine if his mental illness affected his competency to stand trial. The defense, attempting to appeal the conviction, contended that antidepressants Echols was taking in 1992-1993 heightened his manic episodes, creating a "psychotic euphoria" that included hallucinations and the delusion that "deities" were transforming him into a "superior entity."

The problems and limitations were longstanding, Dr. Woods explained. "Mr. Echols' mother, Pamela, was adopted under mysterious circumstances and reared as the only child of her adoptive mother, who was trained as a practical nurse, and her adoptive father, who was an illiterate blue collar worker. When Mr. Echols' mother began junior high school, she developed bizarre behavior that intensified as she grew older. She stopped attending high school because, in her words, it made her 'crazy.' She was unable to cope with the stress of school, stopped leaving her home entirely, and received psychiatric treatment. Her adoptive mother was forced to quit work in order to stay home and care for her. Mr. Echols' mother, Pamela, married Mr. Echols' father, Joe Hutchison, when she was only 15.

"Mr. Echols' mother became pregnant with Mr. Echols during the first year of her marriage. Due to her age and mental condition the pregnancy was high risk and marked by numerous complications. According to her, the pregnancy 'almost killed me.' She remained so nauseated and ill that she lost 50 pounds over the course of nine months. Her diet was very poor; she was not well nourished. Her long, high risk labor necessitated a caesarean section from which she recuperated slowly.

"Not surprisingly, Mr. Echols had many problems as an infant and young child. He was 'fretful and nervous and cried all of the time.' His mother could not soothe him, and he slept fitfully for only three or four hours a night. At a very young age he began to demonstrate troubling behaviors. He repetitively banged his head against the wall and floor until he was three. ...

"Following Mr. Echols' birth his mother suffered a miscarriage and soon after became pregnant with his younger sister. ... Mr. Echols' mother was not able to care for her two small children, so she sent Mr. Echols to live with his maternal grandmother. Although Mr. Echols returned to live with his mother and father, his mother was very dependent on her mother for assistance in caring for Mr. Echols and, later, his sister. Pamela Echols was never able to live on her own or care for her children without a great deal of support. She remained dependent on others for guidance and assistance with child rearing.

"Like Mr. Echols' mother, his father, Joe Hutchison, also appears to have suffered from mental instability. Joe Hutchison is uniformly described as immature, self absorbed, cruel and capricious. He chronically neglected and abused his family. He berated his wife and son, set unrealistic expectations, called them degrading names, destroyed their most cherished possessions, terrorized them by threatening to break their bones and hurt them in other ways, and isolated them from community and family support by moving frequently -- sometimes impulsively leaving a residence only days or weeks after moving in. On one occasion, he forced his wife to leave her hospital bed to move with him to another city. He found sadistic pleasure in donning horrifying rubber masks of hideous monsters and appearing at his son's bedroom window where he terrified Mr. Echols by making gruesome noises. In addition, Mr. Hutchison kept his family anxious with his fixation on the notion that others were trying to hurt him. For example, he was convinced 'people were trying to run him down' and constantly harangued his wife and son about the individuals who were trying to kill him. ...

"Neither mother nor child was equipped to deal with Joe Hutchison's increasingly disturbed behavior. Fearing for her life and those of her children Pamela Echols finally found the courage to divorce Joe Hutchison in 1986."

Damien was the product of two extremely unstable parents. Damien's troubling and often bizarre behavior from an early age worried family members. None of this suggested that the result would be a teenager whose only complaint would be your average case of '"the summertime blues."

Dr. Woods continued: "Mr. Echols first recalls being overwhelmed by distressing and terrifying emotions in the second grade when he was positive there was going to be a nuclear war. He believed he 'had to get back to where something told him he came from before the war started.' As he grew older this obsession evolved into a driving force that consumed him and 'took up every bit of brain space and brain power.' He became convinced that he was 'an alien, from another world, not like any human on earth.'"

Problems at home continued, Dr. Woods noted. "Mr. Echols' mental deterioration spiraled against the backdrop of his unpredictable and troubled home life. His mother's confusion and dependence continued. Within days of divorcing Joe Hutchison she married Andy Jack Echols, an illiterate laborer who worked intermittently as a roofer. The family was extremely poor. They found a shack set in the middle of crop fields that were doused with pesticides at regular intervals. Despite the extremely unhealthy conditions, the Echols remained in the shack for five years. …"

Damien's adoptive father, the since-deceased Jack Echols, gave his impressions of the young Damien on Sept. 4, 2000: "I married Pam Hutchison in 1986, shortly after she split up from her husband Joe. I had known her from the city through friends that we both had. I adopted both of her children, Michelle and Damien. When I adopted Damien, his name was Michael and he had to change his last name to Echols and while he was doing that he changed his first name to Damien. Damien was reading about a preacher named Damien who he liked and that is how he got his name.

"When we first got married, I lived in some apartments in Marion. Pamela and her children moved in with me and we stayed there for a few months. We finally moved into a house that needed a lot of work that was in the middle of a wheat field. Some folks might call it a shack, but it gave us a roof over our heads and a place to go home to. It was only 35 dollars a month and we needed someplace that did not cost very much. I fixed the house up as best I could. We had a toilet in the bathroom and a sink in the kitchen, but they weren't hooked up right so we could not use them at first. I fixed up a pump that was supposed to pump in water, but it could only handle a little bit of water at a time. We learned to use as little water as possible. Since water was a problem we ate off paper plates so we did not have to do dishes. During part of the year, the water would quit running and we had to bring it in from outside. Most of the time we went to Pamela's mama's house and my children's houses and filled up gallon jugs. We tried to fill up enough at one time so that we only had to go every other day or so. We had to haul in wood to heat the place, and it got plenty cold in that part of Arkansas. I got paid okay when I was roofing but if there was ever a storm or other bad weather then I did not work and we did not get a paycheck for that week. I was the only one working in the family so it was real hard when I missed out on work."

In his writings, Damien has described this portion of his childhood with great bitterness.

Jack Echols continued: "Damien was not in very good health while we lived at the old farm house. He was not able to go outside of the house because he got really sick. He had a real hard time with his breathing because of all the crops outside the house. Sometimes his eyes and throat swelled up and he could not swallow or see very good. The place right below his eyes turned to a darkish color kind of like he had been hit in the eye. I think the worst thing for Damien, though, were his headaches. From the time that we moved into that house, he would get terrible headaches. He asked me to squeeze his head so that his pain would go away. I would put my arms around his head, like in a head lock and I squeezed it. I did not want to hurt him but he always asked to squeeze harder, so I did. I think that the pain of the headache hurt more than the squeezing of his head. He got relief for a few moments while I did this but the headache always came back. He took some medicine to help with his breathing and to try and keep his swelling down and it did help a little bit but not near as much as we wanted it to work.

"Damien went through these spells where he could not sleep no matter how hard he tried to. He stayed up for three or four nights in a row without sleeping at all. These periods were very hard for him and by the end of the second day of no sleep, he was exhausted, fussy, and miserable. He cried a lot during these times and no one seemed to be able to help him with what he was upset about. We never could figure out what he was so upset about, but there was no doubt in my mind that he was as miserable as a little boy could be. His sister Michelle went in his room to talk to him and he sometimes fell asleep for a couple of hours or so and then he stayed up for another few days before getting anymore sleep. I was worried about Damien but I did not know what to do. I had to work during the day and every evening when I came home, I hoped that he would be asleep but he was normally still up. After many days of this, Damien finally slept for an entire night. Once he got a full night's rest, he went for a few weeks without having trouble sleeping. I always hoped that these times would not come back but they always did. It just about broke my heart to see how hard Damien tried to handle his problems, but he never was able to figure out what made him so sad.

"Damien never was a really happy boy. He got really sad sometimes and no one, including Damien, had any idea what was wrong. He cried really hard and I asked him what was making him so sad and he told me that he did not know. I never could figure out how someone could cry so hard and not know why they were sad and it was real hard to watch Damien go through this. Damien used to spend a few days in a row where he cried really hard. Sometimes it seemed like he was having trouble with his breathing because he cried so much. During these periods, Damien sometimes started laughing uncontrollably, just like one of those laughs that comes from the belly. It was very strange to me that he went from crying to laughing and I was confused about why he did this. Michelle and his mama tried to get him to stop being so sad but the only thing that ever seemed to help him was time. After a while, he would finally get to where he could stop crying and being so sad. Damien went through this on a regular basis.

"There were other times when Damien had so much energy he did not know what to do. He got really excited and kind of hyper and he always walked at these times. Damien walked to some of the parks in the area, to some of his friends houses, and across town. He told me that he sometimes got confused because he was sure where he needed to go but when he got there he felt like he was in the wrong place. I thought that he meant that he changed his mind about where he wanted to go but he told me that it was not like that. Damien did not decide where he was supposed to walk to but got a feeling about where he should be but, when he got where he was going, his feeling changed and he had to go somewhere else. He was real frustrated at these times and I did not know how to help him. I did not really understand what he meant about not knowing where he wanted to be. I sometimes felt that I should have done a better job trying to figure out what he was talking about and maybe then I could have made things a little better for him.

"I remember that Damien had some strange needs. Some things could never be out of place and had to be put in a place just so. He had the same pillow all his life and if it ever got misplaced, he howled his head off. Damien could not sleep with any other pillow for as long as I have known him. He had a lot of fear about the closet in his room and did not want any of his toys ever put in the closet. If his toys were in the closet, he panicked and thought they would die. Damien had these two fire hats; one was black and one was red. We had to keep the hats under the bathroom sink just so and right beside each other. If they were not in their place, it made him panic and afraid. …

"Sometimes Damien did not have any appetite and he did not eat for several days. It did not seem to matter what Pamela put on the table, he did not want to eat it. After a few days of not eating, Damien looked weaker and I could tell it was wearing on him. I wished that he would eat for his health but when he did not have an appetite there was nothing any one could do."

Dr. Woods wrote: "Going from Joe Hutchison to Andy Echols was like going from the frying pan into the fire. In addition to increased isolation and poverty and being exposed to toxic pesticides, the Department of Human Services (DHS) records show that Andy Echols sexually abused Mr. Echols' younger sister repeatedly until she mustered the courage to report him to her school counselor. DHS intervened and Pamela moved her children out of the shack. Yet, that was as much as Pamela Hutchison Echols was able to do to protect her children from the ravages of poverty, domestic violence, mental illness and sexual abuse. For, no sooner had she separated from Andy Echols than she, Damien and his sister moved in with Joe Hutchison, along with Joe Hutchison's own mentally impaired son. The return of Joe Hutchison, whom Mr. Echols had not seen for years, coincided with Mr. Echols' first psychiatric hospitalization."

Echols' mental troubles did not get better with age, wrote Dr. Woods. "In adolescence Mr. Echols became frankly suicidal. Unable to find a way out of his depression and hopelessness, he thought the only escape from his constant mental, physical and emotional pain was to kill himself. ... At about the age of 16, his mental illness took a sudden turn for the worst. Mr. Echols describes feeling disorganized and out of control of his racing thoughts and emotions. He began to 'laugh hysterically and make other people think I was crazy.' For Mr. Echols 'manic-ness' meant 'everything sped up and became frantic. Others called it hysterical,' but Mr. Echols described it as '... being driven.' When he '... went crazy, everything sped up.' He '... had no thought process.' He could not remember '... all of the weird things I did,' but people would tell him about them later and he was surprised by his actions. For example, he recalled a time when 'some kids threw a hamburger up on the ceiling' and he reached up, grabbed it, and ate it.

"His mania was interspersed with periods of 'waiting' interminably for 'an abstract thing that might come in the blink of an eye.' He was mentally confused and 'did not know what he was waiting for.' Mr. Echols 'tried cutting' himself to 'feel different somehow' and 'to see if it would let some of the pain out.' He felt 'worn-out.' During the one year of high school he attended in the ninth grade, he kept a journal at the instruction of his English teacher. It became more and more abstract -- 'when I wrote about one thing it came out as something else. If I wrote about the moon, I was actually describing the grocery store.'

"Mr. Echols reported that the intense shift between depression and mania 'literally drove me crazy.' He remembered that 'everything hurt, from the smell of water to green grass, brown grass.' He was exquisitely sensitive to 'the way people smelled' and 'the smell of water.' He described manic episodes when his 'brain rolled, like a TV that is not adjusted.' He believed his brain rolled when it rained or when he was near a large body of water. The change of seasons had a strong effect on him also, especially fall and winter, and made 'his brain roll constantly.'

"Mr. Echols' overwhelming depression and other problems with mood during childhood and adolescence caused disabling disturbances in his emotions, thoughts, behavior and physical health. His sleep was irregular; he often had no energy to perform the simplest tasks; his thoughts were paralyzingly sluggish or racing at speeds he could not control. He felt caught in time, and thought it was hopeless even to think about feeling better or gaining control over his life. He ruminated about painful memories and insignificant events. He could not concentrate and became easily confused; it was impossible to make even simple decisions. He cried and 'sobbed all the time without any understanding of what made ...' him so sad. He had no ability to feel joy or pleasure. He became completely inconsolable and isolated, unable to relate to others in any meaningful way. He was inexplicably sensitive to physical sensations and reacted to the slightest changes in his environment. His body 'hurt when the sun went up or when the sun went down, when it rained or when it did not rain.' He could not stop or escape from the pain; it became 'a throb that never went away.' He despised himself and felt worthless; he was consumed with shame and despair."

Dr. Woods added:

"Mr. Echols has been evaluated on three separate occasions by three different psychologists, each of whom administered a battery of tests. A prominent feature of each evaluation was the Minnesota Multiphasic Personality Inventory (MMPI), which was administered on June 8, 1992; September 2, 1992; and February 20, 1994. The independent test results were quite consistent; all revealed valid profiles and strong indications of depression, mania, severe anxiety, delusions and psychosis.

"Test results for the June 8, 1992, MMPI reflected elevations on scores of psychotic thinking, including hallucinations, paranoid ideation, and delusions, as well as severe anxiety and other related emotional disturbances. The suggested diagnoses were schizophrenia, disorganized type; and bipolar disorder, manic. Individual responses on this test revealed that Mr. Echols was afraid of losing his mind, had bizarre thoughts, and had very peculiar experiences. Three months later, on September 2, 1992, a second MMPI was administered. The test results very closely paralleled the findings of the earlier MMPI. Shortly before Mr. Echols' trial began in 1994, he was administered the MMPI a third time for the purpose of identifying mitigating evidence. Like the other two, this MMPI revealed psychotic thought processes consistent with schizophrenia. Specific indicators of a thought disorder included mental confusion, persecutory ideas, acute anxiety, and depressed suicidal ideation. ...

"Prior to and during his murder trial, Damien Echols suffered from a severe psychiatric disorder characterized by enduring delusions, auditory and visual hallucinations and severe mood swings ranging from suicidal depression to extreme mania."

Dr. Woods wrote: "Mr. Echols' accounts of his symptoms since childhood are consistent with severe traumatic stress disorders and mood disorders. He reported periods of dissociation in which he 'lost' long spans of time. He also endorsed numerous physical problems, including frequent severe headaches (for which he was treated with prescription medications as a child), heart palpitations, difficulty breathing (he was diagnosed with and treated for asthma), and chronic sleeping problems. He reported having nightmares from which he awakened in a terrified state as often as twice a night. These symptoms persisted throughout his childhood and adolescence and grew to include periods of psychosis. …

" Although he has received no psychiatric treatment on death row Mr. Echols stated his mental illness has improved significantly since his incarceration. ...

"Prior to and during his trial, Mr. Echols heard 'voices that were not really voices' and he 'was not sure if it was a voice inside' his head or 'somebody else's voice.' He thought it 'was nearly impossible' to tell if it was his voice or somebody/something else. He experienced visual hallucinations that 'were personifications of others. They were like smoke, changing shape but present and constant.' The personifications had specific names and activities. One was 'Morpheus Sandman' who was a hybrid of a human being and a god. Another example was 'Washington crossing the Delaware.' Mr. Echols saw Washington cross the Delaware with 'Hermes on the boat.' Hermes was able to cross with Washington because 'Hermes was moving backwards through time.' Mr. Echols came to believe that he was the same as these personifications, 'made of the same material and from the same place.'

"Mr. Echols stated that at some point in his adolescence he came to believe he was 'something that was almost a supreme being that came from a place other people didn't come from.' This transformation caused him to change physically, the pertinent changes appearing in his 'appendages, hands, feet, hair.' He acquired 'an entirely different bone structure that was not human.' He developed 'stronger senses.' His eyesight was better and his 'ability to smell and taste changed.' He had a different stance, moved his eyes and held his head differently. He grew his nails so that they would be a 'perfect 1 ½ inches long.' When he looked at his hands, he could see his bones. His weight dropped to 116 pounds, consistent with neurovegetative signs seen in mood disorders. This period of physical change began the year before his arrest and lasted for about two years after he was on death row. ..."

Echols' lifelong struggle with mental illness took several violent turns in the year leading up to his arrest.

"A BIZARRE AND UNUSUAL MANNER"

Damien Echols was first referred to family treatment from the Department of Human Services on May 5, 1992, a year to the day before the murders. The family was living in Lakeshore.

The referral form, based on allegations from his sister Michelle, stated: "Child reported her step-father has been sexually abusing her for a long time. Her mother knows about it but has done nothing to stop it. Sexual abuse reportedly occurred periodically from age 7 until present. The abuse included fondling."

Charges were pending contingent on counseling.

According to records from the East Arkansas Regional Mental Health Center in West Memphis, the family was in deep disarray. Gloria Stevenson, the family service worker, reported: "It appears that the Echols family has extreme problems related to an ongoing history of sexual abuse, suspected emotions problems and undefined interpersonal relationship disorders. Mr. Echols admits to being overly affectionate with Michelle and to have been charged for indecently exposing himself to an older daughter, however, Mrs. Echols states that she feels Michelle is lying as she has been skipping school and sexually acting out. Michelle alleges to have had several miscarriages though the mother denies it. Damien Echols on the other hand, holds his adopted father in low regard and feels the allegations are in fact true. Mrs. Echols states Damien is in need of counseling and evaluation as he feels he is 'smarter than everyone else' and will verbalize this fact. He also reportedly has little regard for others and stated he feels people have no true feeling for each other; Their main purpose is to use and bring harm to others around them. Mrs. Echols reports that Damien has attempted to fight with her on occasion."

Beyond the lack of consensus on reality among the Echols family, Damien's mother described his persistent grandiosity and a view of reality typical of psychopathic personalities who have little empathy and view others as objects to be used. His mother gave the lie to Damien's claim that he was not violent as a teenager.

She later told caseworkers that she "was most concerned about son 'not learning to deal with anger and rages.' {Mother} mentioned her belief that son may be responding to outside stimulation. Voiced fear 'son may be crazy.'"

Besides the family drama, Damien's teenage love life took a histrionic turn.

"By the age of sixteen Mr. Echols' depression and hopelessness was written all over his body," wrote Dr. George Woods in his 2001 report. "He wore black clothes, hair and nails. His strange, often flat affect kept him out of step with mainstream life in a small Arkansas town. Yet he found one person, a young girl with problems of her own, whom he felt could understand him. They developed a relationship and became inseparable. Her parents strongly opposed their dating and tried to keep them apart.

"Desperate to stay together, they planned to go to California. Mr. Echols' mother, overtaxed with her own problems, did not intervene to keep the troubled teenagers near their parents. Instead, she gave them no more than $10.00 to $15.00 - the only money she had - as a contribution toward expenses."

Echols and Deanna Holcomb, 15, had broken up earlier that spring at the insistence of her parents. Echols' violent reaction brought charges of terroristic threatening.

Echols promptly found a new girlfriend, Domini Teer, but continued to pursue Deanna. Finally, Damien and Deanna decided to run away together to California. They didn't get far.

The teens were reported as runaways on May 19, 1992. Police found them hiding in the closet of an abandoned mobile home in Lakeshore. The teens were "partially nude from the waist down," according to the arrest report. Damien and Deanna were both charged initially with burglary and sexual misconduct and taken to the county jail. Juvenile Officer Jerry Driver was contacted, and the teenage lovers were permanently separated.

Echols shared a different, infinitely more romantic memory of his final encounter with Deanna in a May 14,

1996, letter to future wife Lorri Davis, as revealed in "Yours for Eternity": " ... When I was 16, I was very much in love. Her name was Deanna. One day we skipped school together. We walked for miles until we found a place that was absolutely beautiful. There were hills, and the grass was so full and soft and green, the sky was grey and overcast. We spent hours talking, telling each other things that we had never told another living soul, our worst fears, our most wished-for dreams, and we made love several times. I never suspected that that would be the last time that I ever saw her. There's no way that words can ever do this memory justice, but it's a day that has returned to haunt me every day of my life." This pastoral interlude set amidst the nonexistent hills of Crittenden County was a far cry from the reality of a rainy night in a ramshackle trailer.

As he was being held in a police car, Echols later told a psychiatrist, he witnessed his girlfriend's father coming toward her as she waited with officers. Damien "states that he was able to work his fingers loose, moved over and was able to slip the safety off of the police officer's gun which had been left in the police vehicle. Damien freely admitted he had plans to shoot the girlfriend's father if he acted in an aggressive manner toward the girl." As part of his rich fantasy life, Echols' thoughts often turned to homicide.

Sheriff's Department investigators searched the Echols home and confiscated a number of items that would show up at his murder trial, including a dog skull that Echols explained was "a decoration for my room" as well as a "Book of Shadows" detailing his progress on the Wiccan path.

"Mr. Echols was taken to a juvenile facility where he attempted to hang himself," wrote Dr. Woods. "Following their arrests and initial evaluations both youths were placed in psychiatric hospitals."

Echols was sent first to the Craighead County Juvenile Detention Center in Jonesboro and then, after the suicide threat, to East Arkansas Regional Mental Health Center.

On May 28, 1992, Echols was given a Millon Adolescent Personality (MAPI) test, designed especially for teenagers, which reported "The behavior of this youngster is characterized by impulsive hostility, an apprehensive distrust of others and an edgy defensiveness against criticism. Fearing that others will dominate and possibly brutalize him, he puts forward a socially blunt and aggressive public posture. He fantasizes being all powerful so as to block others from possessing the means to be belittling and harmful. He believes that only alert vigilance and vigorous counteraction can prevent the malice of others. Closeness to others, displaying weakness and a willingness to compromise are seen as fatal concessions.

"The desire to gain power and demean others springs from animosity and a wish to vindicate past grievances. Although frequently unsuccessful in these aims, this teenager believes that past degradations may be undone by provoking fear and intimidation in others. He often loses his temper, gets into fights and acts in a daring fashion. He avoids displaying warmth, gentleness and intimacy. Defiance and disobedience are rationalized into virtues. ...

"Inadequacy and failure are intolerable to him, and blame is quickly projected outward.

"Disposed to be headstrong and able to inspire discomfort and anger in others, he may use his position in the family to bully young sibs into submission. ... He is rarely able to submerge the memories of past humiliations and this resentment may break though ... in impulsive and irrational anger. ...

"Cool and distant, this youth demonstrates little or no compassion for others, viewing their difficulties as the product of their own weaknesses. He is likely to feel no compunction about ignoring their needs and sensitivities. This lack of empathy may lead this youngster to serve only himself regardless of the consequences for those around him."

Among the statements about himself that Echols designated as "true": "It is easy for me to take advantage of people. ... Punishment never stopped me from doing whatever I wanted. ... I have a pretty hot temper."

He was diagnosed as "adjustment disorder with disturbances of conduct."

Among the therapeutic implications: "Teenager may relate to the clinician in a polite, though passive way. ... Difficulties will be attributed to others who are claimed to be the source of problems.... Efforts to be what may be called a good and cooperative patient will be exhibited, even when restraining strong and angry feelings."

Dr. Woods reported: "Personnel at East Arkansas Regional Mental Health Center described Mr. Echols as very disturbed. He was withdrawn, spoke little, and rarely had eye contact with anyone: 'he stared at the wall or cast his eyes downward.' He appeared 'confused,' and dressed strangely -- 'all in black.' He was preoccupied with his fingernails, which he 'filed to points.' Concerned about the nature and complexity of his problems Mental Health Center staff recommended that Mr. Echols immediately be involuntarily committed to Charter Hospital in Little Rock for more extensive evaluation and treatment."

A request for service dated June 1 recorded a threat "to hang himself while in custody." The intake sheet noted that Damien and Deanna had a pact to commit suicide if they could not be together and that Damien was continuing to express suicidal thoughts, voicing plans to use a sheet to hang himself. Damien admitted to the suicide plan: "It would have been necessary if her parents would not have let us see each other."

Driver had Echols admitted to Charter Hospital in Little Rock for a monthlong stay. Admission papers noted: "He has a history of extreme physical aggression toward others."

Criteria for the emergency admission included:

"1. Fire setting behavior by history."

"2. Potential danger to property."

"3. Excessive irritability and anger that is potentially dangerous and persistent."

"4. Involvement in bizarre and unusual behavior."

A case file from June 1 reported that Echols "admits to having seen suspended 7X this past semester for inciting fights at school, starting small fires, cussing. States in one fight he almost gouged out the victim's eyes."

A report on June 2 stated: "He has been suspended x7 due to negative behaviors in the classroom. Information does suggest that Damien has set fire to his academic classroom on two occasions, that he has also been truant, engaged in physical confrontations while on school grounds and has, often times, threatened to put 'hexes' on school instructors."

Echols admitted to being a "practicing warlock" while denying devil worship. He had a "blood brother" with whom he exchanged blood. Damien said he had one friend: "A friend is someone who would die for you — everyone else is only interested in themselves & what they want."

Deanna was also admitted for mental treatment, at Mid-South Mental Health; Echols had been scheduled to go there but because his girlfriend was there, he had been sent to Charter.

Concerning allegations about abuse in his family, Damien denied he had been abused, an assertion "strongly questioned." He denied feeling violent, saying he saw fighting as a release: "Sometimes I have to do this not because of feeling angry — sometimes I'm confused."

On the home front, Jack Echols was gone, and Pam Echols had reunited with Joe Hutchison after little or no contact over the past seven years.

Damien admitted to using drugs, including speed "over a month ago."

Glori Shettles' "attorney work project" for the Echols murder defense quoted the Charter records: "Information from detention center — Damien and girlfriend to have baby and sacrifice it. Damien denies this. Says he is involved in witchcraft, not satanism. Alleged to have chased younger child with ax and attempted to set house on fire. Damien denies this. States girlfriend's family wants him in trouble. Admits to violence … Suspensions and disruptive at school. Has heart problems, asthma, bronchitis and migraine headaches."

Damien underwent a psychological evaluation.

He also explained his name change. He repeatedly has denied that "Damien" was inspired by the diabolical child in the 1970s hit movie "The Omen," instead claiming he took the name from a Catholic priest who worked with lepers. The name was shared by one of the main characters in "The Exorcist." A character in that book explains, "It was the name of a priest who devoted his life to taking care of lepers on the island of Molokai. He finally caught the disease himself." Among the books found in Echols' room at the time of arrest was a copy of "The Exorcist."

Echols later testified: "… I was very involved in the Catholic church, and we were going over the different names of the saints. St. Michael's was where I went to church at. And we heard about this guy from the Hawaiian Islands, Father Damian, that took care of lepers until he finally caught the disease himself and died." Echols said that was the reason he chose the name and it had "nothing whatsoever" to do with "horror movies, Satanism, cultism, anything of that nature."

Progress notes at Charter indicated depression and bizarre behavior but that Echols was making progress.

Echols was prescribed Imipramine at 50 mg on June 5, increased to 100 mg on June 12. Psychological testing by Lewis F. Bracy, PhD, on June 8 showed that Damien was depressed and did not trust others but was not psychotic.

The psychological report revealed Echols had a verbal IQ of 101, a thoroughly average score. Bracy's battery of tests found no evidence of psychosis but the possibility of a thought disorder. "The most prominent finding is that he has a rather strong depression process going on and has real difficulty making contact with people." The diagnosis: depressive disorder and bipolar disorder.

The assessment of his art produced in the psychological testing could be applied to his current projects: "Damien's drawings reflect rather impoverished, empty appearing figures. They lack enrichment, color, life and emotion. They appear to be primarily depressive, helpless and in poor contact with reality. … He appears to be a very concretistic person who is arrested in his imaginative function. He would be expected to see things in a rather simplistic, overly constrictive manner."

Based on a Minnesota Multiphasic Personality Disorder (MMPI) exam, Echols was given preliminary diagnoses of schizophrenia, disorganized type (paranoid and catalytic types also possible) and bipolar disorder, manic.

It was noted: "These persons spend much time in personal fantasy and daydreaming, often with themes of sex or power."

Dr. Woods' affidavit from 2001 described Echols' first trip to Charter in detail, much of which was echoed in trial records:

"Mr. Echols was provisionally diagnosed with Major Depressive Disorder, single episode and

medicated with Imipramine, an anti depressant drug. ...
The staff psychiatrist who conducted a mental status
exam upon admission described the 17-year old as
'cooperative and polite' with 'an odd stare,' and flat
affect. ... The psychiatrist had 'major concerns that this
young man was exhibiting disturbed, bizarre and
unusual thinking.'"

Dr. Woods continued: "Mr. Echols' delusional
thinking was evident throughout his hospitalization. He
explained that he had 'no feelings about suicide'
because he thought he could 'be reincarnated.' He
indicated to others he thought he possessed special
powers. A social worker reported Mr. Echols 'appeared
to be sniffing the air around him as if he were
responding to an external stimulus.' He smiled
inappropriately and 'cut his eyes in one direction or the
other, as if he were hearing or thinking of something
before he spoke.' The social worker concluded he was
'responding to an outside stimulation' and 'may have
been experiencing auditory hallucinations.' Visual
hallucinations also may have been present. Mr. Echols
said he thought the furniture in the psychiatric unit
'was causing blurred vision.'

"Mr. Echols exhibited 'a bizarre and unusual
manner' of adjustment to the psychiatric unit that was
also reflected in his 'bizarre and unusual thinking
pattern.' He was 'preoccupied with witchcraft' but
consistently denied any involvement with satanic
worship. He was observed 'meditating in his room in a

bizarre and unusual fashion,' 'wrote some very unusual poems,' and remained on 'the peripheral of the group throughout' his hospitalization. He made unusual and bizarre sounds 'with his mouth that sound[ed] like a cat purr.' He had 'trouble making eye contact' and was 'quite paranoid.' He told staff there were 'survelance [sic] cameras behind his mirror and under his desk' and cautioned other adolescent patients that staff were 'constantly watching them.' The hospital staff observed him sitting and 'rocking methodically back and forth,' daydreaming, and staring into space. When interrupted, he appeared startled. He wanted to 'calm down' and said he 'was feeling "jittery" internally.' Hospital staff noted he showed 'no aggressive behavior' in the hospital.

"Mr. Echols' behavior demonstrated 'a pervasively depressed mood throughout most of his hospitalization.' He withdrew from family and friends, had a 'sad facial expression' and 'spent long intervals alone.' He lost interest in eating, had difficulty going to sleep, and planned ways to commit suicide. He repeatedly thought about wrapping the sheet from his bed around his neck and 'trying to hang' himself.

"Mr. Echols' psychiatric care was interrupted by his parents who removed him from the hospital June 25, 1992, and moved to Oregon. His discharge diagnosis was major depression, single episode, dysthymia and psychotic disorder not otherwise specified. He was instructed to continue taking 150 mg. of Imipramine daily."

Driver was designated to monitor Echols. "Family indicated that they were moving to Denver, Colorado. Prosecuting Attorney was in agreement with Damien leaving State. Not felt to be a danger to himself or to others per doctor."

Echols apparently did not leave the state until weeks later as he was referred again to Charter on July 24 for a screening. That intake report noted: "Dresses all in black — T-shirt slacks & shoes, Wears small gold cross stud" earring in left ear. "Nails are clean & filed to points." Damien presented himself as intelligent, generally honest, calm and coherent, expressing mostly his desire to be with his girlfriend. He denied feeling angry or depressed, "but appears depressed — voices apathy — blunt affect."

Damien admitted to the suicide pact: "It can go either way now." "Question of satanic involvement" still lingered.

"Extremely dysfunctional family however."

With Damien diagnosed with major depression, dysthymia and a conduct disorder, the preliminary treatment plan was for a resumption of hospitalization due to suicidal thoughts and a range of other issues. But the case was closed because of his parents' plans to move.

Woods described Damien's patterns of continued drug use: "Mr. Echols's mental illness did not improve after his hospitalization. He remained in excruciating emotional pain, betrayed by his mind and body. The world was an unsafe, unpredictable maze from which he desperately looked for an escape. He finally found relief in his own form of medication. He instinctively turned to inhalants and began 'huffing' gasoline; he thought he 'invented it.' Later he tried marijuana a few times before his arrest, but it did not become a habit. He also used the medication prescribed for his migraine headaches — Midrin — as a means of tolerating stress and fear of attending school. ... Unable to outrun his terror, he withdrew from school in the ninth grade and tried to insulate himself from the external pressures that contributed to his mental illness."

Moving to Oregon would provide no relief.

"SUICIDAL, THREATENING FAMILY, DRUG USE, PARENTAL CONCERN RE: SATANISM"

When Pam Echols and Joe Hutchison picked up Damien from Charter Hospital in Little Rock, Hutchison had not seen his son for years and didn't recognize him at first. "I was in there and turned around to Pam and ask her, 'Is this him?' You know, I was very confused," Hutchison later testified.

In a Sept. 3, 2000, declaration, Hutchison talked about Damien's time in Oregon: "I told Pam I thought we should move to Oregon and we packed up the family and took off. Michael was having a really hard time then. He had just broken up with his girlfriend Deanna and cried the entire ride up there. He was just really, really sad. When we got to Oregon, I set Michael up with a job at one of the BP gas stations that I ran. I thought Michael would do a really good job working there and I was hoping that everything was going to work out."

Echols spent several weeks with the family in Aloha, Ore., just outside Portland, before matters came to a head.

As with many accounts from the Echols family, what actually happened remained unclear. Several incidents led up to Echols being readmitted to a mental hospital.

One medical professional subsequently downplayed Echols' display of symptoms, suggesting he was using alleged mental problems as a means of manipulation.

Indeed, Echols often has seemed able to turn the "crazy" off at will, using his "mental illness" as just another attention-seeking schtick, like dressing up in black, or as an excuse for bad behavior.

Echols was either dangerously mentally ill or doing a very good imitation of a violent maniac in Portland.

As Joe Hutchison later testified, "The altercations that was brought up is two different instances made in one. The first instance was this is —- I was afraid —- he had a habit of shutting his bedroom door and had been by himself and him being depressed as he was, and the medicine that he was taking, I was worried. I went into the bedroom. I opened the bedroom door. He did have a knife. It wasn't an altercation at that time. I asked him one time, 'Hand me the knife.' There was never an argument, never a cross word. He handed me the knife."

Hutchison testified Echols had been talking about committing suicide.

As for the second incident, Hutchison testified, "I am the one who took him to the hospital. ... And the altercation that broke out he did tell me he would eat me alive but it was after I made the first move …. He had —- he didn't want to be there but he went there because I took him there for them to do observation on him and at that time and the way that I am, sometimes my temper gets the best of me. If you say just one little word, you know, it would kind of tee me off. But it was my mistake. I'm the one who cause him to tell me that … He stood up in there and he said somebody is going to get slapped. Well, if anybody had to be slapped, I'd rather it had been me. I stood in front of him and called him names that I shouldn't have called him. I called him a punk and I'm one —- I can't —- it's my fault. He did tell me he would eat me alive but it was after that. I'm the one who caused it."

Hutchison testified that Echols remained in the hospital about two weeks, though records showed he was there just two days. "From there he was homesick for his girlfriend and everything. I had to make arrangements for her to come out there." Echols supposedly had been distraught over his breakup with Deanna but had also reconnected with Domini. Given the time frame, it's not clear how Hutchison would have been able to make arrangements for Domini "to come out there."

"And he was set on coming back into Arkansas, back to West Memphis, and at that time Jack was living down there."

Hutchison testified, "And finally I said, 'Well, you know if that's what he wants, then, you know, let him have him.' And that's when he come back to live with

Jack. … I put him in a cab. I had a cab take him to the bus station."

According to records at St. Vincent's Hospital and Medical Center in Portland, Echols was admitted on on Sept. 2, 1992. Echols was described as "suicidal, threatening family, drug use, parental concern re: satanism."

According to notes from a social worker: "Dad says that Damien has been sniffing gasoline & that at dinner table tonight he talks about drinking a bottle of bleach & that it would be over soon. Pt told sister that he would be killing himself in the next 3 days … has made threats to kill himself by hanging w/bed sheet or tying socks together & told grandmother today that he would cut his mother's throat."

Hutchison later struggled to explain the incident to WMPD Chief Inspector Gary Gitchell and John Fogleman: "There had been some kind of misunderstanding one night, you know, I was in on it. And I was, somebody had uh, a matter of fact, his grandmother had told me, well, you know, he's got a knife. He's got a knife out of the drawer … I went looking for it. I did not find one, you know. And after all this was over with, and there was a big scuffle, um, there wasn't a scuffle. We didn't fight. No, did not fight. Uh, he was took to the hospital. …"

Gitchell asked: "Well why did you have to take him to the hospital?"

Hutchison answered: "Because when I accused him of this, he got a little upset, and again, I haven't been around this boy in 8 years, and uh, so I told him that it's best, let's go to the hospital. Now, you know we all know you know, uh, I'm not going to say he's not right, you know …"

Understandably Fogleman and Gitchell did not know. Fogleman followed up with the obvious, unanswered question: "What, I mean, what happened that it got so bad, he needed to go to the hospital?"

Hutchison's answer did little to clarify: "Nothing, really. I called the police out there. I will tell you what I did do. And you know, he was making his money, and he was spending his money any way that he wanted to spend it. And I didn't care cause I was the one paying the bills … uh, he had bought 3 knives … To me it was just knives in a holster that you wear on your sock. … And, you know, naturally you accuse somebody of something, and he was … he's always been afraid, I won't say more afraid of the police, okay, so, he put the knives on. And he was in his bedroom. … This was at, at, you know, the start. … So, I go into the bedroom, and I sit down on the bed, you know, and I don't picture Damien as hurting other people. … His self maybe. I would believe that more than I would him hurting other people."

Fogleman: "Have you ever seen him try to hurt himself?"

The typically self-contradicting answer: "No, nothing, you know. I've seen him beat his head on a wall. … Other than that, that's all I've seen. …

"So, I went in there, and I sat on his bed, and I just said, what you gonna do with them? He say, they're not gonna take me Daddy. They're not going to take me. I said who is gonna take you? The police. You called the police. I said son, I said I ain't trying to have you locked up. So, I talked to him for a minute there, and I asked him, I said I want to ask you, I said I want the knives. … Without any resistance whatsoever, I got 'em. … But, the only altercation, like I said, that we had, was at the hospital. …"

Fogleman continued to try to get an answer to the obvious question: "Uh huh. Why did you call the police?"

Hutchison said: " … I knew he had a case of mental imbalance. … I didn't want to take any chances. If he exploded then, I wanted to call the police."

Hutchison denied he had concerns about his own safety: "You know, Damien wouldn't hurt me." Hutchison explained again that Damien had offered no resistance and there was no knife taken from the drawer as the grandmother alleged.

Fogleman tried again: "Alright, well then why did you call the police?"

Hutchison: "Because, you know. He does have a temper. You know, he got a little … It was nothing that I couldn't handle, but I didn't want to take any chances.

… He did not do anything. The only thing he said y'all don't believe nothing I say. You take her word over mine … You want to look at it, he was right … You know that he had bought knives, and I took them. At that point, after, before I took the knives, I did call the police. Before they got there, I went in and I took the knives myself."

In his 2000 declaration, Hutchison offered more details: "While we were in Oregon, Michael got really sad, like the time when we were driving up there. Finally he locked himself up in a closet and had taken something in there with him. His grandmom told me that Michael had a knife. I thought that this was really serious and Pam and I made him go to a hospital in Oregon. Michael got really upset with me and I lost my temper and, after I yelled at him, he got even more upset. I feel bad about this whole incident because what started it was when Michael's grandmother told me he had a knife. I do not know why I immediately trusted her, instead of checking it out, but what I found out later was that Michael may have just had a spoon with him."

Unlike in 1993, Hutchison said Echols had locked himself in a closet and he made no mention in 2000 of the three knives in a holster taken from Echols.

Damien testified that he had several knives on him during this incident, including a boot knife.

Pam Hutchison told investigators the trip to the Oregon hospital "was basically for the same thing" as the trip to Charter in June. "He was real depressed. He cried a lot. He didn't want to come out of his room."

In a declaration on Sept. 4, 2000, she said: "Damien was very unhappy in Oregon. I was very worried about him because he would lock himself in a closet and talk about suicide. I finally decided that he had to be placed in a hospital so that he did not do anything to himself. He did not want to be admitted but I insisted because I was very concerned for him. Damien got really upset with me and Joe for putting him in there but I did not feel that I had a choice. After he was released from the hospital, we sent him back to West Memphis on a bus. I wanted him to stay in Oregon with us but I thought that if he really wanted to go back to Arkansas then instead of arguing with him to stay, I should just let him go." Pam made no mention of calling the police, the knives in a holster, the threats to cut her throat, the threats against Joe; in her version, she was the one who made the decision to have Damien hospitalized; she also claimed she wanted him to stay on with them while everyone else said the family wanted him out of the home.

"… He never threatened to kill me. … I'm sure about that. … In my opinion, sometimes he lets his temper get the best of him. And he said, well, I'm fixing to hit somebody, and I stopped him. I said no, you're not."

Echols later admitted he had been drinking that night. At the hospital, he threatened to eat his father alive with a spoon.

The emergency room report said: "The patient ... comes in by way of parents, concerned about his mental health. Apparently, the police were called to the house and after discussing with him his options, he comes voluntarily to St. Vincent Hospital for evaluation. Apparently, the parents were concerned about his thoughts of harming himself and possibly others."

Echols told the staff he had been feeling homesick after talking with friends in Arkansas and that his parents misinterpreted his tears as a sign of depression.

The ER report said: "He apparently has had thoughts of harming himself by his report to the family members, even though he denies that. He has talked about drinking lye or some type of bleach that would kill himself, he has also apparently told his sister that he won't be around much longer. The parents are concerned that he is also into satanism or devil worship. He apparently has a number of items that relates to this. ...

"... He has apparently cut on his hands in the past ...

"The patient denies suicidal or homicidal ideation at this time, however, in talking with the family members, they state that he made it quite clear that he had thoughts of harming other people, i.e. was going to cut the throat of his mother and has said so in the past and also apparently made some verbal threats to his father here at St. Vincent Hospital even."

In the ER, Echols was calm, responsive and lucid, denying hallucinations or delusions. He denied most of the information given by his father, including that he wanted to harm himself or kill others. He denied involvement in Satanism or cult activities.

Echols told the doctors: "Everything is fine at home."

The admission diagnosis? "Suicidal/homicidal ideation. Adjustment disorder."

Echols was placed on suicide watch. He apparently slept well that night.

Notes for his treatment plan: "When seen … this morning, he continues to deny suicidal ideation, but acknowledges that he has been depressed for quite some time related to ongoing legal and family problems and most recently missing his friends in Arkansas." He was described as quietly compliant.

Later, "Parents visited …. visit did not go well. he was tearful & would not discuss visit other than to say 'I no longer have parents.'" Staffers heard Echols beg his parents to take him home. He showed little interest in complying with treatment after that.

Echols filled out a questionnaire of several pages for the patient database.

The first question: "what do you do when you feel uptight or angry?" His answer: "nothing"

He gave the same answer to "who do you turn to when things are not going well?"

On personal qualities, he checked off "cold and not very emotional," "a leader," "bored easily" and "quick tempered." He said it was "easy to make friends."

What he liked best about himself was his "determination" and that he wanted to change "nothing" about himself.

To questions about school, he scrawled, "I don't go to school."

He felt different from other kids: "Other kids are shallow...."

"Neither" parent was the easiest to get along with.

He said his parents had no alcohol, drug or legal troubles and said there were no problems that his family argued about routinely. Asked "how do your parents discipline you?" he answered, "They don't."

He described his mother as having a number of positive traits, adding that she was "stupid." He said his father was "stupid" and bad-tempered. He said his parents had a "warm and affectionate" relationship in which they "enjoy activities together" and "argue often."

He said he was allergic to "everything" and had used "marijuana, speed, acid, gas."

A perceptive progress report noted: "He appears to be an individual who passively provokes anxiety in others including actual petty criminal behavior, now mixed up with suicidal threats entitling him to psychiatric treatment. …

"He is not suicidal, but rather is in disagreement about living in Oregon and on this basis pines for Arkansas and his friends."

A discerning mental health professional had noted manipulative aspects of Damien's "mental health problem."

Echols told doctors: "I'm the only person who stands up to my Dad. My Mom just cries but I don't stand for him pushing me around. I won't want anything to do with either one of them. I just want to be on my own from here on out. I'm not suicidal, that's their way of trying to keep me in a hospital & away from my friends & girlfriend."

Dr. Stanley Sturges in his Physician's Progress Report on Sept. 3 bolstered Echols' self-assessment: "…. There is no evidence of a thought disorder. He is not depressed and his efforts at self harm may be seen more as a manipulation to escape responsibility for a wide variety of behaviors which have got him into difficulty with the law. … Plans for emancipation and return to Arkansas seem reasonable to me."

A social services report noted that Pam and Joe showed up for the assessment, explaining they had recently reconciled after many years apart. "Father maintains that he barely knows his son. …

"Pam stated that she has had difficulty with Damien since he was 10 years old. He always tended to be an angry child and somewhat difficult to manage, particularly through his adolescent years. She is convinced that he is into activities, such as witchcraft and is very concerned about the quality of friends that he developed while living in Arkansas. For this reason, she felt that coming to Oregon would be a new beginning for him. ...

"Because of the circumstances that precipitated the hospitalization and Damien's threats, particularly toward his father and of course his mother, both parents do not feel that they wish to have him return to their home. They are frightened of him and what he can do, not only to them but to other children that reside in the home."

Damien described plans to go back to Arkansas, including making proper arrangements with his probation officer. Jerry Driver had continued to track Echols' whereabouts.

An attending nurse noted that Echols' mother would be picking him up after his discharge and making arrangements for travel back to Arkansas by bus. "Damien has been quiet, but cooperative. He shows little or no investment in treatment."

Echols said he was engaged to Domini, who was still living in Illinois with her father though Dian Teer, her mother, lived in Arkansas. According to Dian, Echols returned from Oregon "to be with Domini."

Domini apparently left the home of her father about this time, because she could not get along with him, to live with her mom. She reunited with Echols soon after his return. They had been boyfriend and girlfriend prior to Echols' final breakup with Deanna.

Meanwhile, Echols' parents planned to remarry.

The discharge summary on Sept. 4 stated Echols had been admitted to the emergency room "because of alleged threats to his parents." It cited "considerable conflict between him and his parents through the years in which he has threatened to harm himself in the context of a host of legal difficulties." Echols offered contradicting claims about his use of street drugs, at one point saying he had not used in four months, at another saying he had not used in a year and in the discharge summary, "He admits ... using street drugs within the past year."

In Glori Shettles' notes about the hospital stay prepared for his defense, she wrote: "Diagnosis — Suicidal ideation, Depression. Admitted through Emergency Room — parents called police — alleged threat to parents. Parents stated he has been abusing drugs. Threatening suicide.

"Information was consistent from Michael. Parents expressed concern that he was involved in satanism. Felt family members were in danger. Michael stirred chocolate with a spoon. Grandmother accused him of having knife, but wasn't true. ...

"Probation officer made phone arrangements for Michael to return to Arkansas and check in with probation office upon arrival. Michael missed friends and parents thought it was best he return without them. Hospital agreed. Did not feel he was suicidal or a threat."

In still another description, Dr. George W. Woods said in his 2000 affidavit: "Mr. Echols' mental illness worsened after his release from Charter Hospital. Within two weeks of moving to Oregon with his family he was voluntarily admitted to St. Vincent Hospital in Portland after his parents observed extremely bizarre behavior that was unresponsive to outside influence. Mr. Echols and his family have different memories of the events surrounding Mr. Echols' admission to St. Vincent's Hospital. ...

"As had staff members at Charter Hospital, those at St. Vincent consistently described Mr. Echols as quiet, compliant and noncombative. The admitting diagnoses were psychotic disorder, not otherwise specified, dysthymia, depression, and suicidal ideation. However, within 48 hours these diagnoses were changed to adjustment disorder of adolescence with disturbance of conduct, whereupon Mr. Echols was discharged to his parents with instructions to continue taking daily doses of 150 mg. of Imipramine. Despite two psychiatric hospitalizations within six weeks, Mr. Echols' parents allowed the disturbed 17-year-old to return to Arkansas."

"BROKE PROBATION ... SUCKING THE BLOOD ... FRIGHTENING TO COMMUNITY MEMBERS"

A homesick Damien Echols returned to Arkansas.

Echols later told friends that a Satanic priestess followed him from Oregon, with the intent of either murdering him or pulling him back into the cult.

In his 2001 affidavit, Dr. George Woods described Echols' circumstances:

"Mr. Echols was completely incapable of caring for himself when he returned to Arkansas. He had no money and his mental illness and lack of skills and experience prevented him from working. He lived on the streets and even stayed at the home of his abusive step-father, Andy Echols, a few nights. Within days he was identified by his probation officer who believed that Mr. Echols should be treated in a long-term residential psychiatric facility. The probation officer had Mr. Echols detained in the juvenile facility for violating his parole by returning to Arkansas. Staff and residents at the facility describe Mr. Echols as losing touch with reality. His behavior deteriorated drastically. One resident reported he observed Mr. Echols '. . . sucking the blood off the scratch that . . .' another inmate '. . . had on his arm.' Mr. Echols was placed in isolation and on suicide watch. The juvenile facility quickly obtained a court order and sent Mr. Echols to Charter Hospital for the purpose of 'determining the appropriate method of referral to a residential treatment facility.' Mr. Echols was readmitted to Charter Hospital in Little Rock, Arkansas, on September 14, 1992, where he remained until his discharge on Sept. 22, 1992."

While driving Echols to Little Rock, Jerry Driver asked about the blood sucking incident. At first Echols told him it was a joke "and then he said that's how you receive power. He said I've been doing this for years ... and generally it's with willing people and he had some scars on his arms and he said he and his girlfriends and other people .... had done that, and that's how they receive power."

Echols' aunt, Patricia Liggett, was given temporary custody so she could admit him to the hospital.

Charter notes from Sept 15 indicated: "Damien's behavior has become frightening to community members in Jonesboro …. Had been suspected of witchcraft and/or devil worship prior to incident involving arrest. … Again, thought to be suicidal, but not afraid to die, per Damien. Knows he can 'come back.'"

Dr. Woods reported: "The provisional diagnoses at Charter Hospital were psychotic disorder, not otherwise specified, and dysthymia. Staff members immediately noticed Mr. Echols' bizarre behavior, including his 'growling' and making other strange sounds. …

"Mr. Echols also had noticeable problems with attention and concentration. He 'stared off into space' and daydreamed in class and group activities. When staff members attempted to bring him back to the task at hand he 'would then act like he was very startled, as if "jolted" back into the group process.'

"Other serious problems noted by staff members include '[a]lteration in thought processes evidenced by delusional thinking and inappropriate social behavior.' His appearance was 'disheveled' and 'unkempt,' and he had consistently 'poor' eye contact. He dressed 'in entirely black clothing, frequently [wrote] poems and [drew] pictures of symbols' which one staff member erroneously interpreted as 'closely associated with devil worship.' Mr. Echols stated that he was 'a witch' not a vampire or devil worshiper.

"Mr. Echols' mood disturbances continued unabated. His affect 'was extremely flat,' he showed 'absolutely no observable evidence of emotion' and he appeared anxious and uncomfortable. Charter Hospital records reflect that Mr. Echols had almost no insight into the nature or severity of his problems.

"Like all other staff who observed Mr. Echols over time, he was described by Charter mental health staff as 'calm,' 'compliant and cooperative." A psychiatrist noted that even though Mr. Echols had 'difficulty with reality testing' he related in 'a very quiet and withdrawn fashion' and 'was actually quite pleasant.'

" Mr. Echols was discharged … with diagnoses of psychotic disorder not otherwise specified, and dysthymia. He was released to the care of his step father, Andy Echols, who lived in West Memphis, Arkansas. Mr. Echols was instructed to continue taking his daily dose of 150 mg. of Imipramine and report to the local mental health center for follow-up care."

The discharge notes included this pledge: "Will not participate in occult beliefs."

The discharge summary added that Echols had stabilized and no longer needed to be in acute care. "Damien 'contracted' that he will not attempt to harm anyone after time of discharge." Mental health professionals considered him a potential risk to others, though his behavior no longer presented immediate problems.

"I KNOW I'M GOING TO INFLUENCE THE WORLD -- PEOPLE WILL REMEMBER ME"

After three trips to mental hospitals, Damien Echols again was wandering Crittenden County. He turned 18 in December 1992, still relying on his much-loathed adopted father for food and lodging.

Echols was referred back to counseling on Jan. 5, 1993.

His medication remained imipramine, the Tofranil brand.

While imipramine effectively treats depression and is sometimes prescribed for panic attacks or anxiety, the medication can cause or worsen emotional problems, such as mood, anxiety, panic attacks, insomnia, impulse control, irritability, hostility, aggression, restlessness, hyperactivity, depression and self-abuse or suicidal ideation.

The intake sheet for Jan. 5 prepared by social worker Sherry Dockins contained extensive notes, noting hospitalizations and that he was on probation.

Dockins wrote: "'Damien reports his problems began at age 8 when his parents divorced and Pam remarried. 'They were constantly fighting — tried to ignore it but finally started fighting back.' …. 3 months ago mother divorced him and remarried father. Sister, mother and father currently live in Portland, Oregon. He has little contact with family. Currently lives with stepfather Jack Echols. 'It's the only way I could live here in Ark.' They do not get along but rarely see each other. Damien is planning to move in with girlfriend and her mother when they get an apartment. Reports he and Domini (gf) have been together for long time?"

Six months before, Damien was threatening to kill himself if he could not be with Deanna; now he and Domini were a longtime item.

The report continued: "Damien wants to live in West Memphis because of his friends and 'it's where I belong.'"

Despite his subsequent disparagement of West Memphis, Damien regarded the town as home; he was willing to risk constant scrutiny to live there.

A further irony was his association with Jack Echols, listed as his parent/guardian on the intake papers, who was allowing Damien to live in his home.

Concerning Damien's state of mind: "Describes self as feeling 'neutral/nothing' most of the time. Denies current suicidal/homicidal ideation."

Dockins wrote: "Reports history of self mutilation — cutting self with knives/razors. Last time was 3 months ago. Denies symptoms of depression. 'I usually don't smile.' He quit school in ninth grade (this year) because he was not allowed to return to his previous school (Marion High School). Reports sleeping most of the day and then goes to Domini's house."

Damien was holding down a part-time job with a roofing company. "Relates that he tends to 'trance out' when by himself. He has done this since the 5th grade."

Dockins wrote: "Reports history of alcohol/drug usage — coke, acid, pot, alcohol. Denies current usage …. Reports being harassed by local authorities as 'they think I'm a Satanic leader.' He admits being caught with Satanic items and with handwritten books about witchcraft. Denies cult involvement. Is interested in witchcraft for past 8 years. He has tried to steal energy from someone else and influence other minds with witchcraft. States he was able to do these things."

Echols believed he could "steal energy" from other people; he later testified that children contained more energy for magickal purposes than adults.

Dockins also reported: "Describes self as 'pretty much hate the human race.' Related that he feels people are in two classes — Sheep & Wolves (wolves eat the sheep).

"Dressed in black, wearing silver cross and earring studs. Intense eye contact."

The "wolf in sheep's clothing" is an ancient concept, cited in the Bible: "Beware of false prophets, who come to you in the clothing of sheep, but inwardly they are ravening wolves."

Psychopaths often describe themselves in wolfish terms. For instance, the sadistic psychopath Eric Harris, one of the two Columbine High killers, described fantasies of ripping apart "weak little freshmen" like a wolf. Charles Manson referred to his followers as "slaves" or "sheep" and recorded a record album "Way of the Wolf."

The theme is also popular in occult circles. The Church of Satan Web site, for example, maintains extensive Web pages devoted to "Lycanthropy: A Handbook of Werewolfism," describing occult exercises for transforming the practitioner into a man-wolf, "a person who has regressed, by force of will and desire, to a feral or wolflike state."

At turns grandiose and pitiable, Damien's wildly fluctuating self-regard was on display throughout the records.

Dr. Woods described Echols' return to East Arkansas Mental Health Center:

"There is an abundance of evidence to show that Mr. Echols' serious mental illness required long term hospitalization and more aggressive treatment than he received in prior hospitalizations. In January of 1993 Mr. Echols again sought help at East Arkansas Mental Health Center where mental health professionals described Mr. Echols' elaborate history of delusions, psychosis, and severe problems with mood and memory. His delusions often were grandiose. ... His mood oscillated between euphoria and severe depression. ... During his worst periods Mr. Echols became psychotic. He felt a 'spirit [was] living within him' that was 'put inside him last year.' The spirit 'decided to become part of him' and was the spirit of a woman who was killed by her husband. ... Though profoundly mentally ill, Mr. Echols has always responded well to the structure of a therapeutic setting. He has never been a management problem and staff members uniformly describe him as passive, compliant and likable."

The quiet and likable version of Echols would consistently show up for TV interviews from Death Row.

In January 1993, Damien told EAMHC staff that his problems began at age 9 with Jack Echols. Damien reported self-mutilation and said he had a history of abusing drugs, though he, as usual, denied current usage.

On Jan. 13, Dockins reported: "Damien reports one of his biggest problems that he would like to work on is being able to forgive others. When questioned about this he reports that he is very angry with family members and with other people that have 'let him down.' He wants to be normal but feels that he has never been normal. ... He discussed issues of power and control. He states that he could make things happen. He believes very much in magic. ... Damien's affect and mood was flat. He did not smile during the session."

For the Jan. 19 session: "Damien relates that he is trying to find a way to live on his own. He does not get along with step-father. Reveals a history of abuse as he talked of how he was treated as a child. Denies that this has influenced him stating 'I just put it all inside.' Relates that when this happens the only solution is to 'hurt someone.' Damien reports being told at the hospital that he could be another 'Charles Manson or Ted Bundy.' When questioned on his feelings he states 'I know I'm going to influence the world — people will remember me.'"

Gloria Shettles' "attorney work product" for Echols' trial correctly reported that the session produced "very damaging notes."

After Echols' Jan. 20 session, Dr. David Erby wrote: " ... three psychiatric hospitalizations. Each has been associated with anger, thoughts of killing other and thoughts of killing himself. He's not currently suicidal or homicidal. He's been on Tofranil 15 mg. at bedtime for about a year. He's found that that's been somewhat helpful. He's not experiencing any side effects with it, he's tried to stop it and had some discontinuation symptoms." Again, a mental health professional noted that Echols had suicidal or homicidal impulses. Though his medication was "somewhat helpful," Echols was trying to discontinue Tofranil.

Shettles noted that yet another session, on Jan. 25, was "very damaging." The "Individual Progress Notes" by Dockins stated: "Focus of today's session is spent talking with Damien about his feelings of death. He brought with him to session a poem that he had written during the past week. The theme of this poem centered around death and power. Damien explained that he obtains his power by drinking the blood of others. He typically drinks the blood of a sexual partner or of a ruling partner. This is achieved by biting or cutting. He states 'it makes me feel like a God.' Damien describes drinking blood as giving him more power and strength. He remembers doing this as far back as age 10. He does not remember where he learned to do this.

"Damien believes that there is no God. He feels that society believes there is a God because society is weak. He wants very much to be all powerful. He wants very much to be in total control. We discussed how some of this is related to his experiences as a child. He acknowledges that some of this is related to his childhood abuse trauma but he feels that it is who he is now.

"Damien related that a spirit is now living with him. The spirit was put inside him last year. He indicates that a month ago the spirit decided to become part of him and he to become part of the spirit. This is reportedly a spirit of a woman who was killed by her husband. When questioned how he feels with this spirit or what the difference is, Damien is able to relate that he feels stronger and more powerful with this spirit. He has not seen this spirit but does hear the spirit. In addition, he also reports conversations with demons and other spirits. This is achieved through rituals. He denies that he is satanic, seeing himself more as being involved in demonology.

"It becomes more noticeable today in talking with Damien that he has many things from childhood that he simply does not remember. This is believed to be a dissociative response to trauma issues. Damien is agreeable to beginning to talk about what he experienced as a child that he remembers. He is also agreed to continue to discuss his issues with power and control as related to his practice of rituals. ...

"... Damien's affect and mood today continued to be bland though there was more emotion when talking about drinking blood."

Echols livened up therapy with discussions about gaining power through drinking blood via cuts and biting.

They also could have livened up sessions by having Echols explain the difference between Satanism and invoking demons through ritual. In theory, a powerful magician would be able to control demons or other disembodied entities through proper ritual and use of the will and use them for his own purposes. Those purposes wouldn't inherently be evil in intent, and many dabblers in bygone eras regarded themselves as Christian and by no means Satanists. Orthodox Christianity, however, has regarded trafficking with demons as evil.

Echols was almost certainly manipulating the mental health staff to qualify for Social Security Disability but his delusions, such as being inhabited by the spirit of a murdered woman, were consistent with statements made when disability wasn't at issue.

Among other noted killers who claimed to have been possessed by some sort of spirit was Ted Bundy, who claimed a "malignant entity" had taken over his consciousness. Other serial killers, such as John Wayne Gacy and "Hillside Strangler" Kenneth Bianci, blamed murderous alter egos for their crimes.

On Feb. 5, Dockins reported that Echols "dressed completely in black and is noted to have cut on his R arm and hand.

"... Damien relates that he cut his arm & hand as a way of permanently marking his skin. The name Domini is cut into his arm. Session continues focused on Damien's self concept and image. Relates feeling very angry yesterday when running into previous girlfriend. 'I controlled it — I can do anything.'

"... Affect and mood —- flat."

Despite his supposed devotion to Domini, Echols still felt the effect of his breakup with Deanna deeply.

On Feb. 11, Echols reported that he was being harassed by local authorities — "They think I'm a satanic leader." He admitted to having Satanic items but denied involvement in Satanism. He said he had been interested in witchcraft for eight years. His diagnosis was changed to depressive disorder. He was prescribed Tofranil in a 150 mg dose.

Dr. Woods described Echols' continued mental health problems and dealings with the Social Security Administration:

"Though he was only 18 years old, mental health professionals at East Arkansas Regional Mental Health Center concurred that Mr. Echols' severe and enduring mental illness made him unable to function without substantial assistance from mental health and other agencies. Staff members assisted Mr. Echols in applying for Social Security Disability Benefits through the Social Security Administration (SSA). After conducting an independent evaluation, the SSA determined that Mr. Echols was 100% disabled and was awarded full disability benefits on the basis of his mental illness. The finding by the Social Security Administration of a mental disability is a significant factor that any competent mental health professional would consider in an objective determination of Mr. Echols' mental state. At the time of arrest and trial, Mr. Echols was still considered severely mentally impaired by the SSA and was receiving full SSA disability benefits."

Echols applied for disability in early February 1993.

In his application, he claimed he was too mentally ill to work, describing his symptoms as "Mentally Disturbed." On another form, he wrote: "I am a sociopath."

Asked "What is your disabling condition?" Echols answered: "I am going through treatment at the

Mental Health Center and have been in several mental hospitals." He explained how his condition kept him from working: "Because when I try to take a time out my employers don't like it. Violent, medicine makes me sleepy, vomit & headaches."

Asked for the reasons for his hospitalizations, on the two stays at Charter, he wrote: "Homicidal, suicidal, manic depression, schizophrenia, sociopathic"; for the hospital in Portland: "Homicidal, suicidal, manic depression, schizophrenia, drug abuse, alcohol abuse, sociopathic."

Echols was deemed totally disabled and began receiving full Social Security Disability payments.

The rest of the Hutchisons moved back to West Memphis around March. Joe and Pam had remarried in February. Joe, 37, had been married at least four times. Pamela, 35, had been married three times.

Echols began sleeping most nights at the Teer trailer, while occasionally staying at his parents' trailer at Broadway Trailer Park. The Hutchisons didn't have a bedroom for him, so he had to "share" a room with his sister. Someone often slept on the sofa.

For his last appointment, on May 5, 1993, he did not talk to Dockins but to Dr. Erby. His imipramine prescription was refilled. The handwritten Physician's Progress Report was difficult to read, having been the only photocopy in 509 pages misaligned on the copier. Fragments are visible:

"… at time he is impulsive … things that may be harmful to … He has impulses to do strange … armful things to himself. He … es suicidal thoughts. He says … kes to read, swim, playing pool, … likes to work with animals, snakes, .. zards & spiders. He is bothered if .. nakes are killed even if they are poison. .. e has not seriously considered a vocation. … he mother seems dedicated, but insecure. He seems to enjoy people being concerned about him."

Later that day, he oversaw the gruesome murders of Michael Moore, Christopher Byers and Stevie Branch.

"I'LL GET YOU, I'M GONNA KILL YOU. YOU'RE GONNA DIE."

Echols was notorious around West Memphis and Marion for walking everywhere, often in a black trenchcoat. He testified that he walked around areas of West Memphis frequently, and was in the area where his victims lived "probably an average of two or three times a week" over "probably at least two years."

Echols would testify that he often had to walk through the neighborhood of the victims to make his way between Lakeshore and his parents' trailer on South Broadway.

Despite having lived in the neighboring Mayfair Apartments, he testified that he had never been in Robin Hood. That claim had no credibility, since the pipe over 10 Mile Bayou offered one of the few pedestrian shortcuts between the Echols/Hutchison trailer and Lakeshore — a route Echols testified he regularly used.

When he moved to Salem, Mass., briefly, after his release from prison, the Lurker in Black quickly gained notoriety as the convicted child killer who was constantly walking around the town. Now apparently based in New York City's Harlem, he is just one amid a vast throng of black-clad hipsters trudging around the big city.

Echols has described this lifelong pattern of obsessive walking in interviews. He told Justin M. Norton of www.metalsucks.net that "When I first got out, I would go and walk and walk for hours, just looking in shop windows and feeling the wind and the rain. I would be exhausted to the core and want to go lay down, but as soon as I'd get back in, I would want to go right back out."

Echols in his 2012 memoir, "Life After Death," described, without a lot of specifics, his dissatisfaction in his relationship in 1993 with Domini and how he sought out his old girlfriend:

"I thought of Deanna frequently, wondering what had happened. Through sheer coincidence (I use that word but don't believe there's any such thing) I found out Deanna's family had started attending church. The possibility of seeing her again plagued me. I couldn't get it out of my head. I constantly wondered what would happen, how she would react, what I would see in her eyes, and I had a plethora of questions I needed answers to. I couldn't understand how she had so thoroughly and completely severed our connection. I needed an explanation ...

"Sunday morning found me preparing to descend into the hellish realm of fundamentalism. ... I knew I didn't belong there but I had to do it or I would get no rest. ....

"Scanning the rows, I saw Deanna sitting in the dead center of the room with her family. ... I couldn't breathe. She looked at me ... and looked away. I didn't even see a flicker of recognition. What did that mean?

"I had been expecting something — anything — but her eyes passed over me as if I were not even there. ...

"When it was over, I walked outside and stood on the sidewalk. I was trying to figure out what this meant as I watched her family get in their car and drive away."

Echols did not give a date for this attempted encounter, but the stalking incident closed a chapter in the book that then opened on news of the May 5 killings.

After his arrest, reports surfaced about Echols, or someone closely resembling him, observing children in an obsessive and secretive manner.

Some reports predated the killings. On March 1, 1993, Jennifer Ball, who lived at Lakeshore, reported to police that she had been threatened by Michael "Beshears" (Beshires), 14, on several occasions. On March 1, she said, someone had threatened to kill her by shouting through her window. The police report described "Suspect B," who was not Beshires, as a slim white male about 18 dressed in a black T-shirt, black jeans and a black jacket. Jennifer saw him make the threats, then enter the fenced-in backyard.

On June 10, she gave police this hand-written statement:

"The first contact I had with Damien Echols was when he was at my window (March 1 93). I had heard about him and heard that he was into devil worshipping. So was Michael & Amanda Lancaster. Well Michael had told her that he was going to blow my house up & stay away from me. Well she didn't believe him & we continued to be friends. Well he called her one day & told her to watch out that he had Mark Beshires & Damien Echols watching us all this was happening in March. About March 1 I was on three-way with Amanda Lancaster & Jack Held. It was storming that day. I kept on hearing something but I thought that it was just the rain. Well I was in the kitchen. I was looking out the window & somebody jumped in front of it shouting 'you bitch, I'll get you, I'm gonna kill you. You're gonna die' I started screaming & hollering I didn't know what to do. I dropped down in the corner of the kitchen. Amanda was hollering at me 'Jennifer what is wrong. Jennifer what is going on.' I told her that someone was at my window & it looked like Damien. She told me stay where I was & she was going to call me right back. I hung up the phone. I looked out the window to see if he (Damien) was still there. He was. He just glared at me & said 'you're dead bitch' & ran off. I was so scared. Amanda called me back & I was crying. I told her what Damien had said. She just sat their like, 'oh my god.' About 5 minutes later she said 'Jennifer, Jennifer was Damien wearing pure black & a black trench coat?' I said 'Yes. Why?' she said 'He's walking down the street and eyeing my house.' She got really scared & started crying & then her house alarm went off. She was screaming & crying. I didn't know what to do. I had a feeling that Damien was going to be watching us & after us. When my mom, Teresa Woodson, got home from work that day, I told her what happened. She didn't know what to do. She waited for my stepdad, Don Woodson, to get home. She told him about it. He really didn't know what to do either. Me & my mom were talking & she asked me to describe Damien. I told her that he had black hair. & these eyes that looked black. He was dressed in a black shirt, black jeans & a black trench coat. She asked me if he was tall. I told her yes. She said she remembers seeing him in Wal-Mart. This was about 10 minutes after he had done passed by Amanda's house & came up to mine. She decided to call the police. Officer Reese came to our house. She asked me to describe Damien. I did she (Officer Reese) asked me if I was sure it was Damien. I told her no. I was scared that if Damien found out I told, he would definitely kill me. So the person at my window was left blank. Well about a month ago I was in Kroger. I had left my mother to go get something. While I was looking I noticed that somebody kept passing by & looking at me. When I looked up, I discovered that it was Damien. I just ran off. I didn't tell my mom because I didn't want her to worry so I let it slide by. About 3 weekends ago I went skating with Amanda Lancaster. We were having a good ol time until Damien walked in. I looked at Amanda & pointed. She just said oh my god. I told her I was going to go call my mom. She told me to just ignore him. (She had told Amy Allison when the 3 boys first got murdered that Damien & some boy named Jason had murdered them. Amy just ignored her.) Well me & Amanda were walking around the skating rink. We decided to sit down & get something to drink. We were about 2 tables over from Damien, Jason Baldwin & his girlfriend Heather. I don't know her last name. Well we were all singing & having a good time. I noticed that Damien kept on staring at me. I just ignored it or at least I tried to. I looked up & noticed that him & Jason were whispering to each other & Pointing at me. Damien whispered something to Jason & Jason looked over at me & said I don't know. Then Jason whispered something to Damien & Damien looked at me. He looked me up & down & said Yep. Then Damien started saying something & Jason kept on saying 'No man. No' Well, we finally left that table & went walking around. We went to the back of the skating rink. I noticed that Damien had followed us. Not w/his body w/his eyes. It was really starting to freak me out! My best friend Shannon Sanders was up there. She noticed that I had been acting paranoyed. She kept on asking me what was wrong. I told her I was just tired. (Finally on Sunday I told her what was the matter). I had lost Amanda & was trying to find her. I went to the bathroom to see if she had walked in there. When I came out Damien was standing there against the wall. I bumped into him. I didn't realize who it was until I looked up. When I looked into his eyes its like I

froze. I just stood there. Its like something clicked & I
came back to reality & I ran off. His eyes followed me
all the way to the back. I didn't really say anything to
Amanda because I didn't want to get her scared. We
stayed at the back for about 10 minutes & decided to go
back up to the front. Well some girl, I can't remember
her name I really didn't know her, asked me to go buy
her some candy & a coke. When I went to give it to her,
I noticed she was at Damien's table. I just ran over there
handed it to her & walked off. I could feel his eyes
following me. Well I later found out that he was asking
some people who I was. Some girl that I don't know
told him I was Jennifer Ball. He sat there for a minute &
then said 'Jennifer Ball, Jennifer Ball, I know her, I really
really know her' & had this evil look on his face. Then
he started asking around what Amanda's phone
number was & where she lived. No one would tell him.
While we were walking out of the blue Amanda started
saying shut up shut up. I looked at her & asked her
what was wrong. She said that she could hear Damien
in her mind saying 'Bitch you're gonna die, you know to
much.' (Last year Amanda had P.E. w/Damien. She said
he would sit there & enter her mind. It really freaked
her out.) Well it was finally time for us to leave & I was
glad. Damien watched us as we went out the building.
Ever since then it feels like someone is watching me.
Friday after everyone had found out who murdered the
little boys I got a phone call. I answered the phone &
someone asked who this was. I said Jennifer They said

well you & your friend Amanda were the next to die by Damien. & Hung up. I was really freaked. I didn't say anything to Amanda about the phone call. I had heard that Damien was going to kill 2 more girls his girlfriend & Jason Baldwin's girlfriend. Well Jason's girlfriend is a girl named Heather whom is Amanda Lancaster's cousin. I don't know her last name. Amanda kept on saying Friday I know those two girls were me & you I knew they were. I just told her not to jump to conclusions - even though after the phone call I was certain it was us. After Amanda read that statement in the Commercial Appeal she kept on saying, 'I have a feeling our picture is in that briefcase. I have the weirdest feeling.' I just wish somebody would find out. Then yesterday some woman that had come swimming w/my aunt told my mom that she heard Damien was going to sacrafice 2 virgins next. I told my mom about the mysterious phone call. She asked me how come I hadn't told her. I told her I thought it was a prank, but now I'm really not for sure. It's just really scary. Know I feel like every where I go I'm being followed. I haven't had any phone calls since Friday."

That was just one example of Echols' curious practice of getting his kicks by intimidating the impressionable.

Her friend, Amanda Lancaster, gave police this handwritten statement on June 10, beginning with information passed on to her by Jason Baldwin's girlfriend:

"Heather Clite had told me that Damean had been asking me question's about me, about where I live & my phone number.

"Jennifer Harrison had said that she thought Damean had done it cause he new way to much, and he went around Horseshoe the same day the murders had happened, and had dog intestents around his neck.

"At the skating rink, he watched me and stuff. He would follow me around, he would like just watch me.

"He would really scare me, and someone had told me that I was next, me and Jennifer Ball were next.

"I was on the phone with Jennifer Ball when Damean apparently was at her window."

Police notes from her interview stated that she thought Echols had a camera, that she felt people in a cult were watching her and that she felt that Echols knew too much about the murders.

Jennifer Ball's mother, Teresa Woodson, gave a handwritten statement to police on June 10:

"On March of 93 When I came home from work my daughter told me that Damin Echols was at our window in the back yard yelling he was going to kill her. When her stepfather came home from work I talked to him & we called the police. Officer Reese came and took our statement. Jennifer was also told that when her stepfather & Mom went to Calif. she better kiss me goodby for good because she would never see me again. She would come home from school and be terrified that something was going to happen to her.

And friends would tell her that Amanda & her were going to be killed & sacerficed. The day he was in the back yard on my way home from work I saw Damin walking down Balfour. Amanda & Jennifer went to the skating ring May of 93 and Damin was there he followed Jennifer and Amanda to the Restroom & would just watch them. And Friday June 5 we had a phone call that Jennifer was told you & Amanda will be the next to die. A boy that lives two doors down would tell Jennifer I will have Damin to kill you Because he Damin is a member of a cult. And Jennifer would come home they are going to kill me and she was always afraid that people were watching her. She would get werd phone calls all hours of the night."

Also on June 10, Karen Beshires McAteer told police that, about two months before, her daughter, Jessica Bryant, 11, and a friend, Heather Smith, had been waiting outside to go to church at about 10 a.m. on a Sunday. The girls came into the house and told her that a man was taking their picture. McAteer gave a handwritten statement on June 11:

"On a Sunday morning approximately 2 to 3 weeks before the triple murder occurred my daughter & a friend were outside playing in my front yard at 515 Belvedere. They came into the house & said there was a man watching them from a bush one house away. I immediately went to the door & when I opened it he got up from a squatting position & started to run toward Balfour Rd. I called my husband & he & I immediately started looking for the man. We looked all over the neighborhood & the Bayou behind Balfour. He just disappeared & we could not see him. The guy behind the bush was Damion Echols. I saw him clearly & there is no doubt. I was told later that at that time he was staying with a family on Balfour. My daughter said the guy had something in his hand. My daughter believed that he was taking pictures of her & her friend at that time."

She said Echols was wearing a long black trench coat.

Jessica Bryant told police: "It was a Sunday and we were just, we were just running around talking to each other and this boy just came up walking down the street and he was dressed in all black and so we were just playing and we looked over there and we saw him. He was behind the bush, and so we went, and so we weren't playing any attention to him we didn't think anything was going to happen, so we continued playing and he was still there so went over and hid behind the car for a few minutes and we thought he won't come out, so he will go away and leave us alone. And we went back and he was still there and so he was looking out of the corner of his eye at us. And so we didn't know what to do, so we went inside and told my mama and he started running off and then we don't know what happened to him. ...

"He had sort of long hair, and dressed in all black and he real black long over coat on, with some black shoes on. And he had something on his face, I didn't get that close to him. He was pretty good in front of me and he had something on his hair I don't know what it was but, it was something weird in his hair. It looked like rabbits feet. ...

"He was just looking out of the corner of his eyes and with his hands like this against him. He was like digging in his pockets, he had his hands in his pocket, but I don't know what he was doing. ...

"It looked like black stuff on his face, I don't know what it was. Its just black stuff on his face ...

"He was squatting down behind the bush. ...

"He was doing something in his pockets. ...

"He was like getting something out of his pockets, or putting something back in."

On May 18, 1993, before the arrests, Laura Maxwell, who had dated Echols, gave a handwritten statement to police in which she described Echols' bizarre personality, including his propensity to issue death threats, stalking and his hatred of small children.

"Dated Damien Summer of 1991. ... After we stopped dating my best friend Ashley Smith told me about Damien talking to her ... He told he used to be a knight in his past life that killed all these people and he has written some books on witchcraft. He told me that he liked to get raw steak meat and suck the blood out. This one boy told me one time Jason Baldwin busted his nose & blood was all over the ground so Damien got down on the ground & started licking the blood up. He used to say that if he was out walking or something & he got thirsty that he would just like to take a baseball ball bat & knock somebody out & take a bite out of their neck & drink their blood. I'm not sure if he ever did this, that's just what he told me. He never liked my brother ... he told my friend he was going to kill him ... he had it all planned out what was going to happen. And he told my friend & I that if we told Donnie about this that he would kill us too, if that's what he had to do. And if our parents found out & they tried to get involved that he would just kill them too. He told my friend that he used to watch my house overnight & he knew everything that happened in my house every night. He also told one of his friends that one night while I was asleep he snuck in my house & came in my room & did all this stuff to me. I'm not sure if any of thats true though. He used to always talk about how much he hated little kids & he used to always say this saying about cutting all of your fingers & toes off one by one. We still talked alot after we broke up but when school started he started going out with this other girl Deanna Holcomb. And when she broke up with him he went to her house & kept saying he was going to kill her if she didn't go back out with him. …

“Garrett told Jason Frazier that Damien & Jason (Baldwin) always have their devil-worshiping meetings in that park & those little kids were riding over there & they saw something they were supposed to of seen so

Damien killed them. Garrett said he heard this from Jason Baldwin who was supposed to of been there."

Garrett Schwarting was a mutual friend of Maxwell, Baldwin and Echols. Jason Frazier was a 16-year-old acquaintance of Schwarting's. Both Schwarting and Frazier were questioned by police —- with confusing results —- about Schwarting's statements to Frazier that Echols and Baldwin had killed the boys.

On June 14, 1993, Barbara Deatteart of Lakeshore told police that two white youths had tried to steal her dog in March. She identified them as Baldwin and Echols from newspaper photos. She had seen an old Pontiac drive by her home, stopping several times, so she asked the two boys inside what they wanted, and they drove off. When they returned, a blond youth got out, looked around and tried to get his hand and arm over the fence to grab her dog's chain. She ran out and yelled at them. They took off again.

On Oct. 5, 1993, Mark Byers, adoptive father of Christopher Byers, gave this statement to police:

"Sometime between end of February 1993 & 1st half of March of 1993. My wife Melissa & myself went to grocery store at Flash Market on Ingram around 4:00. We were gone about 15 to 20 minutes.

"When we returned home Christopher was inside. When we came in he started telling us about a man taking his picture. We asked what did he look like Chris said he was wearing a black coat & black pants & shoes black & had sort of long black hair. He said the man was driving a green car. Chris was playing under car port when man drove up. He said that he ran out into the yard because the man scared him and we asked what happened and Chris said he just took my picture then got in his car and left."

Melissa Byers, mother of Chris, repeated the information in a statement Oct. 5 and testified to the same set of facts in the Misskelley trial.

In his confessions, Jessie Misskelley Jr. described how a photo of his three victims was passed around at Satanic cult meetings led by Echols.

Investigators never found the photo or the briefcase in which it was kept along with weapons and drugs.

In the Misskelley trial, because they had access to Misskelley's confessions mentioning the photo, the prosecution argued that the stalking indicated premeditated murder.

The description of the photo, along with other evidence such as blue candle wax found on the shirt of Stevie Branch, added credence to the theory that not only were the the time and setting part of an occult scheme but the victims were hand-picked.

"WHEN I GO GET ANGRY IT IS USUALLY NOT A PRETTY SITE."

Though Damien Echols routinely and wrongly has been described as "innocent" or even "exonerated," Jason Baldwin in many ways has been more effective with his assertions of innocence than the weird and off-putting Echols.

The perpetually smiling Baldwin projects a whimsical and slightly goofy image for one supposedly mistreated by the justice system. In many ways unchanged from the skinny little murder defendant who looked as if he should still be drawing race cars and airplanes at the back of a classroom, Baldwin continues to speak without self-consciousness of his simple beliefs in justice, truth and loving your mom.

While perpetual poser Echols scowls and sulks in his frequent media portraits, Baldwin today seems positively blithe.

Crime novelist Charles Willeford's description of a heartless young criminal as a "blithe psychopath" sums up many a man lacking a conscience, eager to rob, rape, cheat or kill with never a doubt, qualm or worry.

For those who consider Baldwin's actions on May 5, 1993, "out of character," consider that his very best, his inseparable friend was a violent, mentally ill dabbler in the occult who went to great lengths to project an image of foreboding evil.

In a hearing in 2009, Samuel Joseph Dwyer, a neighbor and playmate of the Baldwin brothers at Lakeshore in 1993, described how Jason began to adopt Echols' manner of dress and distinctive way of speaking after they began hanging out together. Even so, Dwyer carefully characterized Baldwin as someone who was not a follower, but as one who kept his own counsel.

Jason, like the disturbed Echols and the thuggish Misskelley, already had had several brushes with the law prior to his arrest for murder. Also in counterpoint to his reputation as a mild-mannered animal lover with an artistic soul were several incidents of violent acting-out.

There were troubling incidents. On June 5, 1987, the Baldwin/Grinnell clan was living in a rundown section of rural Shelby County when someone set fire to a bedroom with a lighter. Setting fires is one of the earliest and surest signs of budding criminal psychopathology.

Exactly six years later, on June 5, 1993, in the first shock of the arrests, Jason's paternal grandmother, Jessie Mae Baldwin of Sheridan, Ark., expressed doubts about his innocence to the Commercial Appeal. She said, "I thought in my own mind when those boys were killed that my grandson is sorta superstitious about that devil stuff. He was always catching lizards and snakes, something was going on in that child's mind."

Years later, Baldwin testified he first was placed on probation when he was 11. As juvenile records are closed and Baldwin has been stingy with details, the facts surrounding this encounter with the law are not clear.

In a letter to girlfriend Heather Cliett written from lockup, Baldwin wrote: "I have never been in jail before, except for once and I was only there for one hour that was nothing." Most 16-year-olds would count a trip to jail as a life-defining moment, but for Baldwin getting into trouble was "nothing" and going to jail really didn't count as going to jail. His thinking lacked proportion and betrayed a pervading sense of unfairness, hence his complaint that "they keep me locked up in my cell for 24 hours a day. while the other prisoners get to get out of their cells all day long to play games, eat steaks, and all kinds of stuff." He made it sound as if he was not allowed to go to summer camp.

At age 12, Jason, his brother Matt and several other boys broke into a building and went on a destructive spree vandalizing the antique cars stored inside. They broke out the windows on several autos and wrecked the place.

They were caught jumping on the cars by two men who called the police. The boys were charged with breaking and entering and criminal mischief.

The incident often has been framed as harmless adolescent mischief, but prosecutor John Fogleman was concerned enough to recommend that the boys be placed in reform school for two years. They were all placed on probation. Gail Grinnell was ordered to pay a fine of $450 each for her boys. Typically, family members portrayed this as an unfair burden on poor, hard-working Mom, who only paid $30 of the fine.

Jason got into trouble again, at age 15, when he shoplifted potato chips and M&Ms from the Walgreens in West Memphis. He was placed on diversion of judgment for a year with the stipulations that he stay in school and out of trouble. That court order was one reason why Baldwin did not skip school on the day of the murders or the day after.

Meanwhile, his family life was in turmoil.

Jason's mother, known today as Angela Gail Grinnell Scheidmiller, had been involuntarily committed to the East Arkansas Regional Mental Health Center in February 1992. There had been four trips to the emergency room at Crittenden Memorial Hospital in January 1992, where Mrs. Grinnell was treated for self-inflicted wounds to the neck and arms, according to "Blood of Innocents." Probate records indicated she was admitted for a period of up to 45 days because of "paranoid delusions," including "hallucinations of a male voice" and the fear that she was dying of AIDS. Records indicated she had been abusing drugs since her teens.

Around this time, dad Charles Baldwin, long absent, showed up for a visit with his two sons. According to "Dark Spell," the boys so enjoyed their visit that they told their mother they would consider living with their dad for a while. This reportedly prompted a suicide attempt via cutting her wrists. Jason called 911 and his mother survived. This may have been the incident that prompted Jason to write in a school assignment in April 1993: "Once my mother tried to commit suicide and I know how I felt when that happened it was pretty devastating since I was the one who found her and called 911 and kept her alive, but …. my mother is well and happy now and so am I." Despite Jason's sunny spin, his mother was neither well nor happy.

In another writing assignment, Jason described a violent fight with his younger brother: "I am usually a calm person, and can take mostly of anything. But sometimes I get angry, when I do get angry it is usually not a pretty site. One time I had to babysit my two little brothers, one is 8, and the other is 13. I let Matt, the 13 year old go outside to play, or whatever he want, and I let Terry the 8 year old have some friends over. That was a mistake. I let them go in my room and play Super Nintendo, while I watched T.V. in the living room, I thought I had everything under control, but I was wrong. Those kids got to fighting over the game, and tore everything up in my room, it was a mess. I couldn't believe it. I made them clean everything up and leave. Then Matt got home griping as usual, and started aggravating me. He would run up and hit me and say 'You can't hit me back, I'll tell mom' so I said tell mom boy, cause you're fixing to get it. I ran over there and grabbed him into a choke hold and held him there until his face turned bright red and then let him go. I said mess with me again and it'll be worse, so he pick up a broom and tried to hit me with it I grabbed the handle pulled it a little ways then pushed and it knocked him down, he didn't do nothing else but say 'I'm still telling' I said 'so' and he did and I got grounded for nothing."

Several key points: Jason tended to bottle up his anger until it exploded; Jason was deeply resentful over having to babysit his brothers and be "the man of the house"; there was a family pattern of violence with Matt not hesitating to attack with a broom after being choked by Jason until his face turned red; Jason was used to handling defiant younger children; Jason often felt he was not treated fairly, a complaint that has cropped up again and again in his public statements; Jason expressed no remorse about overreacting to Matt's provocation — he "got grounded for nothing" except choking and knocking down his little brother.

A typical psychopath is "usually a calm person" but when a psychopath does get angry, "it is usually not a pretty site." Psychopaths are prone to retaliating over petty grievances that they view as affronts to their grandiose vision of themselves. They never take responsibility for anything unless there is a significant tradeoff in benefit to them. Their view of their own role in their misdeeds is grossly disproportional. Psychopaths experience few qualms about their ruthless disregard for others, and they are highly adept at hiding their lack of normal, healthy humanity behind a superficially pleasing mask.

His family life did nothing but exacerbate Jason's antisocial tendencies.

Their mother's marriage to stepfather Terry Ray Grinnell had long been shaky, marked by violent arguments over Terry's habitual drinking on weekends. Jason often had to call the police, according to "Dark Spell," and his stepfather often slapped not only their mother but Jason and Matt.

A few weeks before he killed three little boys, Jason took a baseball bat to his stepfather during an argument and drove him from their home, according to Leveritt's book. "I took that little bat, and … I hit Terry with it. He hit the ground. I opened the door and said 'leave,'" Baldwin told Leveritt in "Dark Spell."

Soon, a new boyfriend named 'Dink' Dent would move in briefly. Dent had a lengthy rap sheet that included multiple counts of larceny, burglary and auto theft.

The relationship did not last long. Grinnell and Dent broke up the very evening that Jason murdered three little boys. Dent gave key evidence that Jason was not home at the time of the murders.

By the time of the arrests, the stepfather was back on the scene. When officers raided their home on June 3, 1993, Gail angrily accused Terry of turning in their son for the reward money.

Asked by John Fogleman in September why she had reacted with that accusation, she said, "I don't know why I would have said that."

In a case full of inarticulate, lying, confused and confusing witnesses, Gail Grinnell was notably incoherent.

Among her problematic actions was her appearance along with "Mr. Grinnell" at the Hobbs home on the evening of May 6, after the bodies were found, according to a June 9 statement from Pam Hobbs, who had recognized Gail at the preliminary hearing. Terry Hobbs also identified her as a visitor that evening. There was no explanation as to why the Grinnells would have been at the Hobbs home, as they were not friends with the family, or why "Mr. Grinnell" would have accompanied her, as she had just broken up with Dent (who had not yet moved out) and was separated from her husband.

Intended as a sympathetic account of Jason's life, Mara Leveritt's "Dark Spell" inadvertently paints a fascinating portrait of the young killer as a savvy street-smart wheeler-dealer with an eye for the main chance.

The book is rich in such ridiculous fictions as that Baldwin was an often-disappointed believer in old-fashioned truth, justice and virtue who, despite little evident interest in religion, had learned just what Jesus would do and then did that. Because his mama raised him right.

Baldwin quickly adapted to the brutal Arkansas prison system, figured out how to work his way into the trust of prison officials and worked every angle to always put himself in the most positive light. He has portrayed his agreement to get out of prison as a selfless act, saying he agreed to the Alford plea because he feared Damien would die from unspecified causes while incarcerated.

Baldwin's years in prison stand in stark contrast to Echols' story, which endlessly whined about how Damien was sick, lonely and scared. Baldwin quickly learned that he could show no weakness. He survived near-daily assaults for years until he established a solid reputation among inmates and guards as a tough little fighter and standup guy.

Psychopaths often do relatively well in prison, an environment based on who can most effectively wield power. They often do well in other aggressive environments where they quickly size up opportunities. They charm and manipulate others when they can and ruthlessly crush those resistant to their act.

As a convicted child killer facing uncommonly hostile guards and fellow prisoners, Baldwin never backed down, taking "power" as his byword; from the first to the last, he was a cool customer, far from the "Paradise Lost" image of a powerless child.

Baldwin had a knack for duping others into believing he was trustworthy; he projected an air of innocence, easily fooling old ladies in the trailer park into thinking he was a nice boy. His air of assumed humility and guise of open-hearted sincerity pervade "Dark Spell."

But who is Jason Baldwin?

Those who believe he was guilty see a child killer who claimed he was innocent when his sentence was being handed down. They see no shame, no regret, no doubt, no remorse.

Even those who believe him innocent will acknowledge that he was Damien's best friend.

What does that tell us about Baldwin?

Contrary to cliches about "nice guy" killers, longtime criminologist Stanton Samenow in "The Myth of the Out of Character Crime" states that any crimes that a person commits are in keeping with his character. He notes that "what a person presents publicly often differs radically from what he is like privately."

Echols was grandiose to an extreme. Echols lied with abandon, seeming to spin untruths just because he could. Lying offered an illusion of control. Echols enjoyed playing cat and mouse with the police, though his arrogance and blatant falsehoods were key to his conviction.

On the surface, Baldwin could not have been more different. From the first, he said little to authorities and what he said did not implicate him in any way. His whole defense was built around saying nothing, hoping he would be exonerated because of the paucity of evidence. Like Echols, Baldwin had an arrogant illusion of control but he had a better grasp of reality.

Echols talked and talked, as did Misskelley, but Baldwin was tightlipped from the start, with one possible, crucial exception.

Another detainee in juvenile lockup, Michael Carson, testified in gruesome detail about Baldwin's confession to him while they were in custody. The testimony offered a foundation for finding Baldwin guilty.

The key to his guilt was his association with Echols. Read "Dark Spell" and then wonder how a straight-arrow regular fellow who professes adherence to Christian values and the American way could have been blood brothers with a blood-drinking boogeyman. Baldwin acknowledged that Echols and his mother were mentally ill; what he didn't explain was his easy camaraderie with a boy viewed by everyone as weird and sinister.

Echols has the childish view that the only thing worth doing is the thing that is forbidden, and he flaunts his contempt for mainstream values. By feigning his embrace of those values, Baldwin has made his own lie, behind a perpetual smile. The two are mirror opposites, one as sick as the other.

"… The normal are inclined to visualize the psychopath as he is in mind, which is about as far from the truth as one could well get … These monsters of real life usually looked and behaved in a more normal manner then their actually normal brothers and sisters, they presented a more convincing picture of virtue than virtue presented of itself — as the wax rosebud or the plastic peach seems more perfect to the eye, more what the mind thought a rosebud or a peach should be, than the imperfect original from which it had been modeled." — William March, "The Bad Seed," as quoted in "Without Conscience: The Disturbing World of the Psychopaths Among Us" by Robert D. Hare, PhD.

Hare explained in his preface: "Psychopaths are social predators who charm, manipulate, and ruthlessly plow their way through life, leaving a broad trail of broken hearts, shattered expectations, and empty wallets. Completely lacking in conscience and in feelings for others, they selfishly take what they want and do as they please, violating social norms and expectations without the slightest sense of guilt or regret."

There you have the link between Echols and Baldwin: two of a kind.

Echols had psychological problems, such as depression and anxiety, since early childhood. In addition he displayed many qualities of the classic sociopath, or psychopath, a label he embraced.

According to Hare, "These often charming — but always deadly — individuals have a clinical name: psychopaths. Their hallmark is a stunning lack of conscience; their game is self-gratification at the other person's expense. ... The most obvious expressions of the psychopath — but by no means the only ones — involved flagrant criminal violation of society's rules. ... These pieces of the puzzle form an image of a self-centered, callous, and remorseless person profoundly lacking in empathy and the ability to form warm emotional relationships with others, a person who functions without the restraints of conscience."

That describes Echols well enough. Jason has shown a similar though more lighthearted ability to disregard the consequences of his actions.

Criminologist Stanton Samenow found that habitual lawbreakers feel that they are different from other people, that the usual rules do not apply to them and that they will continue in their evil ways unless highly motivated to change.

Samenow has explained that many parents use the excuse that their suddenly delinquent child fell in with the wrong crowd. Not so. "Criminals seek out one another for their own purposes," said Samenow in "Inside the Criminal Mind." "In radar-like fashion, they hone in on others who have similar interests. They are not enticed into crime against their will. If a basically responsible youngster makes an unwise choice and misjudges another youth who he discovers is up to no good, he will eventually extricate himself from that situation and most likely from the entire relationship."

Contrast the actions of Murray J. Farris and Baldwin. Despite a common interest in witchcraft,

Farris and his good friend Chris Littrell quickly and consistently kept Echols at arm's length; they were not drawn into crime. Similarly, Deanna Holcomb, despite deep romantic ties to Echols and their shared belief in "magick," broke cleanly from him when the full implications of his plans to ritually sacrifice their possible child became clear.

By contrast, Baldwin, with no apparent interest in witchcraft, was easily drawn into Damien's world, a world totally at odds with Baldwin's public statements.

Also contrast Baldwin's seemingly guileless lack of remorse with the criminally inclined Misskelley, who expressed shock, shame and disgust over his involvement in the killings. Misskelley, though often cruel, hardened and callous, was capable of empathy, guilt and shame, unlike his partners in crime.

Psychopaths are smooth liars who bend and break the truth in breathtaking fashion and continue to lie even when exposed. Drawing heavily upon the research of Hervey Cleckley in the classic psychiatric text "The Mask of Sanity," first published in 1941, Hare notes: "Phrases such as 'shrewdness and agility of mind,' 'talks entertainingly,' and 'exceptional charm' dot Cleckley's case histories" … as well as media presentations of Damien and Jason.

Cleckley stated: "The (psychopath) is unfamiliar with the primary fact or data of what might be called personal values and is altogether incapable of understanding such matters."

Despite this lack, psychopaths are experts at weighing circumstances for maximum self-advantage and then saying or doing whatever is necessary to fit their purposes. They are masters of manipulation.

With Baldwin, there is a pervading sense of "something's wrong here but I can't quite put my finger on it," which is how Hare describes a characteristic impression of the psychopath. As described in "Dark Spell," Baldwin's journey through some of the roughest prisons in the United States was that of a cold-blooded opportunist who seized upon the feelings of others, such as the jail workers who left illicit food for him or the series of prison officials who found him relatively cushy jobs.

Baldwin quickly sussed out the "soft touches," just part of his special knack.

Hare said of psychopaths: "To some people … they seem too slick and smooth, too obviously insincere and superficial. Astute observers often get the impression that psychopaths are play-acting, mechanically 'reading their lines.'"

Mechanically reading their lines, such as in these quotes from Baldwin in "Dark Spell": "I didn't think there was any possible way they could find us guilty when we didn't do it. Not in America. … People thought we did drugs because we looked wild, but we didn't. We didn't need them. … Jesus didn't judge people. He pretty much forgave everybody, unless they were misusing religion or being hurtful. It was all about the love. That's what Jesus uses. You've supposed to love people, to uplift people, to make people better. That's what I learned from Jesus's teaching. That's why he's the guy. He's the big radical. ... I tried to forgive them because I knew that if they knew I was innocent — if they knew the truth — they wouldn't be reacting to us that way. And knew that that was the purpose of this trial: to get to the truth of it. ... I did my best to show them that I wasn't afraid, that no matter what, we must stick together as a family, to not lose hope and to have faith in God and what is right. ... Our love would get us through this, and God would work out a miracle for us. ... I can see where they might think I'm in a cult because I wear Metallica T-shirts and stuff like that, but I'm not into nothing like that. I couldn't kill an animal or a person."

Baldwin consistently delivered this sort of hypernormal spiel with the smile of the practiced prison scammer.

Concerning Echols' highly incriminating answers to police questioning and incriminating testimony, Baldwin said: "They took what he said in innocence and twisted it on him, and they did it because he was Damien."

About a possible plea deal, he said, "I was not tempted. It was wrong. It was against everything I was brought up to believe in."

And in "Dark Spell," Baldwin described his first day in prison: "... My mantra is born: 'I am tough.' I say that out loud. ... The old man is looking at me again and smiling that dirty smile. I tell him he better get me some boxers that fit and do not play any games with me because I do not play ... He says that I do not look like a killer to him. I tell him that is what I am in here for so he better not mess with me. I wasn't lying. ... It works and he gets me some boxers that fit."

Thus did a 16-year-old kid establish his dominance over the first longtime inmate he encountered. As he said, "I never wanted to incur any disrespect or loss of respect."

Offered a romance novel, the connoisseur of horror movies and the heaviest of heavy metal offered a "by gosh" memory: "I can't read this stuff. A kid going through puberty? No. I didn't need to be reading that."

Early on, Baldwin refused a prescription of the antidepressant Zoloft from a Department of Corrections psychologist because "there wasn't anything wrong with me." He already had decided that he would rather risk being placed in general population rather than the Diagnostic Unit or the Suicide Prevention Unit. He supposedly told prison officials, "I refused to be so doped up that I cannot even think about fighting for my freedom."

Baldwin claimed he did not allow himself to experience fear over the prospect of prison life. He told Leveritt: "I'd already experienced so much in my short little life — so much bad — that I'd ceased to be afraid.

And I'd ceased to be shocked." One defining trait of psychopaths is the absence of fear.

Explaining that he deferred going to school in prison, instead earning the respect of the guards and inmates on work details, he said, "As limited as my choices were, I wasn't going to make one that would reduce my chances around here."

After being beaten unconscious, he supposedly pulled a "Cool Hand Luke" and walked out of the infirmary with an untreated fractured skull and broken collarbone after regaining consciousness.

After being robbed by a fellow inmate, Baldwin, again in "Dark Spell," said, "So being the hothead that I was, I went into the dayroom and started kicking things over, like big stacks of plastic chairs. I yelled, 'All right, you bitches, you're going to wake up!' I went over to the first rack and yelled 'This is a shakedown!' Then I went to the second rack, and lo and behold, I saw a bunch of my stuff there. I said to the guy, 'All right, you and I are going to the shower and we're going to fight.'"

Thus stood revealed the hard man hidden in the waif with the ruddy cheeks.

As for his relationship with Echols, it was reminiscent of two other devotees of the cult of the black raincoat, Dylan Klebold and Eric Harris.

The shooting spree of Klebold and Harris at Columbine High School in 1999 that left 13 dead and 20 injured was the culminating atrocity of a dynamic duo not unlike the unnatural bond of Baldwin and Echols.

As the myth of the poor, persecuted trailer park "throwaway kids" persisted and grew in the West Memphis case, the Columbine killers have been portrayed as misunderstood, picked-upon teens who lashed out in frustration at their tormenters.

In both cases, the killings were carefully planned by cold-blooded killers hoping to leave their mark upon the world.

After the murder-suicides of Klebold and Harris, the often-ignored truth appeared in their writings — Eric Harris was a grandiose psychopath carrying out his fantasies of killing for pleasure while Dylan Klebold was a depressive with cripplingly low self-esteem who often fantasized about suicide.

Harris was often described as intelligent, well-spoken and even "nice" — much like Baldwin. Harris was a cool customer able to slaughter acquaintances and classmates in a detached manner, taunting them as they begged for mercy. Similarly, Baldwin had no problem knifing, beating and drowning helpless children and then, a few hours later, dickering with a friend over music tapes.

Meanwhile, Echols was exhibiting bizarre behavior and insane thought patterns. Back in 1992 and 1993 he was consistently diagnosed with various forms of depression, much like Klebold.

Dave Cullen, in an excellent book on the Colorado case, "Columbine," explained the Klebold-Harris pairing as a dyad, "murderous pairs who feed off each other," citing such other similar pairs as Bonnie and Clyde, Leopold and Loeb and the Beltway snipers. Other well-known examples would be Fred and Rose West, the Hillside Stranglers, the Menendez brothers, Charles Starkweather and Caril Fugate, etc.

Cullen writes: "Because dyads account for only a fraction of mass murderers, little research has been conducted on them. We know that the partnerships tend to be asymmetrical. An angry, erratic depressive and a sadistic psychopath make a combustible pair. The psychopath is in control, of course, but the hotheaded sidekick can sustain his excitement leading up to the big kill."

If there ever was "an angry erratic depressive," Damien Echols would be one.

Consider the likelihood that Echols was never "the ringleader," a role he clearly relished, but merely "the hotheaded sidekick" who kept his cool-headed little buddy on track toward a long-planned, very special evening in Robin Hood Hills.

As Deanna Holcomb explained, Damien was too much of a coward to do the killing himself. In the May 5 attack, Echols exhorted Misskelley and Baldwin to beat their captives but it was Baldwin who pulled out his knife and began carving up Little Stevie and Chris.

According to the only first-hand witness who has talked, it was not clear that Echols did more than beat, truss, sexually molest and drown the boys. Baldwin viciously mutilated two of them.

As John Fogleman described the utter lack of conscience at the heart of the case: "You see inside that person, and you look inside there, and there's not a soul in there.

"I'M GOING TO KILL YOU, I'M GOING TO RIP YOUR EYES OUT"

In his book "Life After Death," Damien claimed that the only act of violence he ever committed was a fight at school. Echols minimized the attack as just a typical schoolyard confrontation. Not so.

It was serious enough that, months later, in February 1993, when the other boy in the fight, Shane Divilbiss, had gone missing, foul play was suspected because Echols had made threats on Divilbiss's life. Eventually Divilbiss turned up unharmed.

Divilbiss, 18, gave a statement to West Memphis Detective Mike Allen on June 17: "Alright, I was going to school and met Deanna Holcomb and in turn Damien Echols. Because they were boyfriend, girlfriend at the time, I began to hang around with them.

"I spoke with Damien Echols on several occasions just like friends, then emotional things began to develop between me and Deanna Holcomb. She broke up with Damien and soon went out with me, which led Damien to believe I had stolen Deanna from him. He threatened to kill Deanna, threatened to kill several of my family members, just not my uncle, but several others. He threatened to kill me and then later came up behind me in the hallway while I was at my locker.

"I knew he was back there so I just started to walk. I didn't look at him or anything. He jumped on me from behind draggin' me down to the ground and clawing at my face with his fingernails. He uh, people was saying he was trying to rip my eyes out and my the scars is what it looked like. When I got up I turn around and I was going to fight but he was being held down by several of the people that were in the hallway witnessing it so I didn't have to."

Echols routinely filed his fingernails into one and a half inch-long points.

Echols was suspended while Divilbiss was allowed back in class.

"One of the threats was against my uncle, whom had told him that if he had fought with me that my uncle would jump into (the fight)," said Divilbiss.

Echols "threatened him by say if he jumped in, he cut him to pieces and bury him in Deanna's front yard." The uncle was 16-year-old Kyle Perkins, also a student at Marion High.

"Most of (the threats) were generally just short, you know, like, I'm going to kill you or you know, like, when he had me down on the ground he said, I'm going to kill you, I'm going to rip your eyes out and all this stuff, you know, generally, you know, just short phrases. There was no long drawn out threats," said Divilbiss.

Concerning Echols, Divilbiss said, "He was a very imposing person ... when he was around ... quote friends he could silence them with just a glance. I mean, he could look at them and they would be quiet. You know, if they were saying something he disagreed with or if they were disagreeing with him, he would just have one look and they would be quiet. It seemed to me that all his friends feared him including Deanna Holcomb. The way it seemed to me that she was around him because she was afraid that if she left he would kill her. ...”

"She did tell me that he scared her, that she thought he was crazy. ... She didn't tell me anything about sacrifices or anything but she did tell me that at one time they had sexual intercourse in a room full of people watching them, she told me of, you know, that is the main thing she told me, about like a circle of people were watching them, and that is with candles around and everything like that. ....”

Sexual intercourse between ceremonial leaders is a longstanding practice in Wicca, dating back to the witch cult founder Gerald Gardner’s proclivities for flagellation, nudity and exhibitionism.

Divilbiss said Echols was highly intelligent and “he know a lot about things; he knows how to work with a person’s mind; he can manipulate (a person’s) mind to ... what he believes in.” Divilbiss described Baldwin and Holcomb as “susceptible to another person’s mind.”

Divilbiss said Holcomb “said that he proclaim himself to be the son of Satan occasionally, that he did some strange things that led her to believe he was (demonic) ... He let off the image that he was generally, people would think like he was a Satan worshiper just by looking at the time I know him. You know, because of the way he dressed .... just his general outlook. ..."

Divilbiss added that "if he were in black magic there would be bi-sexual tendencies ... because in all magic ... there are ceremonies which include bi-sexual sex magic is what it is called. It does include, you know, bisexual intercourse."

Divilbiss said Echols wore "necklaces and things like that with bones on them" and had given Deanna a golden coin and a crow's foot when they broke up. "The crow's foot was generally used in black magic, was suppose to be a hex ... the crow's foot was supposed to represent pain. Okay, I mean that he did things that represent black magic." The crow's foot often was used in death spells in witchcraft.

Divilbiss admitted he had "done a little study in that area and ... looked up quite a few things."

"I have meet a ... priest who gave me information and told me about things you know so that is one way I know things about like ceremonies. I've never been in a ceremony but I do know how ceremonies are run sometimes. I do know about the ... use of pentagram and I do know the ... white magic use of a pentagram which are exactly two different things ...

" ... there is a downward pointing pentagram but it used for warding off, for, you know, that is what it's supposed to be used for, it suppose to be used for ward that is a warding pentacle, and if it's right side up it's suppose to be invoking pentacle."

Divilbiss ended up in the news again in a November 1998 appearance by his wife on the MTV show "Sex in the '90s: It's a Group Thing." April Divilbiss, 21, said she had two husbands, Divilbiss, then 24, and Chris Littrell, then 22, and was thinking of making it a foursome because having sex with two men was tiring her out.

The appearance prompted a custody battle over her 3-year-old daughter with the child's grandparents (the father was not one of the two "husbands").

Mrs. Divilbiss told the Associated Press that this was an attempt to deny her freedom of religion, describing herself as a pagan. ``The government feels they have the right to impose their own morality on us. We practice Wicca and within our religion this is a very moral situation. It's a highly thought of way to raise children.''

The Divilbiss story was featured in Time magazine on Nov. 7, 1999, detailing their lifestyle after the child had been removed from the home and then returned.

The article about polyamory noted: "The poly community is rallying around April, Chris and Shane, whose case may provide the tale of injustice every movement needs. The case could well be the first of its kind; it's surely the first to debate explicitly the worthiness of polies as parents."

The case was also cited in "Feminist and Queer Legal Theory: Intimate Encounters, Uncomfortable

Conversations" and in a July 17, 1999, story in the Salon Web magazine.

Marc Perresquia, one of the authors of "The Blood of Innocents," and Shirley Downing, who had done extensive reporting on the "Satanic Panic" phenomenon, reported on the connection with the West Memphis 3 case in a Commercial Appeal story Jan. 15, 1999.

They wrote, "Divilbiss and Littrell, then both Crittenden County teenagers, weren't considered suspects but were among scores of youths police interviewed.

"The pair, however, was among a smaller circle of young people who dabbled in the occult and associated with Damien Echols, one of three teenagers convicted for the murders.

"Statements by Littrell and Divilbiss helped shape prosecutors' controversial contention that the slayings were ritual murders orchestrated by Echols and two followers involved in a teen 'cult.' ...

" .... They attend Summerland Grove Pagan Church, which meets in a clubhouse of a Bartlett apartment complex."

Summerland Grove Pagan Church recently still maintained a Web page, which noted the church was organized around Mayday 1994. Their bulletin board indicated a "Court Spell for West Memphis 3" posted in November 2010.

Divilbiss and Littrell did not know each other at the time of the murders but met about a year later. Neither testified, though Littrell was subpoenaed.

April Divilbiss "expressed surprise at a story she said she's never heard fully before."

The polyamorous relationship did not last. On Friday, March 23, 2012, Shane Divilbiss died in his sleep, leaving a new wife among his survivors.

"JESSIE TOOK A KNIFE OUT OF HIS POCKET AND PUT A KNIFE TO MY THROAT"

Even more so than Echols, Jessie Misskelley Jr.'s name was linked to a number of violent episodes, often aimed at younger children.

John Earl Perschke Jr., a 14-year-old eighth-grader living at Lakeshore, confirmed to Detective Bill Durham on Sept. 6, 1993, that he had been attacked by Misskelley.

Perschke said the incident in January 1992 on the railroad tracks northwest of Lakeshore was witnessed by at least five others. "We heard someone coming up ...," said Perschke's handwritten statement. "We tried to hide. ... Jason, Damien, Jessie, Buddy and four other boys were with them and so Jessie shoved me against the side .... Jessie was first talking to me and then after a while Jessie took a knife out of his pocket and put a knife to my throat and he said would you like to be dead and so he shoved the knife harder and so he put the knife up and then Jessie hit me and Buddy too and ... I couldn't tell who all was hitting me. Damien and Jason and the other boys were still on the railroad tracks and there he was yelling at me and then they all left. I walked home. I was coughing up blood." The incident was another example as well of Echols, Baldwin and Misskelley hanging out together.

A girl at that scene, Tiffany Allen, was a 13-year-old Lakeshore resident when she gave a statement on Oct. 7, 1993, about another violent attack by Misskelley: "We had gotten into an argument and he had been spreading a rumor around that he was having sexual intercourse with me to all these people and I confronted him with it and he kept saying all this stuff so I slapped him ... For a year I didn't hear anything from him and ... somebody came up to me and said that he had been looking for me and so I just didn't worry about and one day I was walking through the park and he was at the road and .... he came up to me. He started running at me and my boyfriend stepped in front of me and he hit Carl. ... He hit Carl and then he hit me and we started to walk away and he started coming after us again, so we ran ... until one of my friends' parents came and got us and took me to my house." She had a busted lip.

Ridge had a copy of the complaint dated March, 12, 1993, the day after, that gave essentially the same account.

Her mother, Gayla Allen, was present during the interview along with the child's grandmother, Vera Hill. Gayla Allen told Ridge she had gone to the Misskelley home after the incident. Jessie Jr. ran out the front door while she was knocking on the back door. When she returned later, "OK, I knock on the door. Jessie Sr. was sitting in there and he said that he just could not do anything with his son."

Tiffany said Susie Brewer, Misskelley's girlfriend, had made threats: "She just said that if I put Jessie in court or in jail or anything like that I better watch my back because they were all going to be after me, and all this stuff, and um, his cousins confronted me with it, and everything and I never ever, ever heard nothing from Jessie. It was always somebody else."

Tiffany, identified as a cult member by Misskelley, denied any direct knowledge of a Satanic cult at Lakeshore but said that if one did exist, it would be meeting at nighttime in a field behind the old sewage plant. Ridge reported: "Tiffany admitted that she was aware that a cult like group did exist in or around the trailer park but she did not know any of the members nor had she attended any of the meetings. She seemed afraid for her safety and reluctant to give any information concerning these activities because of the fears she had for her safety. Tiffany stated that she did not know Jessie to be a member of a Satanic group, however she also stated that she has been with people that she had heard were in the group and she was unaware that they were members as well."

She also described a fight she had witnessed between Jason Baldwin and John Perschke. "John hit him hard and he started bleeding and then after the fight and everything Damien bends down, put his finger in, dips into the blood and then sticks it in his mouth."

Misskelley repeatedly told a similar story, widely told around the trailer parks, that contributed to the belief that Echols was a blood-drinking Satanist.

Little Jessie had long-term problems with violent acting out.

Misskelley recently had been involved in an incident in which he threw a rock at a little girl aged about 5 or 6, hitting her in the head, prompting a call to police. He was on probation on those charges when he was arrested for the murders.

Years earlier, on May 4, 1988, when he was about 11, Misskelley had been accused of hitting another girl in the head with a rock or brick after Misskelley began beating up her abusive boyfriend; when Misskelley attacked her boyfriend, she had jumped in to defend the boyfriend.

Even earlier, Misskelley had stabbed a fourth-grade classmate in the mouth with a pencil.

His problems dated to early childhood; counseling and hospitalization had been recommended but there was never follow-through from his parents.

"Blood of Innocents" described a June 1987 report from a social worker based on a court-ordered exam.

The social worker quoted Shelbia Misskelley, his stepmother: "He gets so mad, he's capable of hurting someone." She said he had a habit of punching out windows, once requiring several stitches to his left hand. When blood was found on one of his shirts after his arrest, Misskelley said it was his own, shed after punching out soda bottles.

According to "Blood of Innocents," the social worker's report stated: "Mrs. Misskelley reported Jessie does not own up to his wrongs, that he always blames someone else. She denies Jessie becomes physical with she or her husband but will clinch his fist and take his anger out on someone else or something like breaking the window."

Shelbia Misskelley told the social worker: "I don't think he can control" his temper. "He needs some help."

Years later, a former FBI profiler, apparently oblivious to the history of violence common to all three killers, weighed in on the case.

In "Law and Disorder," John Douglas wrote, "Damien and Jason had no indicative violence in their pasts, and while Jessie was known for a hot temper, he channeled his aggressions into pursuits such as wrestling. ... Though the three were raised in a culture in which corporal punishment was common, none were abused ... In sum, I found ... nothing in the behavioral backgrounds of Damien Echols, Jason Baldwin or Jessie Misskelley to suggest that any were guilt of murder."

Douglas was hired by the defenders of the killers. Douglas did not respond to questions about the case.

"HE STATED THAT THE BOYS PROBABLY DIED OF MUTILATION, SOME GUY HAD CUT THE BODIES UP, HEARD THAT THEY WERE IN THE WATER, THEY MAY HAVE DROWNED."

In late afternoon but long before sunset, Jessie Misskelley Jr. stuck his bottle of Evan Williams whiskey into his pants and began the short walk from Highland Park to Lakeshore.

His friend Jason Baldwin had called him that week and set up a rendezvous for Wednesday.

Damien Echols was waiting with Jason along the road just outside Lakeshore. Jason had just gotten through cutting his uncle's lawn. They had beer.

Jessie and Damien had little in common. Jessie thought Damien was weird. Damien thought of Jessie as crude, simple and thuggish. Nonetheless Jason and Damien had talked Jessie into going along with their plan to go into West Memphis and beat up some boys.

The three walked about two miles to woods behind the Blue Beacon truck wash, one of many businesses along the service road where Interstate 40 and Interstate 55 joined briefly in West Memphis.

The afternoon of May 5 was warm and humid.

It was cooler in heavily wooded Robin Hood Hills. They drank and waited on their victims.

Echols was well-acquainted with the woods, having lived in the Mayfair Apartments, just across the 10 Mile Bayou.

He walked through the area frequently in his travels between his parents' trailer and Lakeshore, and had been seen exploring the woods recently.

Michael Moore, Stevie Branch and Christopher Byers lived in the lower-middle-class neighborhood of single-family homes just south of the woods. The second-graders were all just 8 years old. Chris and Michael lived across the street from each other, right next to the school.

After a typical Wednesday at Weaver Elementary School, Michael and Stevie began pedaling their bicycles around the neighborhood. Michael, proudly wearing his Cub Scout uniform, was riding a 20-inch black Renegade bicycle. Stevie was riding a green bicycle he had received two weeks earlier from his grandfather, Jackie Hicks.

Stevie's mother, Pam Hobbs, had picked up Stevie earlier at school, around 2:55, and walked home. Michael showed up at the Hobbs house and asked if Stevie could come over to play. Pam told Stevie that he needed to be home by 4:30, before she left for work. He did not return home at that time. Stevie's stepfather, Terry Hobbs, drove his wife to her shift at the Catfish Island restaurant shortly before 5 after a brief search for Stevie.

Terry looked further for Stevie after dropping Pam off at work; Pam first learned Stevie was still missing when Terry picked her up after work at 9.

Michael's mother, Dana Moore, had first seen her son around 3:10, 10 minutes after school got out. She saw Michael with Stevie occasionally throughout the afternoon. She saw all three together around 6 p.m. Chris and Stevie were sharing a ride as they tooled around East Barton and 14th Street; the Moore family lived at Barton and 14th. The Hobbs family lived several blocks south, at 1601 South McCauley. Michael's father Todd was out of town on his trucking job.

Mrs. Moore asked her daughter Dawn to tell Michael to come eat supper. He was supposed to be home "before the street light comes on," around supper time, around 6 p.m. Dawn saw Michael in the distance, but couldn't catch up. When Dawn failed to bring Michael home, Dana first searched for Michael and then stayed home, hoping he would arrive, meanwhile contacting the other families and the police

While running errands, Mark Byers had spotted his adopted son Christopher skateboarding in the street, taken him home, spanked him with a belt and ordered him to clean up the carport. Mark left on another errand about 5:30. Melissa Byers had last seen Christopher around 5:30 or a quarter to 6 under the carport. When his mother found Christopher gone, she thought he had just gone next door to play.

Mark quickly grew alarmed when he discovered his son was missing. Byers was first to call the police, soon followed by the other two families. Byers searched intensively all evening, into the early morning hours.

Neighbor Deborah O'Tinger saw the three boys walking through her yard between 5:45 and 6, pushing a bicycle.

Between 6:30 and 6:45, another neighbor, Brian Woody, saw four boys going into Robin Hood Hills. Two of the boys were pushing bicycles, another had a skateboard, and a fourth trailed behind.

Concerns grew as the sun set with no sign of the boys. Parents, relatives and friends, joined for a while by police, searched much of the night.

They would not find them.

Jessie Misskelley later described what happened:

When the boys entered the woods, Jessie and Jason hid while Damien lured them by making noises. When the children were close, the teens jumped the boys and began beating them viciously. The attack occurred on the banks of a muddy ditch, about two feet deep after recent rains. Their screams and cries for help were muffled by the embankment, woods and noisy interstate. Shirts were stuffed into the boys' mouths. The little boys did not offer much resistance; they were overwhelmed. They were like whipped puppies.

Michael tried to escape but Jessie ran him down and brought him back, quickly beating him unconscious.

The boys were stripped.

Jason pulled out a knife and gouged a huge cut into the left side of Stevie's face, as Jessie later told it; then Jason fell upon Christopher and castrated the boy, who quickly bled out.

Jason and Damien began sex play with the little boys, Misskelley told police; Damien masturbated over one and ejaculated onto the boy's pants.

The boys were bound with their own shoelaces, left wrist to left ankle, right wrist to right ankle, and thrown into the muddy ditch. Christopher had already bled to death. Stevie and Michael, mortally wounded but alive, drowned.

Jessie ran from the scene, fell ill under an interstate overpass and angrily broke his whiskey bottle against concrete. He walked the rest of the way home.

Jason later called Jessie and asked why he left so early.

Jason showed up at home around 9.

Damien was spotted walking along the service road near the crime scene in muddy clothes at about 9:30.

The search for the boys widened the next morning, with police and other agencies joining. The West Memphis Police Department held a briefing about 8 a.m. and sent out detectives. The Crittenden County Search and Rescue Unit was heavily involved.

Around 1:45 p.m., searchers discovered a small tennis shoe floating in a ditch that drained into Ten Mile

Bayou, an irrigation canal that eventually drained into the Mississippi River

Mike Allen walked along the bank where the tennis shoe had been found. He noticed that one area of the bank was cleared of leaves, while the rest was covered with leaves and sticks. He described the cleared area as "slick," but having "scuffs."

Opposite the slicked-off bank, toward the Blue Beacon and the interstate, was a high bank, a kind of bluff.

Allen awkwardly positioned himself to get the shoe and fell into the water. To his horror, he felt Michael's body rise to the surface.

Policeman John Moore saw blood in the water, but none on the bank.

Detective Bryn Ridge volunteered to methodically search the ditch by hand, soon finding the corpses of Christopher and Stevie, about 25 feet downstream.

Ridge described the search: "I got into the water north of the bodies, north of the victim that had been located, who was, we'd discovered was Michael Moore, and I proceeded to work my way through the water through the ditch, and being careful not to destroy any evidence, I was searching the bottom of the ditch as I made my way to the body. I found some clothing items." The clothes, jammed into the mud with sticks, were piled on the bank.

The bodies had been submerged for 18-19 hours. Michael's body was discovered about 1:45 p.m. About an hour after its discovery, the body was removed from the water. Ridge discovered the bodies of Stevie at 2:56 and of Christopher at 2:59.

The bodies were placed on the bank, covered in black plastic.

Coroner Kent Hale received a call at 3:20. He arrived at 3:55 and pronounced the boys dead one by one. Their bodies had been exposed to heat, insects and the elements for about an hour. Heat combined with immersion overnight in cool water made the use of body temperature to determine time of death problematic.

The bodies of Chris and Stevie were found face-down in the trash-strewn muck; Michael's body came up left-side up, and he was apparently placed lying on his right side. Ridge collected the clothes, three tennis shoes and a Cub Scout cap floating in the water. Most of the clothes were jammed into the mud; one stick, for example, had a shirt wrapped around the end stuck into the mud. There was little other physical evidence.

Police quickly set up barrier tape at the perimeter and made a new path to the site to preserve possible evidence.

The bodies were sent to the state medical examiner's office in Little Rock.

All three corpses' right hands were tied to their right feet; their left hands were tied to their left feet by black and white shoelaces.

Michael Moore's body had wounds to the neck, chest, and abdominal regions apparently caused by a serrated knife, as well as scalp abrasions that could have been caused by a stick.

Dr. Frank Peretti, a state medical examiner, reported Michael was still alive when he was placed in the water, as there was evidence of drowning. Michael had several deep gouges in the top of his skull, with more traumatic head injuries than the other two, though he did not show other extensive wounding. There were no stab wounds. There was little evidence that he struggled with his bonds. There were few defensive wounds, indicating he was quickly rendered unconscious.

Stevie's corpse was covered with wounds, including head injuries, chest injuries, genital-anal injuries, lower extremity injuries, upper extremity injuries and back injuries. The body had multiple, irregular, gouging wounds, which indicated that he was moving while being stabbed. The anus was dilated. Penile injuries indicated oral sex had been performed on him.

His wrists and ankles had abrasions where he struggled against the bindings. Injuries to his neck indicated his face had been stomped into the mud. He also had drowned.

Chris's corpse also had injuries indicating that he had been forced into oral sex. His head had scratches, abrasions and a punched-out area; one eyelid had a contusion. There was a scrape on the back of the neck. The inner thighs had diagonal cuts. The back of the skull appeared to have been struck by a stick the size of a broomstick. The skin of the penis, the scrotal sac and testes had been removed. There were cuts around the anus, apparently made by a serrated blade while he was still alive.

Unlike the other two, Christopher had defensive wounds and had bled to death before being placed in the water.

The bicycles were found nearby after investigators dragged Ten Mile Bayou for evidence.

Talk of Satanic rites held in Robin Hood Hills began to circulate immediately among the crowd gathered at the dead end of North 14th Street near the crime scene.

Residents mentioned strange groups of people hanging out in the woods, possibly cult involved. Some described occult signs and markers.

Steve Jones, the assistant juvenile probation officer who first sighted the floating tennis shoe, and his supervisor, Jerry Driver, had been concerned about occult activity and had investigated a number of reports with occult overtones. Among Jones' clients had been Baldwin and Echols' girlfriend, Domini Teer.

Jones was convinced that the murders "appeared to have overtones of a cult sacrifice," an opinion shared by WMPD Lt. James Sudbury.

On May 7, the day after the bodies were discovered, Jones and Sudbury visited the Echols home and talked to Damien in his bedroom after receiving permission from his parents, Pamela and Joe Hutchison.

Sudbury's notes gave no specifics on Echols' responses, though he noted that Echols had a "tattoo on his chest of a five pointed star or pentagram." Jones observed that tennis shoes and boots habitually worn by Echols were caked in mud but the items were not taken into evidence at that time.

Police received a tip, also on May 7, that the pastor at Lakeshore Baptist Church, Dennis Ingle, was concerned about devil worshippers at Lakeshore. On May 9, Ingle told Officer Shane Griffith that Damien Echols, who had a girlfriend named Domini Alia Teer, was "supposed to be involved in cults" and wore boots with "666" written on them.

A Lakeshore resident familiar with Echols, Narlene Hollingsworth, reported on May 9 that she had seen Echols and Teer, dressed in dirty clothes, walking in the vicinity of the murders on May 5. She also reported suspicious activity that night by L.G. Hollingsworth, a teenage relative who was friends with Echols and Teer.

Shane Griffin and Bill Durham talked to Echols, Baldwin and Teer on the afternoon of May 9 in the front yard of the Baldwin home. West Memphis police were using a behavior analysis interview guide furnished by the FBI to help identify possible suspects during initial questioning. Some of Echols' answers fit the profile of a guilty suspect. Echols, for example, shared his insight that the killer would be "happy" about his crimes, as well as a number of other responses consistent with those of a guilty suspect.

Baldwin's interview was cut short when his mother arrived and angrily refused to let her son talk to police. This also raised officers' suspicions.

On May 10, four days after the bodies were found, Ridge questioned Echols about how he thought the boys died. "He stated that the boys probably died of mutilation, some guy had cut the bodies up, heard that they were in the water, they may have drowned. He said at least one was cut up more than the others."

During Echols' trial, Ridge testified that the fact that Chris had been cut up more than the other two was not known to the public when Echols made that statement.

Echols claimed he learned about the injuries from reading newspapers, a statement easily proven false.

A front-page story in The Commercial Appeal the day after the bodies had been found had quoted an Arkansas State Police bulletin saying that a sharp instrument had been used to sexually mutilate the three boys. The West Memphis PD had deliberately let the misinformation stand, with the idea that it would help investigators weed out false confessions.

On cross-examination at trial, Echols admitted that none of the newspaper articles mentioned one victim being more mutilated than the others. He admitted he had not read such a fact in a newspaper.

Echols had not been considered a suspect prior to the May 10 interview but, according to Ridge, his answers on May 10 turned him into a suspect. Those answers and his explanations of them at trial helped convict him.

Echols said the boys had been placed in water possibly because the assailant urinated into their mouths. West Memphis police did not find out about urine in the stomachs of two of the boys until Gary Gitchell was informed of this by phone on May 16. The information was deliberately withheld from reports to minimize information leaks.

Echols gave conflicting statements about his whereabouts on May 5. He told police on May 9 that Jason, Domini and he had gone to Jason's uncle's house so Jason could mow the lawn and that Damien had called his father to pick all three of them up at 6 p.m., when all three were taken home. On May 10, Echols said he and Domini had left Jason at the uncle's house, gone to a laundromat to call his mother, who drove Domini to her mother's house and then drove Damien, his father and his sister over to visit family friends Randy and Susan Sanders from 3 to 6 p.m.; Damien said he then was at home talking on the phone with a girl living in Tennessee, Holly George, until 11 p.m. The 13-year-old would tell police that she did not talk to Echols that evening. On the stand, Echols admitted changing times on the Sanders visit to fit whatever narrative he was trying to build.

On May 10, Echols described the probable motives and reactions of the killers with such insight that investigators felt he had special knowledge about the crime. Echols' explanation of occult beliefs and ritual practices closely fit investigators' developing theories that the murders had ritualistic and perhaps occult ends. Echols then underwent a polygraph exam. Deception was indicated in his "no" answers to five of the 10 questions:

"At any time Wednesday or Wednesday night, were you in Robin Hood Hills?"

"Were you present when those boys were killed?"

"Did you kill any of those three boys?"

"Do you know who killed those three boys?"

"Do you suspect anyone of having killed those three boys?"

Despite the results, Echols at first continued to deny involvement in the killings and then ceased to deny his involvement, which Bill Durham considered "admission through absence of denial." Durham, who administered the polygraph, asked him what he was afraid of. Echols replied, "The electric chair."

Echols told officers: "I will tell you all about it if you will let me talk to my mother." After talking to his mother, he again denied involvement and agreed with Durham's assessment that he would never admit to the crime.

Police also talked that day to L.G. Hollingsworth, who named Echols as a likely suspect. Police also recorded an expanded statement from Narlene Hollingsworth concerning how she and her family had seen Echols near the crime scene.

In just the first few days of investigation, Echols had fueled suspicions in his initial interviews with police by making provocative statements and showing special knowledge and insight into the murders. Then he failed a lie detector test and further manipulated and taunted investigators. Then an eyewitness placed him near the scene of the crime.

As the investigation continued, new evidence, including a confession to a friend, continued to grow against Echols.

"DAMIEN AND JASON WERE ACTING A LITTLE STRANGE THAT NIGHT."

Several of their friends told police about the three murderers attending the all-night skate at the West Memphis skating rink the day after the bodies were found.

Baldwin's girlfriend, Heather Cliett, said she saw Baldwin that Friday at the skating rink with Damien Echols and Jessie Misskelley. She just said hi to Jason.

Jason Crosby told police that Echols and Baldwin came in together while Misskelley arrived later with Dennis Carter.

Misskelley approached Crosby and said he had heard Crosby was telling people "that Jessie had not whipped him." Misskelley had beaten up Crosby after he retrieved a bicycle stolen by Misskelley. Crosby told Misskelley that he was not looking for a fight and then went to sit with Echols and Baldwin. "Damien told him that he would watch his back for him." Crosby told police that Misskelley "likes to get people from behind."

The police report from Crosby continued: "States that Damien & Jason both had girls with them and Jason seemed to really be down in the dumps. States that he asked Jason what was wrong with him — he told him nothing — he just didn't feel good."

Crosby left around 10:30 or 11 p.m. Echols, Baldwin and Misskelley were still there.

Dino Perfetti, a close friend of Misskelley's, described a closer interaction among Baldwin, Echols and Misskelley in a hand-written statement on Jan. 12, 1994. Perfetti, 17, said, "I can remember I'd seen him at the skating rink in West Memphis, with Jason and Damien. Jessie did come in with them but when he noticed some other people he knew he left the other two so he could be with his other friends. Even though Damien and Jason were acting a little strange that night, I thought Jessie was calm and he didn't show any signs of being scared or anything but I can't be sure that he wasn't."

"IT IS OUR OPINION THE CRIME HAD TAKEN PLACE WHERE THE BODIES OF THE VICTIMS WERE RECOVERED."

Despite fake news that authorities had no evidence against the WM3, investigators found physical evidence at the scene that linked the murders to the murderers. Other physical evidence pointed to the West Memphis 3. None of the evidence was conclusive, but none offered grounds for exoneration.

Other evidence, such as inadmissible Luminol testing and a blood-spattered pendant discovered too late to be entered into evidence, didn't make it to the courtrooms for various reasons.

The killers did not leave a great number of forensic clues. Because of submersion in water, no fingerprints were found of anyone, including the victims. Similarly, clothing items tested negative for traces of blood. Virtually all of the DNA recovered and tested matched the boys. Several imprints from tennis shoes were found, but none matched the killers and may have been left by searchers or others walking through the woods.

By the time the bodies were found, a number of searchers had been over the woods, where the gumbo soil was muddy from several inches of rain earlier in the week.

The crime scene itself had been cleaned up, with the banks washed and smoothed over.

The killers had gone to great lengths to obscure the location of the bodies, which were found only when a boy's tennis shoe (a Scout cap in some versions of the story; two shoes, according to Allen's testimony in the Misskelley trial) was spotted floating in the water.

The West Memphis case has been influenced by the "CSI effect," in which the public has come to expect a higher level of forensic evidence than often exists at crime scenes. As a corollary to the effect, the value of circumstantial evidence has been discounted.

Television shows focusing on DNA and other forensics in investigations necessarily rely on such evidence to figure into the plot. Consequently the public is largely unaware that DNA from killers is found in a relatively small fraction of all murders, with latent fingerprints or any kind of biological trace found in much fewer than half of cases. Further contributing to the relative lack of forensic evidence in the West Memphis case were the cleanup at the scene, the submersion of the bodies in dirty water over an extended time and their exposure to heat and insects in the open air for about an hour, contamination by search efforts and subsequent recovery of the bodies, etc.

As a result, for example, two samples of apparent bodily tissues found in the ligatures of the shoelace bindings on Christopher and Michael were too small and degraded to yield DNA results.

"CSI: Crime Scene Investigation," the prototype of the forensics-based crime shows, premiered in October 2000, so the series and its many offshoots and imitators would have had no effect on the original juries. Even the O.J. Simpson murder case in 1994-1995, the breakthrough case for public awareness of DNA testing, followed the WM3 trials.

Even so, forensic science played a role in perceptions about the case from the beginnings.

The initial "Paradise Lost" film, while leaving out much about evidence against the killers, included the strange episode of a knife that Mark Byers gave one of the "Paradise Lost" cameramen as a gesture of goodwill. Remnants of blood were found in the knife. Testing revealed the blood could have been a match for either Byers or his stepson — an example of the ambiguous results often obtained from DNA testing. Byers had told police, "I don't have any idea how it could be on there." Byers ended up giving testimony during the defense portion of the Echols/Baldwin trial about his fold-back Kershaw knife.

Byers testified he could not say for sure that Christopher had never played with the knife. He testified he had used it to trim his toenails. He recalled cutting his thumb with the knife while trimming venison for Thanksgiving 1993. During a Jan. 26, 1994, interview, he told Chief Inspector Gitchell that he had not used the knife at all but had said he had used it to cut venison. He also told Gitchell he might have used it to trim his fingernails. He told Gitchell he did not remember cutting himself with the knife but recalled during testimony that he cut his thumb. The inconsistencies were mostly the consequences of not answering questions carefully, along with an apparent slip of the memory about cutting his thumb.

Much of the second film, produced in 2000, again focused on Byers, with a new angle in supposed bite marks, implying that Byers left the imprint of his teeth in the face of Stevie Branch. Byers had had his teeth pulled since the murders, a commonplace necessity framed as suspicious. A check of the supposed bite mark against his dental records found no match; the state's medical examiners thought the mark may have left by a belt buckle. The mark also could have been left by a blow from the end of a survival knife such as the "lake knife," a type of knife commonly carried by Echols.

Though long viewed by adamant "supporters" as the primary alternative suspect, with much of the "Devil's Knot" book casting suspicion, Byers' place as the imagined "real killer" has been supplanted by Terry Hobbs.

All that was required for the change was DNA in a single hair that might have come from Hobbs found in one of the boys' shoelaces.

Stevie's stepfather has acknowledged that the hair could be his, with the commonsense explanation that his stepson or one of the other boys could have picked up the hair during Hobbs' interactions with the kids.

That possible DNA match quickly took the heat off Byers and set 2011's "Paradise Lost 3: Purgatory" and 2012's "West of Memphis" on the scent of Hobbs.

Coupled with a dearth of ironclad DNA evidence linking Echols, Misskelley and Baldwin to the crimes, that hair has been the slender thread holding together the case against Hobbs.

On the other hand, the considerable circumstantial evidence against Echols has been ignored, with an increasing focus on the supposed lack of physical evidence.

One of the most telling pieces of evidence has been routinely discounted or explained away. In his May 10 report, Ridge noted about a statement from Echols: "Steve Jones told that testicles had been cut off and someone had urinated in mouths and the bodies had been placed in water to flush out."

Gitchell did not find out until May 16 that urine was present in the stomachs of two victims. Jones could not have revealed that information to Echols because he did not have that information; only a killer would have known about the urine.

The urine finding was one of the mostly closely held secrets in the investigation, with references to the stomach liquids deliberately obscured in written communications between Little Rock and West Memphis. Gitchell had been informed of the findings over the phone, with no mention of the urine in autopsy documentation received long after Echols' May 10 revelations.

Further clouding most of the evidence are media misrepresentations, the cult of victimhood surrounding the killers and second and third opinions disputing original investigative findings.

Experts hired by the defense even claimed the mutilations were the result of animal predators, particularly snapping turtles, though Christopher bled to death before being placed in the water. While it is possible, even likely, that small fish or turtles left superficial wounds, it is not possible that a team of highly trained snapping turtles killed Chris.

The ditch was drained immediately after the bodies were found; there were no snapping turtles.

Stains found on one of the boys' jeans were analyzed by Genetic Design. Michael DeGuglielmo, the DNA testing company's director of forensic analysis, testified they were able to recover a small amount of DNA.

DeGuglielmo said the sample was most likely sperm cells, though he could not confirm that. Misskelley in his later confessions described Echols masturbating over the body of a victim and wiping his penis on the boy's pants. There has been no other explanation offered for how sperm wound up on jeans owned by a prepubescent boy.

Some fibers retrieved from the scene were found to be microscopically similar to items taken as evidence from the Baldwin and Echols homes.

Green fibers found on a pair of blue jeans and on Michael's Cub Scout hat were microscopically similar to fibers found in a shirt from the Echols home. One polyester fiber was found on the hat. The fiber found on the pants was cotton and polyester. The shirt from the Echols home was a child's shirt. Lisa Sakevicius, a criminalist with the state crime laboratory, testified that the presence of the fibers suggested a secondary transfer, as the blue size 6 Garanimals shirt, which belonged to Echols' half-brother Tim Hutchison, was much too small for Echols. In an "O.J." style tactic, defense attorney Val Price asked Echols to attempt to put on the shirt, which he was not able to do.

Three red cotton fibers similar to those found in another T-shirt from the Echols home were recovered from Michael's Scout shirt, a pair of blue pants and a bag of items found at the crime scene. The fibers were also a match for a red shirt found at Michael's home.

Items from the bag recovered from a pipe, where it had been either discarded or cached near the crime scene, included a pair of Jordache size 33-34 blue jeans, a black medium-size thermal undershirt, a pair of white socks, two Bic razors, a plastic bag and a tan short sleeve shirt. The items were wet and moldy.

There was no clear evidence linking the bag and its contents to the crime, other than its presence. Despite a similar red thread potentially linking Michael, Echols and the bag, investigators were not able to establish a positive link.

The bag was from Road Runner Petro, where Echols's father was employed and that shared parking space with Alderson Roofing & Metal. Echols told police he worked as a roofer for Anderson. The businesses were not near the crime scene.

A red Rayon fiber matched a bathrobe owned by Baldwin's mother. That fiber was found on a black and white polka dot shirt, which, like the blue pants, was found turned inside out. Sakevicius again suggested secondary transfer, and later explained that such transferences commonly occur when clothes are washed together.

The polka dot shirt worn by Stevie was the source of residue of blue wax similar to candle wax. A small blue candle was found on a table in Domini Teer's bedroom, and similar wax was found on a witchcraft book, "Never on a Broomstick," from Echols' bedroom. Similar wax was also found in a bar of soap from the Baldwin bathroom. Jurors cited the wax as evidence against Echols. Candles are routinely used in occult ceremonies.

Sakevicius also testified that submersion in water was "very detrimental" to the recovery of trace evidence.

Sakevicius testified that a Negroid hair had been recovered from the sheet covering Christopher. The presence of that hair was never explained. One obvious and irresistible theory attributed the hair to "Mr. Bojangles," the bleeding black man who commandeered the restroom of a local restaurant shortly after the probable time of the killings.

The hair could have been from a police officer or other searcher, but no hairs from officers were submitted for comparison.

Bolstering the idea that more than one assailant was involved were the varying knots used on the shoelaces to tie arms to legs.

The text used by local witches, "Buckland's Complete Book of Witchcraft," contained a section on knot magic and how knots were used to bind magical spells. The magic number for knots was nine. Michael, Stevie and Christopher were tied with eight, 10 and four knots respectively.

The knots used on Michael: Square knot on the left wrist and ankle, three half hitches on the right wrist, four half hitches on the right ankle. Only one shoestring was used to bind Michael, by contrast with both shoelaces used on the other boys, in another deviation in the patterns of bindings. In a later confession, Misskelley described helping pull shoestrings from the shoes; his involvement would explain not only the single strand but the variance in knots used to bind Michael.

The knots used on Stevie Branch: three half hitches on both the left ankle and left wrist, three half hitches with the loop tied twice around the right leg, half hitch with figure eight on the right wrist.

On Chris Byers: double half hitches on all four knots.

The knots used were square knots, half hitches and double half hitches, with one knot being looped twice and a figure eight thrown on top of a half hitch —- at least three different knots, suggesting that three people tied up the boys. It is extremely unlikely that one person would have used three different knots to tie up the boys, particularly in a high-stress situation such as a murder scene. The forensic evidence showed that Chris and Stevie struggled against their bindings, while Michael, with deep and traumatic wounds to the head, had no such signs of struggle.

Michael also showed few if any signs of sexual molestation, fitting with Misskelley's description of a quick, violent pounding of the face and head but subsequent protection from further predation by Baldwin and Echols.

A pagan "ax" necklace belonging to Echols was discovered to be speckled with blood from two DNA sources as the Echols/Baldwin trial neared the end. The prosecution had already rested its case when questions arose about the blood spots.

The prosecution weighed the implications of entering the necklace as trial evidence. Judge David Burnett made it clear that the prosecution would be dealing with "two basic remedies, either a mistrial or a continuance."

At the least, the new evidence would have resulted in a continuance while the defense was allowed to examine the evidence.

Besides the possibility of a mistrial, prosecutors were concerned that it could result in a possible severance of the Echols and Baldwin cases.

One DNA source was compatible with Echols, while the second was compatible with both Stevie and Baldwin. The prosecution was prepared to argue that Stevie was the source, seeing little benefit from arguing for a match with Baldwin.

The necklace, taken from Echols at the time of his arrest, prompted a hearing on March 17, 1994, out of the presence of the jury, while the case was on continuance as the result of the discovery.

Prosecuting Attorney Brent Davis explained to Judge Burnett that "questionable" red spots had been found as Deputy Prosecuting Attorney John Fogleman and some police officers were reviewing evidence. Fogleman first noticed the spots.

A deleted scene from "Paradise Lost" footage available on DVD and YouTube showed a meeting between Fogleman and the Baldwin attorneys concerning the necklace. Though marked by jovial banter, the conference illuminated the difficulties posed by the "blood necklace" for both defense and prosecution.

The necklace had been sent to the crime lab, where the red spots were discovered to be blood, and then was sent to Genetic Design in North Carolina.

The prosecution learned late on the afternoon of March 15, just as preparations for closing arguments were under way, about the two DNA sources. The lab attempted an "amplification process" to further differentiate the DNA, which was successful on the larger sample from Echols, to not much effect, but was unsuccessful on differentiating Baldwin and Stevie. The prosecution learned of that in late afternoon on the 16th.

The prosecution hoped to present to the jury the DQ-Alpha match with Stevie Branch, consistent with about 11 percent of the white population.

Because Baldwin was also a match, Echols attorney Val Price explained in a court conference: "Part of our defense in this matter would be that sometime during the time period approximately a month or two before the arrest that besides my client having access to this pendant that also Jason Baldwin had access to this pendant. If that is indeed Jason Baldwin's blood on this pendant and not Stevie Branch's then this evidence is of no value at all and not relevant, it should be excluded and not considered by the jury at all."

Baldwin attorney Paul Ford argued that the evidence should apply to Echols alone since he wore the necklace and presumably there could be no proof of a link to Baldwin.

Prosecutor Davis said his understanding was that a mistrial for Baldwin would result from entering the necklace into evidence but the case could proceed against Echols. Without a counter-ruling, Davis did not plan to enter the new evidence.

Judge Burnett pointed out that among the potential complications was that Echols and Baldwin could cross-implicate each other, rather than engage in a common defense, if the necklace was introduced.

Because the matches were so common, the blood spots could not have been definitively linked to either Baldwin or Stevie. The spots did raise the question of why Echols' necklace would be splattered by two or more sources of blood.

Years later, Baldwin testified, "The necklace that had been acquired by Damien Echols at the time of his arrest was one that I believe my girlfriend Heather had given me. … I don't recall specifically how the necklace had come into Echols' possession."

As with all things in the West Memphis 3 case, facts about the necklace were disputed.

Echols had more than one necklace: Ridge noted in his May 10 report that "Damien was wearing a necklace that he claimed that he had just bought at the Mall of Memphis on the Saturday before the interview. The necklace had a pentagram as a pendant that Damien explained meant some type of good symbol for the Wicca magic that he was in." The blood-spattered pendant was a tiny axe, not a pentagram.

Echols had the axe pendant before the trip to the mall on May 8. Echols routinely wore this necklace. For example, Echols was filmed wearing the necklace at Skateland on May 7, two days after the killings. He continued to wear the axe pendant after purchasing the pentagram pendant. He was photographed wearing the axe necklace on May 9.

Because testing used up the original sample, retesting was not possible, giving the defense another possible objection since they would not be able to order tests.

A blood stain found on a shirt gathered as evidence at the Misskelley home similarly showed a possible match for both Misskelley and Michael. The HLA-DQ alleles had an expected frequency of 7.9 percent in the general population.

Misskelley said he gotten the blood on the T-shirt by throwing a Coke bottle into the air and smashing it with his fist, showing off his toughness.

The shirt was not entered into evidence at trial.

Besides the hair commonly linked to Hobbs and the Negroid hair, about four other hairs from the site were determined not to have originated with the victims. Because the DNA sampling from Hobbs was obtained by stealth via three discarded cigarette butts and a Q-tip, resulting in three variances after DNA testing, the link between Hobbs and the hair was even more questionable.

Another hair found in a tree trunk was a near-match for David Jacoby, a friend of Hobbs. There was no conclusive evidence that Jacoby was the source, that the hair dated from the time of the crime or that Jacoby or someone else did not leave a hair during the search. Jacoby said he was not in the area, but his memory was spotty.

Other hair included a dyed hair recovered from the sheet used to cover Stevie, a hair recovered from the Cub Scout cap and a hair from beneath Chris' ligature. It's possible, given the imperfections of the testing procedures, that the same person was the source of all three hairs.

There was no DNA testing on a number of items from the site, including other hair and tissues.

Among the many misconceptions about the case is that no blood was found. Since Stevie and Chris bled extensively —- Chris bled to death — the seeming lack of blood generated theories that the crime scene was a dump site, that the boys had been stashed down a manhole before being placed in the water, etc.

Blood was spotted in the water after the initial discovery but the site, which had been washed down, seemed surprisingly clean. Subsequent testing with Luminol revealed areas where blood had been spilled.

There was little testimony about blood. The jury did not hear the results of Luminol testing. Since such testing was not considered valid as evidence, the defense teams successfully sought motions to suppress Luminol results.

Kermit Channel and Donald Smith of the Arkansas crime lab, in the company of Mike Allen and Bryn Ridge, spent two days studying the effects of spraying Luminol, working in the dark, running a black light over the sprayed area to pick up glowing traces of iron in blood residue.

Testing May 12 yielded traces of blood on both sides of a tree near the ditch bank with more blood on the right side of the tree, facing the stream bed; in the areas where the bodies were placed; in a concentrated area on the east side of the ditch in a pile of sticks and a depressed area in the soil, and in a large area of concentration near tree roots. Other traces were visible where the victims were placed on the bank.

The areas with the pile of sticks and the tree roots were cited as likely locations of attack.

"There were no visible signs or indication of blood at any of the locations we investigated," their report said. The testing was begun a full week after the bodies were found. It had rained at least once. The testing was in less than optimal conditions as any light sources, such as stars and ambient light, compromised results. Some evidence would have been compromised in the search, recovery and investigation, the report noted, citing numerous reasons why investigators were unable to document findings with photographs.

Nonetheless, "It is our opinion the crime had taken place where the bodies of the victims were recovered."

On May 13, with tenting using plastic over canvas, Luminol was freshly applied, and a "less than perfect" photograph became possible. "These photographs still documented the areas of interest, showing luminol reaction in respective areas," reported Smith.

Soil samples were taken May 14; tested four months later, no Luminol reaction was noted, a result considered inconclusive given the age of the sample.

At the time of the Luminol report, investigators did not have the Misskelley confession. His descriptions of the attacks accord with the blood evidence.

A tree near the crime scene had the initials "ME" carved into it. Echols was sometimes known as "Michael Echols"; while in Oregon, he went by "Michael," and was in the process of changing his name to Michael Damien Wayne Hutchison. His family called him "Michael."

Much of the second-guessing of investigative findings by defense "experts" began with the hiring of Brent Turvey of Knowledge Solutions LLC in 1998, as Misskelley attorney Dan Stidham sought a new trial and as the second "Paradise Lost" was filming.

In his book, "The Unknown Darkness: Profiling the Predators Among Us," former FBI profiler Gregg O. McCrary characterized Turvey as a "self-proclaimed profiler."

McCrary wrote: "Not only has Turvey never completed any recognized training programs, such as those run by the BFI or the International Criminal Investigative Fellowship (ICIAF), he doesn't even have the basic qualifications to apply for those programs. As a matter of fact, he has never even completed even a basic policy academy training program anywhere. He had, however, authored a flawed textbook on 'profiling.'"

Turvey, working pro bono, examined photos of the bodies and other evidence and determined that the ditch was a dump site. He claimed at least four crime sites: abduction site, attack site, dump site and the vehicle used to transport the bodies, based on his contention that the attack would have required light, time and privacy.

He based this claim on darkness in the woods, lack of blood and the screaming of the boys. (The attack occurred before sunset in woods well away from any homes and in an irrigation ditch depression that would have muffled sound. The crime scene was not far from busy interstates and service roads. Echols told police how background noise obscured the screaming. The boys were quickly subdued and gagged.)

Turvey also formulated the "bite marks" theory featured in "Revelations: Paradise Lost 2," continuing to fuel baseless suspicions about Mark Byers. Despite how Turvey was presented in the film, he testified he was not an expert on human bite marks. The "new evidence" uncritically presented in the movie consisted of no evidence.

The huge amounts of money pouring into the defense fund — estimated between $10 million and $20 million — yielded nothing of value.

The fibers from the crime scene matching items from the killers' homes, Echols' statement about urine in the stomachs, the blood necklace, the knots used on the shoelace bindings, the semen stain on the pants, blood traces matching Misskelley's descriptions of the attack and blue wax residue all pointed to the West Memphis 3.

A SWIRLING CAULDRON OF SUSPICION

In the days after the bodies were found, the murders of Christopher Byers, Stevie Branch and Michael Moore had everyone around the greater Mid-South speculating about motives and suspects.

Early on, West Memphis police had lists of potential suspects. They checked out numerous tips and investigated violent felons and sex offenders, as well as surveying records on truckers. They surveyed Vietnam veterans based on an FBI profile of potential suspects (supposedly the wounds were similar to those inflicted on American soldiers).

Over the following weeks, police continued to pursue a long list of potential suspects, talking to over 70, clearing many through alibis or polygraph examinations.

Shortly after the boys were found, the department issued radio calls about a bearded transient on a bicycle headed toward Forrest City and two young male hitchhikers around Osceola.

As tips came flooding in, names, including that of Damien Echols, popped up again and again. Some had alibis while others could only guess at what they did that evening. Police relied heavily on polygraph tests. Because of the evidence piling up against him, Echols remained a person of interest.

Investigation yielded a wealth of puzzling episodes and sightings, most notably "Mr. Bojangles," a disheveled, bleeding black man who stumbled into the women's restroom at a fried chicken eatery, leaving bloodstains and excrement upon his departure an hour later, on the night of the killings. Police made a number of miscalculations and missteps in handling the matter. Police failed to collect evidence initially, lost a blood sample collected the next day and failed to determine the identity of "Mr. Bojangles." As a result, a fairly typical nuisance call became a crucial component of the myth of the West Memphis 3.

There is no evidence that the apparently intoxicated man with a cast on one arm had anything to do with subduing three 8-year-olds, but the incident provided a wealth of material for speculation and denigration of the police for several decades.

The "tattooed man" also prompted speculation. A Little Rock man named Ken Govar told police on May 8 that he had picked up a white man in his mid-20s while traveling eastbound 20 miles outside Little Rock on Interstate 40. The man, angry because his prior ride had stolen gasoline and was drinking and using drugs, had a large tattoo of a devil on his left forearm —- "… he had the face of a traditional devil, like you would draw a devil with a pointed chin and you know the horns and everything. That's what the face of the thing — but it was a terribly terrifying tattoo, I mean you looked at it you were terrified. It was horrible."

Govar said the hitchhiker had a "kinda sick" tattoo of a bone with blood as the background on his right inside forearm. Around 3:30 p.m. on May 5, the "tattooed man" asked to be dropped off at a convenience store in West Memphis on the south side of the interstate. "... He wanted to go specifically to the south side of the freeway and he wanted off right in this — at this one place," at a truck stop across from the dog track. The man supposedly was traveling to Knoxville. Govar was willing to take him further but the man insisted on being dropped off there, near the site of the murders. "... This guy was wired. He was angry. He was angry."

Govar said the hitchhiker would not give his name, seemed to be more familiar with Little Rock than would be expected, seemed too pale and too knowledgeable about mechanics to be a tree trimmer and was neither drunk nor smelly like the usual hitchhiker. The man has never been identified. There was no evidence linking the "tattooed man" to the murders.

Police quickly began checking out other leads, with much of the early focus on reports of a white van — a vehicle mentioned around the world in "urban legends" about stalking and kidnapping children. Investigators were dispatched door to door in the nearby neighborhood, as well as the Mayfair Apartments. Police checked out weirdos, anyone wearing a uniform and manifold hot tips, as well as a variety of transients. They brought in a local schoolteacher for questioning. One of the strangest stories was of a man with long hair and cutoff jeans who told a Memphis cab driver he had been in West Memphis and wanted to go to Nashville before finally paying $390 to be dropped off in Centerville, Tenn.; that lead led nowhere.

In another tangential aspect of the case more extensively covered than much of the evidence against the killers, young Chris Morgan and Brian Holland came under suspicion for leaving Memphis for California shortly after the killings. Morgan's parents and a former girlfriend lived in West Memphis. Morgan once had an ice cream route in the victims' neighborhood. He knew the little boys.

Morgan voluntarily showed up when he learned police in Oceanside, Calif., wanted to question him.

When deception was indicted in polygraph tests, he underwent hours of interrogation. After 17 hours, the frustrated Morgan "confessed," suggesting that maybe he had killed the boys after he "blacked out." Morgan immediately retracted the statement. Police soon ruled out Morgan as a suspect. Echols' defense lawyers wanted to present him on the stand. The prosecution said Morgan had no relevance. Morgan threatened to invoke his rights against self-incrimination if forced to testify. Judge Burnett ruled that he would not compel Morgan to testify.

From start to finish, the Morgan matter was much ado about not much.

Three knives were confiscated early in the investigation from Richard Cummings, considered a possible suspect. Cummings first drew attention May 9 on a tip that he had been drilling peep holes into walls to spy on a female neighbor in the Mayfair Apartments.

On May 10, Cummings, 23, told police that he was home until 10 p.m. on May 5, when his mother picked him up to take him to his job as a janitor at the Iron Skillet restaurant.

Police investigated possible links between Cummings and a murder-rape of a 12-year-old boy on a bicycle near Ithaca, N.Y., in 1990, not far from Cummings' hometown. The body was found nude, bound with duct tape at wrist and ankles, gagged and bound to a tree. While the murder had strong similarities to the West Memphis case, possible connections never panned out. After investigation, Cummings was not considered a suspect.

Vicki Hutcheson on May 28 gave West Memphis police the names of several associates of Damien Echols: Shawn Webb, also known as Spider or Red; Lucy, or Lucifer; Robert Burks (actually Robert Burch aka Snake); "some little boy named Jason" who lived in Lakeshore, and Jessie Misskelley.

She described the mysterious Lucy, or Lucifer, as an older guy, about 30, who drove a older, beaten-up car such as an Impala or Caprice painted with primer. He had brownish hair and a big nose and wore glasses. Other than his age, the description did not match an unnamed Lakeshore resident who gave orders at devil worship sessions organized by Echols, as described by Misskelley.

Investigators turned up others who described an adult with name variations on "Lucifer" who seemed to be leading cult activities, though physical descriptions were wildly at variance.

According to Hutcheson, "Robert Burks" had told a girl that he had killed the three boys and that if she opened her mouth, she would be next. The rumors about who said what circulated around West Memphis, often circling around a small set of suspicious persons, often including Echols and/or Baldwin, with rumored suspects spreading rumors about other potential suspects.

For example, a Joni Brown reported on June 28 that Whitney Nix had told her on May 14 that Robert Felix Burch, aka Snake, had said that he and Echols had committed the murders and would commit two more. Shortly before he confessed, Misskelley told police of rumors that Echols and Burch had committed the crimes.

Police had arrested Burch in July 1991 on charges of burglarizing Skateworld of about $200 and in August 1991 for criminal trespass and fleeing from a police officer. Among his friends were Jason Baldwin, "not the one that lives at Lakeshore," and "Ricky Climmer," who had moved away. After the arrests, Ricky Climer gave a lurid statement about his own involvement in violent occult activities with Echols, the Lakeshore Baldwin (the "other Jason Baldwin" lived in West Memphis) and Misskelley but named no other participants.

Police talked to Burch on May 15 about the murders. Burch said he got home from work about 4:10 p.m. on May 5 and couldn't remember going anywhere.

Burch said he had been at SkateWorld on May 14 and had talked to the Lakeshore Baldwin there. Baldwin had told him that "some detectives" had said that he and Baldwin were the killers. Burch knew Baldwin from when he had lived at Highland Trailer Park.

Burch didn't know any of the Lakeshore Baldwin's friends except Misskelley and Charles Ashley Jr.

Burch reported on rumors he had heard about the Wren brothers and Frankie Knight.

Burch was an associate of the Wrens. Michael Wren was an inmate at the time of the killings; David Shane Wren, his brother, lived at the Mayfair Apartments; Frankie Knight, the Wrens' stepbrother, also lived there.

Shane Peden told police that he had heard that Michael and David Wren were part of a cult that required them to kill an animal and a human.

Michael Andrew Griffin said he had heard that Michael and David Wren committed the murders to get into a cult. He said Chris Littrell and Murray Farris were in a group of white witches.

Damien Echols pointed to L.G. Hollingsworth Jr. L.G. Hollingsworth Jr. pointed to Damien Echols.

Echols also named "the other Jason Baldwin" —- not his friend from Lakeshore but the obese teen who lived in the neighborhood of the victims and who was friends with Robert Burch and Jerry Nearns — as a potential suspect.

Police prepared a photo spread for professed 8-year-old witness Aaron Hutcheson on June 2, the day before the arrests, that included Frankie Knight, Jerry Nearns, Murray Farris, L.G. Hollingsworth, Tracy Laxton, James K. Martin and Michael Leiter —- some of whom had been cleared as suspects or had alibis of varying strength. Though WMPD has often been accused of focusing single-mindedly on Echols, their photo spread contained no photo of Echols or Baldwin.

It already had been established that Farris was at a church at the time of the killings.

Hollingsworth would continue to raise suspicions, gaining notoriety as "the fourth suspect."

The police had questioned Nearns on May 14 after a former neighbor, a West Memphis High teacher named Beverly McCarty, had claimed that Nearns had a history of intimidating children and boasted openly, including in a class paper, of "stealing from his friends and killing people." Nearns had been arrested the previous year for breaking into her home.

This tip, with no evidence of any link between Nearns and the killings, was duly followed up by police.

Nearns authorized police to search his home. Nearns told police he had not been in Robin Hood Hills in eight or nine months, and said he was friends with "the other Jason Baldwin." Nearns had seen signs of suspicious activity at the old Dabbs School in West Memphis before it burned down but gave no indication he was involved in a cult. Nearns passed a polygraph test and was not considered a suspect.

Laxton emerged as a possible suspect May 15 after a caller reported "three kids 8 or 9 years old" running away from "a white male on the railroad tracks" behind the Goodyear store on Missouri Street in West Memphis. The children were not found but police did find the callers at the bowling alley at the Holiday Plaza Mall, also on Missouri —- David Sims, 22, Dennis Carter, 15, and Jessie Misskelley Jr.

They told Mike Allen that Laxton had approached them and asked if they want to come to his camp and drink beer. Misskelley and friends professed to be scared because of the murders and called police. Laxton, son of Crittenden County Chief Detective Ed Laxton, was stranded after his car had broken down; he was unaware of the murders and was in eastern Mississippi on May 5.

Police received a tip May 12 about Michael Leiter, who lived with his mother in the Mayfair Apartments.

The tipster told police "He drinks a lot & is into drugs. Hasn't seen him since this happened." Leiter was arrested on a warrant for hot checks on May 25. He passed a polygraph exam and told police he was staying at the 8th Street Rescue Mission at the time of the murders. Records confirmed that. He encouraged police to check out "a strange looking guy" living in the Mayfair Apartments.

Police also checked out James Kenny Martin, a petty criminal and registered sex offender who had served time and had washed out of sex offender treatment programs. He told police he knew at least one of the dead boys by name, though it was not clear which boy.

The polygraph indicted deception in his denials that he knew what was used to tie up the boys and who killed them. He denied any role in the killings; the polygraph did not indicate deception about that. Martin explained that logic told him that shoelaces would be used because they were already there; the shoelace bindings were not public knowledge.

A police memo described Martin in one word: "Nuts." But, much like Echols, he had put a lot of thought into how the killings were carried out.

He thought that Stevie's father may have killed the boys (in a later interview he specifically alluded to Hobbs and outlined a scenario that sounded much like later allegations about Hobbs). Martin's wife Darlene told police that Martin had been with her all May 5 until he went to work from 10 p.m. to 6 a.m. at the Flash Market on Broadway. Martin was on vacation from his regular job at W. B. Davis Electric Supply in Memphis. Martin was cleared as a suspect on May 18.

Martin also described hearing about the boys from his girlfriend, Barbara McCafferty, at about 6 p.m. on May 5. More credibly, McCafferty told police she had gone to Martin's home to borrow a drill about 5 along with her 14-year-old twins. She said his wife pulled up and they talked "until about dark," about 7:30. McCafferty passed along a rumor about a white van circling the area.

Ridge and Sudbury interviewed Martin on May 19 with the ostensible aim of gaining insights on sex offenders, and got more than they bargained for. Martin saw himself as a Hannibal Lector character, a "psycho nut" helping out the law. Martin described how the boys could have been led into believing that being tied up was part of a game.

Because of the apparent lack of blood, Martin believed the boys were killed nearby, with the ditch as a dump site. He described how sex offenders would molest boys from behind without anal penetration and how, with their hands tied, boys could be coerced into giving oral sex — much in line with how Misskelley described the assaults. To solve the case, Martin advised, "you got to think, sick."

Martin's obsessive talk about child molesting prompted police to drop off a copy of his interview with a Memphis psychiatrist for further evaluation. Martin, now living in Johnson City, remained on the Tennessee Sex Offender Registry as of July 2016, where his status was listed as "ACTIVE" and his classification "VIOLENT." His most recent offense continues to date back to 1988.

Investigators talked to Frankie Knight on May 11. He passed the polygraph test. He had been in Robin Hood Hills the day of the search talking to the search and rescue team. Knight had not gone to school the day of the killings but offered no strong alibi. He knew two of the boys by sight, and described several suspicious characters in the neighborhood. He had heard rumors about his brother, which he claimed were spread by a black youth named Dewayne Newsom.

Knight thought Echols was the killer, that Echols could kill the boys himself or have someone do the deed. He described Echols as "crazy" and involved in black magic.

A week before the homicides, he had seen Echols in Robin Hood Hills shooting snakes.

David Wren passed a polygraph test on May 13. He said he had been with a Beverly Houston at the time of the murders, and she confirmed his story. Wren admitted knowing Echols and some of his friends.

Police had the names of other possible cult members. In an otherwise undated note stamped July 30, 1993, were listed Danny Berrero, Jason Baldwin, Jeff Looney, Christy Looney, Daniel Warrick, Tino Berrero,

Kevin Mike Riggs, Tim Harbin, Bo Manuel and Roger Conley. The note contained no mention of Jessie Misskelley Jr., Damien Echols, Domini Teer or Deanna Holcomb, L.G. Hollingsworth Jr., Murray Farris or Chris Littrell. It was not clear if the Jason Baldwin listed was the Lakeshore Baldwin or "the other Jason Baldwin."

Police talked to Jeffrey Looney on May 27. Looney, a 19-year-old West Memphis youth who worked in maintenance at a motel, told police he had lived in the Mayfair Apartments when he was in 10th grade and had not been in Robin Hood since he was 10. He said he "doesn't mess with cults" and knew some people at Lakeshore but not Damien or Domini.

Looney said he had seen a girlfriend at the Mayfair on a Wednesday or Thursday at about 6 p.m. about two weeks before the murders. He took a polygraph test; no deception was indicated.

Other than Jason Baldwin, there was no record that police talked to anyone else on the list of "possible cult members" nor is it clear how the other names ended up on the list.

The "witch-hunt" of cultists was a bust.

Around and around the rumors went. The police checked them out as best they could.

"I CAN'T FATHOM WHERE YOU WOULD GET THAT."

The primary "alternative suspects" have been parents of the victims, John Mark Byers and Terry Hobbs, though Byers' whereabouts were well-documented and evidence against Hobbs rests on meager and tenuous DNA findings.

West Memphis police clearly talked to the parents when the boys went missing and after the bodies were found. Police did not extensively interview the parents or file lengthy reports on conversations with them.

 On May 10, police obtained brief, sketchy explanations about the parents' whereabouts on May 5 and 6. Todd Moore said he did not return home until 5-5:15 a.m. on the 6th and had not gone across the pipe into Robin Hood Hills. Mark Byers said he had begun searching around 6:30 on the 5th and was behind the Blue Beacon Truck Wash around 9 and again at 10. Pam Hobbs said she had gone into the woods briefly around 10 a.m. on the 6th but did not stay long because she had a bad feeling about the area. Terry Hobbs was not at home for the 2:30 p.m. visit by police.

Some of the siblings of the victims were interviewed more extensively.

Police took a statement on May 8 from Dawn Moore, Michael's 10-year-old sister, that included her account of seeing three teenagers, one white and two black, coming out of Robin Hood on May 5 as she was searching for her brother.

On May 12, Ryan Clark, Christopher's 13-year-old half-brother, gave a detailed rundown on his search efforts. Ryan gave another interview to Mike Allen in which he described Christopher's circle of friends and passed along a rumor about a white van following children in the neighborhood.

Police eventually checked out the whereabouts of Christopher Byers' biological father, Ricky Lee Murray, who was living in Henryville, Ind. Police in Clark County, Ind., extensively interviewed Murray on May 24 and he gave a rough accounting of his whereabouts on May 5. (Murray died in 2013 at age 52.)

Little Stevie's dad, Steve Branch, was told his son was missing the morning of May 6. Branch immediately drove down from his home in Osceola to help search. While Pam Hobbs initially suspected Branch had taken their son, he has never been a suspect and has staunchly denounced Echols, Baldwin and Misskelley as the killers of his son.

Melissa Byers gave police some background on Christopher's activities and named possible suspects in a May 25 interview. There was no indication that she was questioned about her or her husband's activities on May 5.

Police extensively interviewed Mark Byers on May 19. Byers gave a detailed accounting of May 5 and

6 and offered possible leads. Toward the end, Ridge and Sudbury confronted Byers.

Ridge told him: "… I may have information, this information suggests that you have something to do with the disappearance of the boys. And ultimately of the murder. Okay. What is your response to that?"

Byers: "My first response is I can't fathom where you would get that …. and it makes me so mad inside that I just kind of got to hold myself here in this chair."

Byers couldn't imagine who could be making such an accusation and affirmed that he had nothing to do with the killings.

Gleaned mostly from his statements to police, though often corroborated, Byers' schedule for May 5 ran like this: Around 5, Byers picked up Melissa from her job at a jewelry supply company in Memphis and dropped her off at home. Then Byers left to get Ryan, who was testifying in a reckless driving case at the courthouse. On the way, he spotted Christopher skateboarding down 14th Street. Byers took the boy home, spanked him with a belt and instructed Christopher to clean up the carport. Byers left again for the courthouse around 5:30. Byers and Ryan returned around 6:15. Byers first realized Christopher wasn't home around 6:30 p.m. Melissa had last seen him around 5:30-5:45. Back home, Mark talked to Melissa about Chris's whereabouts and sent Ryan to look of him. After Ryan returned, the family drove around for about an hour. Around 7:30, Byers alerted a police officer in a parked patrol car that his son was missing. The officer told them to wait until about 8 and then call in a report. Back home, Byers called the Sheriff's Department because they had a Search and Rescue Squad. The dispatcher there told him to call the West Memphis police. He called the West Memphis police.

Officer Regina Meek showed up shortly thereafter, at 8:10, and took a report, then called it in. As she was preparing to leave, Michael's mother, Dana, knocked on the door and told them that Christopher was with Michael and Stevie. She had seen Michael riding his bike along with Stevie and Christopher shortly after 6.

Dana had been looking for her son for about an hour and a half. She said Terry Hobbs had been looking for Stevie since 4:30 or 5.

After 8 p.m., Ryan and Byers began door to door queries. A little girl and boy told them that they and their mother had seen the boys going into Robin Hood about 6:30. Ryan and Byers returned home; Dana continued looking for the boys, and, according to Byers' May 19 statement, Terry Hobbs "had come up by then," around 8:30.

As search parties converged around the entry to the woods, darkness began setting in. Hobbs told them "he was going to spread out down, you know, woods where they were found. I don't know how far down that way he went, but he was going to look that way," said Byers. Ryan's friends Richie Masters and Britt Smith helped search.

Byers, dressed in shorts and flip flops, walked two blocks home to change into coveralls and boots. Then, "I made a pass. I went all the way back to the back, and walked up the gully to where it makes a real steep washdown." He decided to borrow a flashlight from a neighbor, Robert Fountain.

Before he could leave the scene, around 9:40 p.m., Officer John Moore (no relation to Todd and Dana) encountered Byers and agreed to search with his flashlight. They walked back up the trail. Byers said of Moore: "He went down the bank and looked around in the water with his light. And he said, it don't look to me like anybody, you know, has been down in here." They continued to search, finding two sets of bicycle tracks.

They came out of the woods. Moore got into his car. Byers estimated the time at 10:30 or a quarter to 11. Moore told Byers to go home, call the police station and check up on the status of the report filed by Meek. Byers got home at 11. He talked to Meek, who put out an alert. Byers called the sheriff's department again before continuing to search.

Then, Byers said, he and Ryan drove to the Blue Beacon, where they honked the horn and yelled into the woods. He talked to Blue Beacon employees. Byers returned home, where he met Stevie Branch's grandfather, Jackie Hicks, who had driven down from Blytheville, Ark. Byers, Melissa, Dana, Hobbs, Jackie

Hicks and a friend of Hobbs with a beard (presumably David Jacoby) stood out under the streetlight and talked over the possibilities.

"You know, we just kind of felt helpless," said Byers. "So we stood there talking, then we just went back to the woods and said let's make another pass through."

About 1:30 or a quarter to 2, a police sergeant pulled up and told them a search was under way. Byers checked out an abandoned house. A friend, Tony Hudson, arrived. Hudson, Byers and Melissa drove up on the service road to where the Mid-Continent Building was being rebuilt. They checked out the site, then returned home.

Hudson said he was going to make a few more rounds. Byers estimated the time at 2 or 3 o'clock.

"So, we just sat there waiting for daylight. And then just as soon as it got daylight, Terry Hobbs and I think Dana and maybe Todd, you know, knocked on the door, and then I got my boots on. And then we took off looking again." Joining in the morning search were Todd Moore and Steve Branch Sr.

Those who viewed Byers as the culprit generally claimed he had time to kill the boys and clean up the kill site when he went home to change clothes or that he killed them, hid the bodies in a manhole (or killed them elsewhere) and deposited the bodies in the ditch late that night.

It's even been suggested that when Ryan and Britt Smith were spooked out of their search of the woods, the splash-splash-splash sounds and noises that sounded like gunshots were the result of Byers disposing of bodies.

Those ideas border between the ridiculous and the impossible. Byers' presence was well accounted for virtually all evening; the few interludes when he was by himself would have given him little opportunity to commit the crimes and cover up the site.

Byers drew suspicion because of his flamboyant words and actions before the cameras, his history as a drug dealer and police informer, giving a knife to a member of a film crew that held a dollop of dried blood matching both himself and Christopher and having his teeth pulled in a murder case in which defense experts brought late into the case alleged the bodies had bite marks. Based on dental records, Byers' teeth did not match the supposed bite marks.

As for Hobbs, Byers cited his presence around 8 or 8:30 and around 1-1:30 a.m. with Jacoby as well as at first light of day on Thursday. Dana told Byers that Hobbs had been searching since around 4:30 or 5, corroborating Hobbs' statements about early contact with Dana. Byers described Hobbs continuing his search after their encounter around 8:30. In courtroom testimony, Melissa named Hobbs as a searcher.

When Stevie didn't come home at 4:30 as scheduled, Pam and Terry made a quick search by car, starting around 4:50, before Terry dropped Pam off at work. When Terry arrived to pick Pam up around 9:25 p.m., he told her Stevie was still missing. The police were called. Terry told her that the three boys were together and that Mark and Dana had called the police.

Officer Moore arrived at Catfish Island to take statements. Then Terry and Pam began patrolling the neighborhood, with an emphasis on Robin Hood Hills, first entering there around 9:30. The family, including 4-year-old Amanda, rode around until Terry dropped off Amanda and Pam at home, then joining Jacoby and Jackie Hicks Sr. on a search until late that night.

Between 5, when Terry dropped off Pam, and 8, when Terry showed up at the Byers home, Hobbs searched for Stevie. Not interviewed formally by police until June 21, 2007, Hobbs gave a voluntary statement to Lt. Ken Mitchell and Detective Chuck Noles of the WMPD about that evening from 14 years before.

Hobbs said his typical workday running an ice cream sales route over a broad territory began about 5:30 a.m. He got home around 3 or 3:30 p.m. that day and found Pam and Amanda home, but not Stevie. The boy had left with Michael. Hobbs recalled walking out along the driveway to see if he could spot the boys.

Hobbs drove Pam to work, with Amanda in the car. They checked at the Moore home to see if anyone there had any idea about where the boys were. He was told they were riding bicycles.

Terry and Amanda rode around from street to street for "probably 30 minutes," maybe an hour. He was uncertain about times. They went home and walked around the neighborhood, hoping to hear the boys in the distance. Soon Dana drove up and asked if Michael was at the Hobbs home. She drove home. Terry followed her.

Dawn told them she had seen the boys go by on their bicycles.

At the Moore home, Hobbs encountered "a big bully-looking dude," Mark Byers, for the first time. They figured out that Christopher, Stevie and Michael were together.

Hobbs discussed calling the police and assumed Dana would make the call.

Hobbs said he drove around with Amanda before dropping her off at the Jacobys'. David Jacoby agreed to help in the search.

On June 21, 2007, Jacoby gave his first full interview to police, varying in details from Hobbs.

Jacoby said Hobbs came over to his house with Amanda around 5:30 or 6 p.m. on May 5. They played guitars together "I'd say at least an hour." Hobbs left to look for Stevie. Jacoby could not remember if Amanda stayed or left with her dad. Jacoby saw Terry "a couple more times that night uh at one point that night when he came back uh I thank I went with him to look for the kid uh we rode down the road towards I thank that's Barton street? Going out towards those apartment where what's that place there's Robin Hood apartment what every they call it. ... I just I can't I'm just really not sure I mean if was uh I know at one time me and him did go look then his wife had come by and she was hysterical ... we wound up walking through those woods with her dad and some people was from out that neighborhood. Uh I was out until like 3 o'clock that morning with em. Uh not all together everybody was kinda of branched off."

It was getting dark when he began looking: "really close to dark. ... well yeah it was because when I first went out there uh we what'n there long and I told em I had some flash lights and ... I was thanking Terry brought me back home to git some flash lights and we went back looking. Man it's just so hard to remember how it went down."

Jacoby remembered going into the woods, seeing footprints, bicycle tire prints in the ditch and muddy footprints along the pipe. He remembered Byers, Hobbs, Jackie Hicks Sr. and others calling the boys by name. A police officer was part of the search.

Asked about Hobbs' demeanor, he stated, "... I can just thank of Terry is normal low keyed you know every time I seen him. And best I can remember that night you know uh that he came over he was fine you know I mean I didn't notice anything unusual he just like normal he come in sit down you know and we pick up a guitar play a little bit before he picked his wife up uh like I said he got up and left said he had to go check see if Steve had made it in or man I really can't remember."

So, according to Jacoby, Hobbs was at his home from around 5:30 or 6 until at least an hour later, which would have been 6:30 or 7. Jacoby did not recall going with Hobbs at that point, only later when it was getting dark.

According to that statement, Hobbs' whereabouts had no verified witnesses between 6:30 and 7 — possibly later — to around 8 or 8:30 over at the Moore home. He would have had an hour — perhaps more — to locate the boys, kill them, bind them, place them in the ditch and then get cleaned up enough to pass muster before Dana Moore and Mark Byers. He may or may not have had his small daughter along with him.

Three days after the June 21 interview, on June 24, Jacoby gave a declaration in a defamation lawsuit that Hobbs had filed against Dixie Chicks singer Natalie Maines that varied from the earlier statement.

He stated that, although unsure of the time, he believed Hobbs came over to his house about 5-5:30, though it could have been as late as 6.

He said he saw Stevie Branch and two other little boys riding bikes, with one on a skateboard, in the street outside his home, giving no clear timeframe.

Jacoby said he and Hobbs played guitars for "up to one hour" and that between 6 and 6:30, Hobbs told Jacoby he was leaving to check if Stevie had gotten home, that Stevie was expected home before dark.

Jacoby was "90% sure" Amanda remained with his wife and himself.

Jacoby said Hobbs was gone "for awhile. Terry returned to my house later and asked if Stevie had come by. When I said no, I volunteered to go out with Terry to ride with him to look for Stevie.

"Terry and I drove around the neighborhood for approximately 10-15 minutes looking for Stevie. We drove near some apartments. We did not stop at any houses or talk to anyone at this point.

"Terry then dropped me off at my house and said he was going to check a few other places for Stevie. I believe Terry again left alone, with Amanda staying at my house.

"After awhile, Terry came back to my house. I again went with Terry to ride around and look for Stevie. We drove two more times nearly the same route we had driven before." They talked to children playing at the apartments and a little girl told them some boys had been riding bikes in the woods.

"Terry again dropped me off because it was getting dark and I was going to change clothes and get flashlights to search further. I do not know where Terry went, but I expected him to come back to get me. I believe he took Amanda with him. I changed clothes, but Terry never showed back up."

Jacoby, on June 24, said Pam came by the house looking for Stevie and he drove her around, finally meeting up with other searchers, including Dana, Byers,

Hobbs and Hicks. Jacoby continued to search until nearly 3 a.m.

He said he had not been searching either alone or with Hobbs in the woods near 6 or 6:30 p.m., only when it was already dark.

So, according to Jacoby in the later statement, Hobbs left the Jacoby home around 6 or 6:30, returned after a bit, drove around with Jacoby for 10 or 15 minutes, dropped Jacoby off, returned again to the Jacoby home and rode around again until it was getting dark, which would have been closer to 8:30 or 9, before dropping Jacoby off for the final time.

The second statement, though inexact on times, left no time for multiple murders in the woods followed by a meticulous cleanup. The statements from Hobbs and Jacoby taken 14 years after the murders — with both uncertain about times, sequence of events and other details — didn't offer as clear an alibi as the Byers timeline. They did indicate, between hanging out with Jacoby, looking for Stevie and conferring with other parents and police, that Hobbs did not have time to commit the crimes.

Critics of the timelines offered by Hobbs and Jacoby focus on the differences in stories, claiming that Hobbs in particular should remember times and the exact sequence of events because of the significance of his stepson's killing. That's an unreasonable expectation, given the selectiveness of memory, even for once-in-a-lifetime events.

In his statement of June 21, Hobbs said Pam came out from her workplace around 9 or 9:30 with her usual treats, a piece of candy each for Amanda and Stevie. "I said Pam we haven't found him yet. And she says he's dead. I said Pam don't say that, don't even think that. I was getting nervous a little bit before I could come up because it was starting to get dark."

Hobbs could not remember if they first went home or began searching in Robin Hood Hills. He had not been aware of the woods until neighbors described seeing the boys entering there. He said it looked like "the jungle. ... I couldn't see 8 year old boys hanging around."

He entered the woods with Officer Meek, exiting quickly because Robin Hood was hot, muggy and full of mosquitoes. He said he had gone into the woods earlier, around 6 or 6:30, with Jacoby, which didn't accord with his or Jacoby's earlier statements. He wasn't sure how long he had been in the woods then. "I don't know cause we would drive around looking and then go down the service road looking and stuff in there and walk out in there from both sides."

Hobbs followed leads about possible sightings. Hobbs saw Mark and Melissa driving around.

Hobbs was unclear about times on most of the night. "David was still with me and then Pam got with me, but Pam was also with her mom and dad that night." Hobbs said he was in the company of Jacoby for much of the night.

Hobbs said he and Pam went home at some point to change clothes, with Pam wanting out of her work uniform. They put on mosquito repellent.

They returned to Robin Hood Hills "all night long."

Hobbs said that by daylight Pam was accusing Steve Branch Sr. of having something to do with the disappearance. "She thought he might kidnap Steve." Branch, who arrived that morning to help in the search, has never been a suspect.

Hobbs recalled a black "bum" walking down 7th Street near Catfish Island. "And he's wet and looking terrible but he walks all … on the railroad tracks and starts going west." Hobbs particularly remembered the "bum" because "he's coming from that area."

They went to Weaver Elementary that morning to see if the boys showed up for school and continued riding around and walking through Robin Hood.

"… Me and Pam is riding round to git something to eat and we couldn't eat. And I go somewhere and we heard somebody say they found three boys and they tell us it's on that road by the apartments over there and so we fly back over there … we git back over there see the crime scene tape right there and we don't know what's going on but there's a lot of people there. We park our vehicle get out we start running up to the tape Pam faints and I help her git back to the car, and I go up to the crime scene tape … I get there Gary Gitchell standing there I ask him I says

have you found I didn't know Gary and I asked him
have y'all what you find? He said three boys. He said I
thank it's a homicide or it look like a homicide or
something like that. I asked him what? He said it look
like they been murdered. And I just fall on my knees
and start crying I look and there's Pam she's they're
trying to get her woke up ...." Hobbs' collapse into
overwhelming shock and grief was captured on video
and was clearly authentic.

Hobbs described the resulting pressures within
the family. "… After this happen for some reason Pam
and some of her family turn around start telling people
Terry Hobbs killed them kids. I don't know why they
done this."

He told police that Pam's brother, Jackie Hicks Jr.,
threatened to kill him. Terry admitted that, during a
1997 argument, he backhanded his wife across the
mouth, they wrestled over keys and he hit her with his
elbow. Pam called her family. Terry called the police.
During an ensuing altercation, Hobbs claimed he shot
her brother in a warning shot. Jackie Hicks Jr. died in
2006 from a blood clot released during one of many
followup surgeries for the abdominal wound. The Hicks
family has blamed Terry for the death.

Pam told police on July 19, 2007, that Terry did
not get home from work until close to 4:30 on May 5. As
for his mood, "Just seem to be normal every day how he
was. He wasn't in a bad mood or he wasn't real real
cheerful he just Terry." She had to be at work at 5 so

they left a little after 4:45 to see if Stevie was at the Moore home.

When Terry came to pick her up, he went straight to the phones, while she took two pieces of candy to the car. Upon learning from Amanda that Stevie was missing, "I knew something was terribly, terribly wrong that at 9:30 that he still couldn't be found. So my first instinct and my first thought is he's dead."

Terry called the police from the restaurant. By the time the officer arrived, Pam had formulated the belief that Steve Branch Sr. may have kidnapped their son. She then called her family and Philip Palmer, son of the manager of Catfish Island, since she was training to do the night closing.

Pam described Terry's account of that evening: "... he said that uh when he went back home that he was fixing to get out and walk the neighborhood him and Amanda and he said Dana Moore come to the house, so I'm gone ah say this is around little bit after 5, 5:30 maybe that Dana came to our house and was looking for Michael and he said that he told Dana that ah I'm looking for Stevie also, and I'm fixin to walk the neighborhood. So Terry pretty much told me that he walked the neighborhood and uh he started looking into the wooded area and because I guess someone had said that's where saw the boys go at the last home so they were kinda ah looking in the wooded area."

Robin Hood Hills was their destination " ... as soon as we uh got off work and there were several people there. I was still in my uniform too and there were several people there and a lady told me she said I'll stay here and watch Amanda if you wanna walk through. … And we started walking through this wooded area and the fear was really on me hot and heavy because how all the woods and stuff was growing up. And I said God son surely you're not out here. I started yelling Steve name. Steve son are you here, son are you here, son you're not in trouble if you're here just come out and then Mark and the rest of em start hollering Michael's name, Chris name and stuff like that and … "

She said from 10 to 15 people were involved in the hunt, many unknown to her, "just neighborhood people."

Like Terry, she had no prior knowledge of the woods.

She said Terry took her home and left without telling her where he was going. He left about 10:30 or 10:45 and returned about 11:30. She went to the Jacoby home. Jacoby accompanied her and Amanda back to their house, by which time Terry had returned. Terry and Jacoby left together to search. Terry returned again and left with Jacoby and Hicks to search again.

Her account of the rest of the evening and the events of the next day was largely in accord with Terry. She said she was extremely angry with Terry for five or six years for not notifying her sooner about Stevie being missing.

Much of the material in her 2007 statement was repeated in declarations on May 20, 2009, in the Hobbs vs. Natalie Maines Pasdar libel case. Pam has stated that she believes it was possible Terry was involved in the murders. Much of her belief appears based on personal grievances with her ex-husband. She has "doubts" and "questions." Generally she has fallen short of outright accusing Terry.

Meanwhile, in an ironic twist, Mark Byers, no doubt relieved to have someone else be the "alternative suspect," has loudly proclaimed Terry Hobbs as the killer.

"L.G. STATED ... THAT THEY WERE TALKING ABOUT HIM THAT HE WAS THE 4TH SUSPECT."

Like Heather Cliett and Vicki Hutcheson, L.G. Hollingsworth Jr. is an oddly ubiquitous character who popped up in the strangest places in the West Memphis 3 story.

L.G. was listed among possible teenage suspects just days after the killings. Two lists were compiled by Lt. James Sudbury from information from Steve Jones and Jerry Driver, familiar with the teens as Juvenile Court officers. One list had Damien Echols at the top, followed by Jason Baldwin, L.G., Domini Teer and, further down, Murray Ferris. A similar list had Echols at the top, followed by Baldwin, L.G., Domini and, further down, Ferris and Chris Littrell. While all the others were often listed as members of a Satanic group or witch cult, there's little evidence that L.G. was involved in occult activity. Jessie Misskelley. though well-known to law enforcement, was not on the lists.

Like Jessie, L.G. was in frequent trouble with the law. Investigators soon discovered he called or visited Domini, his "cousin," regularly and was well acquainted with Echols. Hollingsworth also had formed a friendship with an older man that officers found questionable.

L.G.'s aunt, Narlene Hollingsworth, called in a tip on May 9 that added to early suspicions about L.G. Besides stating she had seen Damien and Domini walking away from the murder site on May 5, she said "L.G. made a statement on Thursday that he knew about what happened before anyone else. L.G. has 666 on the side of his shoes." Narlene made a similar claim about Echols' boots.

In a case loaded with confusing family relations, the Hollingsworth connections were particularly elaborate. When asked on the stand during the Echols/Baldwin trial to identify L.G., Narlene said, "... He's my ex-husband's son, which is -"

The attorney asked, "So it'd be your step son -- at one time he was your step son then."

Narlene: "No."

Scott Davidson: "No?"

Narlene: "No, I'm - I'm his aunt through marriage. It's just by marriage."

Davidson: "You're his aunt by marriage. But he's your ex-husband's son?"

Narlene: "Yes sir. I know it's confusing."

Davidson: "I'm confused on that one. Now, L.G. is you -"

Narlene: "- Ex-husband's -"

Davidson: "-Ex-husband's son, but you're his aunt by marriage, how did that happen?"

Judge David Burnett: "Is that really relevant? Let's don't try to sort it out," prompting laughter in the courtroom.

Narlene wasn't just L.G.'s aunt. She had once been married to L.G. Sr., divorcing him after he became involved with her best friend. Narlene then married L.G. Sr.'s brother, Ricky Sr.

Narlene was also related after a fashion to Domini, whose mother, Dian Teer, had a sister, Dixie Hufford, who was divorced from the father of Ricky Sr. and L.G. Sr. Domini named Dixie Hollingsworth (Hufford) as one of her relatives in an early interview. Hufford was tied in with the Echols sighting, as well as reports of the puzzling activities of L.G.

Narlene continually referred to Hufford as Dixie Hollingsworth and described her on the stand as "my ex-husband's use to be step mother" (Narlene and Ricky divorced between the time of the sighting and the trial). The Teers rented a trailer in Lakeshore from Pamela Hollingsworth, who was Narlene's sister and had married into the Hollingsworth family.

L.G. Jr. spent much of May 5 riding around with Narlene and hanging around Domini before showing up late that evening at the Flash Market laundromat on Ingram Boulevard, managed by his grandfather's ex-wife, Hufford.

After Narlene's tip, West Memphis police made contact with L.G. the next day, Monday, May 10. Hollingsworth was a dark-haired 17-year-old ninth-grade dropout recently employed as a sacker at the Big Star West grocery. He had "little gangster" tattooed on his right biceps and a cross on his left first finger. The use of "little gangster" drew on his name, L.G.; the initials did not stand for anything.

No record seems available on the May 10 interview, but apparently L.G. said little that would allay suspicions. At the time that police were talking to L.G., down the hall they were interviewing Echols, who named L.G. as a possible suspect.

Police promptly searched the Hollingsworth home on McCauley Circle, just around the corner from the murder site, and confiscated a knife in a sheath and four pairs of tennis shoes.

That afternoon, L.G.'s name appeared in a tip from an anonymous caller taken by Mike Allen "who stated she had overheard that a Dominick & a Damion killed the three little boys & that L.G. last name unknown took and laudered there clothes. Caller stated that Damon had body parts in a box from the children. The caller stated that she didn't want to give her name & that she heard that L.G.'s mother was going to lie about L.G.'s whereabouts."

Information about "body parts in a box" persisted well into the investigation, though nothing conclusive was determined about the notorious "stinky box." L.G. said the box contained test papers from a vo-tech class.

Also on May 10, police interviewed Narlene at her trailer in Lakeshore. She told Detective Charlie Dabbs and Lt. Diane Hester about sighting Damien and Domini walking along the service road near the Blue Beacon about 9:30 p.m. on May 5. She and her family had gone to pick up Hufford. "… So, then when I talked to Dixie Hollingsworth, I got to the laundry mat, she said that L.G. Hollingsworth had just left from there in some car. And, I said uh, that's funny, she said that it is and she never did say why, and I thought it was funny, but I thought that he had just left from there and they were coming down the street."

"She never did say why, and I thought it was funny" would sum up the episode of L.G. at the laundromat.

Narlene had found out about the missing boys the day after the killings while driving L.G. to his first day of work at Big Star, describing intuitive suspicions and hunches in her distinctively vivid style. "It was late, well, when I come back over in this area, again Thursday, because I promise L.G. that I would take him to work, cause he didn't have no way but me, OK, when I come back down the street, I seen a white car that belonged to a policeman or an undercover car, you know and they were two others out there too, and there was a crowd of people gathered around and I said, that's unusual."

This occurred at about 10 a.m. at Barton and 14th. "Cause they were all gathered up there and I didn't know what was going on, so I went down there and L.G. was saying, get me on to work. So, anyway I went on and got him on to work, so then later on that day he got off early ... I know he come to my house about 2:40 or a quarter to three and I thought that he would be working a little later than that on Wednesday, but anyway my kids started hollering about those kids, you know ... and later on that night, he came over there in a yellow car with some boxes in them, now what was in the boxes I don't know. The kids said that the box was about this big and some thing like this and they didn't know what was in the box, but he said don't look at it, don't touch it, don't step on it or I'll hurt you. ..."

Narlene had seen L.G. earlier on May 10, much to the surprise of her interrogators.

"...The day I run into L.G. the day at the police department, he begged me to go in there and sit down with his mother and I said, I can't do that. He said that I wasn't at no laundry mat Wednesday night, I said, yes you was, he said, naw I wasn't, I said yes you was, cause Ricky Hollingsworth" — so says the transcript but Narlene was referring to Dixie, not Ricky — "said that I had just missed you. I said, you better stop lying or they are going to get you for murdering these children, and they are going to want to know why you lie, he said alright, I was there, I said I know you was."

Narlene told Dabbs and Hester that the encounter had not been on Thursday, as they first assumed, but that day at the police station.

Narlene explained, "I went there to pay my husband's fine of $25 that he got in trouble and he got a DUI, I think .... Today I went down there to pay on his fine, L.G. come running out of the building where the police department, he said you go in there and tell them that you are mommy and I said, no, I won't. I said where is your mother and he said, I don't know but she won't come up there with me, I said, well, I said, they will ask you some questions and you answer them, I said, they will let you go. And then if you start telling a bunch of lies and they catch you in them, he said well uh, I wasn't over there in that area that day, I said, yes you was L.G., and then he said, I was, I said, I know you was.

"He said, if you start saying that about Damien, you're going to get in trouble, I said, well, the mommy is up there saying stating that he was, Damien was with her all the time. I said, well the mommy is a liar ain't she. ..."

Police didn't take a statement from "the mommy," apparently referring to the never-credible Pamela Hutchison, until two days later, May 12.

Narlene continued: "He said, you seen him coming down the street, I said, yes L.G. and I am not lying for him. I am not scared of that boy. He said, well don't you put yourself in that kind of trouble, well I'm going to take care of L.G."

As Narlene predicted, L.G. remained under suspicion long into the case. Suspicions still linger.

The next day, May 11, police got another tip about L.G. from Robin Taylor, a third-grade teacher in Horn Lake, Miss., just south of Memphis. According to the report on her phone call, "This date a 8 year old student told her that she needed to talk to her about the murders in West Memphis.

"The girl said that her cousin came home that he is 19 and that he had blood on his clothes and himself.

"That her cousin had something concealed in a box and put it in his car and told his family that if they even went near the car he would kill them.

"Her Aunt said she would lie for him if he was involved and tell the police he was with her at the time of the murders.

"That the police had already talked to her cousin.

"Teacher advised that this was a good and usually quiet student and it would be out of character for her to lie."

Notes indicated the student was Sara Hollingsworth, daughter of Debra Hollingsworth, The cousin was L.G., and two of the aunts were L.G.'s mother Linda and Narlene. Also, "Sara was afraid her dad would find out she told."

The notes also indicated that L.G. was thinking about going to Georgia and that he had arranged children's clothing on the table at the laundromat. L.G. was talking about getting out of town, but to Kentucky not Georgia. There was no other mention of L.G. having children's clothing at the laundromat. Most of the victims' clothing was found stuck at the ends of large sticks thrust into the ditch bed. Police did not contact the Horn Lake Hollingsworths until well after the arrests.

Detectives made a number of attempts to contact Debra Hollingsworth on June 15 and drove to her home

June 16, only to find no one there. A neighbor said they were at a church camp. Police left a note asking her to call.

Durham finally talked to Sarah on June 17. "The interview took place at the Christian church camp near Sardis, Miss. Mrs. Debra Hollingsworth, mother of Sarah, was present. Sarah denied ever seeing L.G. Hollingsworth with blood on his clothes and said she did not see him put anything in his car or threaten anybody. She denied knowing anything about this alleged incident."

Other than rumors and anonymous tips, there was little evidence that L.G. did more at the laundromat than drop by briefly to get a telephone number. Questions about the "stinky box" may linger forever.

The primary evidence, the confessions of Misskelley, made no mention of any involvement of L.G. or anyone other than the West Memphis 3.

Questions about Hollingsworth's involvement remained purely circumstantial for decades. Then a couple of career criminals serving long terms in Arkansas prisons on rape convictions gave sworn statements in 2013 that L.G., Buddy Lucas, Terry Hobbs and David Jacoby killed the boys after being discovered at a sex and drugs orgy in Robin Hood Hills. The story got some play in the news, but investigators did not take the wild story seriously.

Back in 1993, however, Hollingsworth's inability to come up with a consistent, corroborated alibi caused serious doubt about his professed innocence.

Soon after his first interview with police on May 10, L.G. was given a polygraph test. The results of the polygraph show up in a brief report on the www.callahan.8k.com Web site: "Didn't know boys had been killed until Thursday 3 p.m. when his aunt told him"

And "Last time in Robin Hood Hills was Jan. or Feb."

"Says he suspects Damien." The notes indicate deception in the answer about Damien.

While it seems unlikely that L.G. would gone out of his way to help Echols, L.G. was on friendly terms with Domini. He told investigators he went to the laundromat to get Domini's number. Her standing alibi was that she was home all evening with her mother and not on the telephone until 10 p.m., when she and Damien began a long telephone argument.

On May 20, police had received a tip that Dixie "Hubbard use to be Hollingsworth" had told "someone" that two boys and a girl came in the laundromat where she worked on Ingram at 10-10:30 p.m. on May 5 to clean mud and blood off their clothes. "Boone," the tipster, said she was related to one of them, whose name was Hollingsworth.

Bryn Ridge and Gary Gitchell visited Hufford, 50, on May 20 at her townhouse apartment.

Ridge wrote: "She reported that L.G. Hollingsworth came to the Laundry where she works on 5-5-93 in a small light colored car and asked her for Domini's number. This occurred at about 9:00 to 9:30PM. Dixie stated that Narlene and Ricky Hollingsworth picked her up from work at a few minutes before 10:00PM that night and took her home.

"Dixie came to work later and Linda Hollingsworth came in asking about where L.G. had been during the evening on 5-5-93. When Dixie told her of him coming in to the laundry in the small car she asked if she was sure that it wasn't Richard Simpson's car. Dixie stated that she knew Richard's car and that it was not his....

"Dixie stated that we need to talk to Linda Hollingsworth but for us to know that she believes she will likely try to protect L.G.

"Dixie believed that L.G. had on a white shirt and tie that night he came to the laundry."

Hufford made no mention of L.G. — or anyone else — washing mud and blood off clothes. Linda was L.G.'s mother, and there is no record of the police talking with her.

L.G. said he was at Simpson's home in the evening; Simpson initially denied that. L.G. was driving a car unfamiliar to family members. Why was he wearing a white shirt and tie to visit a laundromat? Simpson did remember loaning him a tie, and

Hollingsworth was scheduled to start his new job on May 6.

The L.G. story took a brief detour to Kentucky, where L.G. traveled with Simpson to see L.G.'s "fiancee," Liza McDaniels.

West Memphis police received a message from Sgt. Jim Dorrow in Caldwell, Ky., on May 16, concerning Simpson and L.G., who had been riding a yellow 1979 Ford LTD around Princeton, Ky., in a suspicious manner.

They had rented two rooms in a motel.

Liza's uncle and aunt alerted police about the tryst. Liza was found in bed with L.G.

Simpson produced an ID showing he was a building inspector with the West Memphis Police Department. The car was registered to Tri-State Word Ministries of West Memphis. Simpson identified himself as a 49-year-old building inspector for the City of West Memphis as well as a nondenominational minister.

The sheriff's office there checked out Simpson's ID with Gitchell and sent L.G. and Simpson back to West Memphis.

Ridge conducted another interview on May 26 with Hollingsworth, who gave permission for blood and hair samples to be taken. Said Ridge: "LG stated that he didn't know anything about the murders and that on Wednesday he was with Richard Simpson at his house from 05:30 PM until about 9:30 PM. He stated that after that he went home just before his mother arrived home. He stated that he got on the phone with Domini and was talking with her about the problems that she and Damien were having and that is when his mother came in about 10:00 PM. …

"I next interviewed Richard Simpson who stated that L.G. was not with him during that period of time until Thursday evening."

L.G. seemed highly interested in Domini's troubled relationship with Damien; by her own account, she argued with Echols that evening as well as the next day.

Ridge first talked to Simpson on May 13, following interviews with L.G. on May 10 and 11. While Simpson's statements did little to bolster the various stories from L.G., Simpson was inconsistent about L.G.'s activities on May 5, other than stating that L.G. had not been at his home that evening.

Simpson gave permission to search his home and his yellow 1979 Ford LTD (which supposedly contained the "smelly box"). Police found nothing suspicious. He denied direct knowledge of the murders.

Simpson had met L.G. after the teen introduced himself at Blockbuster Video. He felt sorry for the boy. "His family very hard on him."

Notes on the interview stated: "… Believe that LG told of incident on Wednesday month to 6 weeks ago left & came back from someone very strong in satanic belief. Boy apparently hated L.G." The somewhat cryptic note made a clear reference to Echols.

Simpson took a polygraph test May 14 and said he knew nothing about the killings. He told police "L.G. thinks Damon may have done it." No deception was indicated.

Simpson talked to Ridge again on May 26, after another unsatisfactory interview with L.G. Ridge reported: "He advised me that he could not remember for sure but that he did not have L.G. Hollingsworth over at his house on 5-5-93. Wednesday evening, however he stated that L.G. called him at about 6:30 PM and requested that he come and get him. He stated that he thought that L.G. was at his home when he received the phone call. He again stated that he was not with L.G. at that time.

"Richard stated that he was with L.G. on Thursday evening and that L.G. spent the night with him. He further stated that L.G. spent the weekend with him and that on Friday evening he and L.G. went to a restaurant on Poplar in Memphis. He stated that L.G. did drink some beer and a margarita at the restaurant and that he also drank a margarita while at the bar. ...

"Richard stated that he did remember L.G. borrowed a tie and shirt from him but that he couldn't remember when exactly he borrowed the tie. Richard stated that if L.G. stated that he borrowed the tie on that date, 050593 he wouldn't argue that but that he didn't think that this occurred on the Wednesday 050593."

Simpson took another polygraph examination. Durham's note on the session said "Wed 5-5-93 said L.G. came over sometime after 5 pm to borrow a white shirt — he loaned L.G. a shirt & a tie and then gave L.G. a ride back home around 9 p.m. or 9:30 p.m.

"Said L.G was at his house from 6:30 p.m. to 9:15 p.m. — Richard then gave L.G. a ride home. ...

"Says not sure of date."

This time Simpson failed the test.

Durham noted, however, that "Subject moved during test — yawned and appeared to be attempting counter-measures to distort the test." Simpson told him he had taken pain pills because he had a kidney stone.

He then changed his story and told police that L.G. had not been at his house May 5 but had come over that Thursday and spent the weekend. Simpson did not clear up questions about L.G.

Ridge interviewed a Simpson house guest, architectural engineer Laszlo Benyo, on May 27. The statement from Benyo, a 45-year-old married architect from Budapest, did not clear up questions about L.G. Ridge reported: "When asked about the date of Wednesday 5-5-93. He stated that he was living with Richard Simpson during that time and that he is certain that he was at home during the evening. He knows L.G. and another young black/male who used to come over. He didn't remember L.G. coming over on that Wednesday. He stated that he heard of the murder on Thursday evening when he was discussing with

Richard his traveling plans and Richard brought up the murder of the three boys. He remembered that on Friday morning Richard took him to the airport for a flight he made to New Orleans. He stated that some days ago Richard became upset about L.G. calling quite late at night. This occurred last week. He stated that Richard sometimes cooked for L.G. He stated again that on the night before the conversation came up about the boys that L.G. didn't come over.

"On the night before the conversation. He stated that he once … answered the phone and it was L.G.'s mother." She asked him to tell L.G. to call her back. So Benyo seemingly remembered L.G.'s mother seeking him on May 5 and not finding him either at home or at Simpson's.

In a May 20, 1993, story in the West Memphis Evening Times, contradicting his account of hearing about the murders from Simpson, Benyo said he had been out of town when he heard about the murders.

Benyo continues to work in his own firm as an architect in Budapest.

Domini made no mention in any of her statements about talking to L.G. on the evening of May 5. She said she talked to Damien on May 5 starting around 10 p.m.

Why would Hollingsworth go to the trouble of going to the laundromat to get her phone number if he didn't call soon after? He had seen her earlier that day and would see her several times the next day but he apparently was feeling an immediate need to call. Why would he not act on the information? While he gave contradictory versions of other events, there was no contradicting evidence suggesting that he had not sought out Domini's number.

On Sept. 2, 1993, L.G. gave another statement, this time to John Fogleman. L.G. had moved from 724 McCauley Circle and was living with Simpson.

Asked about his job search on May 5 with Narlene, he said: "Well, we went, uh, she was supposed to come over to my house, and she never did, so I borrowed Richard's car, and I went over to her house …. OK, and I come over there too early, so I took her kids to school. … And then, I left there, no that was the day after, I'm sorry. She come over to the house, and got me, and we went over there. She took the kids to school. And then we went job hunting. …"

He got a job at the Big Star West Broadway, near the high school. Then "we got tired and went to Sonic, and then we got tired, so we was going to go home. … And on the way, she took me to my house and there wasn't nobody there. … So, I told her to take me to my mom's work … So on the way there, she had a wreck, and we stayed there at the wreck and after we left the wreck, we went to her insurance company … And then I went over to her house. No, I didn't. I went to my mom's work and got the key, and then I went home. … Well, I stayed there until my mom got there."

He said Linda got home about 8:30 p.m., or "7:30 somewhere around there." He said he had stayed at his aunt's until around 5 p.m.

He had seen Damien that afternoon. "Well I went over to Domini's and he was there, and I seen him before I left. ... It was about 3 hours before I left my aunt's. ... Yeah, I'd say about 1:00." He stayed "about 20 minutes."

He said Domini and Dian Teer and Echols were there, making no mention of Kenneth Watkins. Dian told Fogleman that L.G. had been at their trailer on May 5 and May 6.

Fogleman asked L.G.: "Did you see them again at any time?"

L.G.: "Yes, I was, I said I was going to go ahead and walk home. So I was going over to my old aunt's to see if she was going to give me a ride." This "old aunt" was Pam Hollingsworth, Dian's sister.

L.G.: "And then I seen Damien right there at the corner, and ..."

Fogleman: "OK. Was he by himself?"

L.G.: "Yes, uh well, I seen him before that, I was walking over to my aunt's, and him and Domini was out there arguing. ... And Domini went her way, and he was standing on the other street ... Like he didn't know what to do. ... And then I left there and went to my aunt's to talk to her."

Fogleman: "About what time was that when you saw them arguing?"

L.G.: "I'd say about 4:30. ... Anyway then my aunt said that she couldn't give me a ride, so I walked outside, and I seen Damien standing at the corner, and I asked him where he fixing to go, and he said my mom's coming to get me, and this was at 5 minutes till 5:00. ..."

Fogleman: "Alright, are you sure that it was that day?"

L.G.: "Yes. ... Anyway, then my aunt took me home."

Fogleman: "OK, was Damien, when you saw him, was he out there standing by himself?"

L.G.: "Yes." L.G.'s story about seeing Damien at Lakeshore contradicted accounts from the Echols and Teer families and seemed to explain part of what actually happened — Echols being at Lakeshore, instead of going home, for a meeting with Baldwin and Misskelley later that afternoon.

L.G. said he did not know the name of the street but it was on a corner near where Baldwin lived..

Fogleman continued: "OK, then what happened?"

L.G.: "My aunt come around the corner and she said, well come on, and I said alright. So I got in the car and she took me home."

L.G. said his mother and a female friend were home when he arrived, and they were "fixin to go to" the home of Mona Robertson. This contradicted some of his other stories.

Fogleman inserted: "Let me stop here and ask you, how are you able to remember all of this so well? You just ...."

L.G." "Well everytime you say another word, it becomes clear."

Fogleman: "But I'm talking about that particular, how do you remember that this happened on that particular day?"

L.G.: "You're talking about Wednesday. I know what happened."

Fogleman: "Well, I know but it was ..."

L.G.: "A long time ago."

Fogleman: "Yes, it was a long time ago. How do you remember that so well? Is there anything in particular about that day that makes it stand out?"

L.G.: "No, it was just a day. See I've been done with this so many times."

Fogleman: "With the police."

L.G.: "Yeah."

L.G. told Fogleman he had not gone over the story with anyone except the police, and "an investigator." Fogleman asked: "Do you remember the guy with the beard, that dresses real fancy?" in reference to Ron Lax.

L.G.: "If he's an investigator, that's who I talked to."

Fogleman asked L.G. what happened after his mother and her friend left.

L.G.: "Well, I stayed there for a little while, then I called my buddy Richard. Richard Simpson. ...Then I went over to his house .... We sat there for a while, and uh, I don't really remember. I think he was tripping out or something.... Then, uh, I went over to go to another friend's house. And, he wasn't home, so I stopped at my aunt's work. Anyway, I left Richard's and he dropped me off home. ... I believe, I'm not for sure. I get the days mixed up, but I know what happened."

So much for L.G.'s incredible memory.

Fogleman: "OK. Let's talk about, now before you said that you went to Dixie's place of work. That's a laundromat."

L.G.: "Yeah."

Fogleman: "Alright, which day are you saying that is."

L.G.: "Uh."

Fogleman: "Alright, before, you said it was that Wednesday. Now, how did you get there?"

L.G.: "Richard. I had his car. Richard's car. ... Richard was in the car on the other side, and I was driving."

Fogleman: "Now, L.G., this is where we're going to start getting into some problems. Um, Richard says, that he saw you that night and it was just for a few minutes, and that he didn't go with you to any laundromat."

L.G.: "Yeah, he did."

Fogleman: "And your aunt says that she knows Richard's car, and the car you came in wasn't Richard's."

L.G. "Yes it was."

Fogleman: "Why did your aunt say that it wasn't and Richard said that it wasn't?"

L.G.: "I don't know. I have no idea."

Fogleman: "You're going to stick with that?"

L.G.; "Yes sir."

Fogleman, bearing down: "Who was it, L.G.?

L.G.: "It was Richard."

Fogleman was moving into some of the toughest questioning in the the case, though ultimately to not much effect: "Do you know why he wouldn't say that it was him?"

L.G.: "I have no idea."

Fogleman: "Why would he have any motivation not to say yes, I was with him, I took him up there?"

L.G.: "I guess you'll have to ask him, because all I know is that we was together, and he knew it and I knew it. And we're still friends, and he didn't say nothing about it."

Fogleman: "What about your aunt?"

L.G.: "I couldn't tell you nothing about that. I don't know why she said that."

Fogleman: "You're digging a hole, L.G."

After a long pause, L.G. responded: "That's the truth, man."

He went on to deny seeing Damien, Jason or Jessie that evening.

Fogleman: "And you're sure about that?"

L.G.: "Yes sir, cause I left there and I went home."

Fogleman: "And what did you do there at the laundromat?"

L.G.: "I walked in and asked for Domini's number."

Fogleman: "Why?"

L.G.: "Because I forgot her number."

He explained that Dixie Hufford would have the number because they were all related.

Fogleman: "OK. What happened the next night? The next day?"

L.G.: "My aunt came over to get me, no ... my aunt came over and got me and took me to Big Star, and I went to work." He started about 9. This roughly agreed with Narlene's account of taking L.G. to work the next day.

Fogleman continued to express skepticism about L.G.'s story, alluding to Hufford's account: "I've got her saying that you came in there, but weren't with Richard. You weren't in his car, it was a different car. And then I've got Richard saying, no, it wasn't me that he was with. Now what would you believe if you were me?"

L.G.: "Well, I don't know, I have no idea. I don't know why somebody would say that."

Domini told investigators that she and Damien "took out stress on each other" the day after the killings.

Multiple statements concurred that the teen couple had a major argument over the phone late in the evening May 5.

Were they arguing that Wednesday afternoon? It doesn't seem unlikely.

One of Damien's complaints about L.G. was that L.G. had suggested that they swap girlfriends, which presumably would have paired L.G. with Domini. Despite being "cousins," they were only loosely related. L.G. showed up at Domini's house regularly for months and continued to call her after the arrests.

Dian Teer explained to Fogleman about L.G.'s visits: "… He used to come over fairly often because he was going out with Domini's best girlfriend, Liza McDaniels … and they would come over sometime and if they'd stayed out too late and if her mother had locked the door on her, they'd come over to our trailer and spend the night."

Asked about L.G.'s visit on May 5, Dian answered: "I don't know exactly what time he left , but they was supposed to be going to see about a job. And uh, his Aunt Narlene and his Aunt Pam both live in the trailer park too and he went I believe with Narlene, to see about the job. … He went over to her house. … It was probably about 12, something like that." She had no recollection of any calls that evening from anyone except Damien around 10 p.m.

Domini was also questioned about L.G. during Fogleman's interviews with the Teers on Sept. 20.

She did not mention L.G. visiting her trailer either day.

Fogleman: "You confide in the L.G. don't you?"

Domini: "That's my cousin."

Fogleman: "You talk to L.G. don't you?"

Domini: "Yeah. ..."

Fogleman pressed her: "OK. Are you sure there's not something you want to tell us?"

Domini: "Uh uh. Nope. I've told you just about everything I know."

Fogleman concluded the interview with this cryptic remark: "Alright ... Well, I'll just let you and L.G. work that out."

In a October 2016 phone interview, Domini Ferris lightly dismissed any significance to her friendship with L.G. "We grew up as cousins and he went out with my best friend. That's about it. Nothing more to it than that." She said she did not talk with him the evening of May 5 and had no idea why he was seeking her phone number that night.

According to Kenneth Watkins, who spent much of May 5 hanging around with Domini, Damien and Jason after he had skipped school, "We went to Wal-Mart to play some video games, and L.G. came to Wal-Mart then we went back inside Wal-Mart to get away from him." This description of events on May 5, which agrees with no one else's account, would have occurred between 3:30, when Baldwin got out of school, and 5:30, when Kenneth went home to babysit.

According to Watkins, in a Sept. 16, 1993, statement: "L.G. came over earlier that morning to talk … He just talked to Domini, I didn't really know it, he was just talking to Domini about moving to Kentucky or something like that, with his girlfriend. …" He said L.G. gave Domini "a little necklace. A black one, with a little green ball."

Bryn Ridge asked Watkins: "OK, and what happened at Wal-Mart?"

Kenneth: "We started playing games, then L.G. came up. We went inside and looked around at some tapes …"

Ridge: "Alright — you said L.G. came up and y'all went inside to look at some tapes. There a conflict between L.G. and somebody?"

Kenneth: "I think Damien said he didn't like L.G. They're always talking about him."

Ridge: "So, when L.G. came up, was it Damien's idea to go in and go somewhere else?"

Kenneth: "Yeah, he didn't want to talk with him."

Watkins said he thought L.G. left during the time they were walking about Wal-Mart over a period of about 30 minutes.

Watkins' account of events at Domini's trailer earlier on May 5 corroborated closely with other statements; his story about the late afternoon was largely uncorroborated and contradicted most other witness statements.

The case records at callahan.8k.com contain a recorded phone call between L.G. and Domini on Feb. 10, 1994, made after a Commercial Appeal article raised questions about L.G. During a preliminary hearing, it was revealed that Echols had named L.G. as a potential suspect. The headline: "Inquiry, trials haunt L.G. Hollingsworth."

L.G. was concerned because Baldwin and Echols had tried to implicate him, according to the story.

L.G. complained: "My name's in the paper."

Domini: "Oh really, about what?"

L.G. "What's, what's that guy uh with Damien? Michael or somebody … Jason, that's the name …. Jason, Jason is trying to say I killed them kids."

Domini: "What?"

L.G. asked: "Now you know I didn't do it, don't you?"

Domini: "Little Jason?'

LG.: "Mm-hmmmm."

Domini: "Don't worry about it."

L.G.: "Now you know I didn't do it, now don't you?"

Domini: "I don't know. I ain't saying nothing. I don't know who did it. I don't have an idea what's going on or what."

She told L.G. to not worry. Domini reassured him that she knew nothing about the allegations and that Damien had said nothing to her about L.G.'s alleged involvement.

Then, in March 1994, with the Echols/Baldwin trial under way, a prisoner named Tim Cotton, who had been in jail with L.G. in February after L.G.'s arrests on burglary and forgery charges, passed a note to jailers tipping them off about a major break in the case, if it panned out.

Timothy Robert Cotton, 26, was among those questioned in the first days of the investigation after drawing attention during the search. Like many others, but unlike either Echols or Misskelley, he passed a polygraph examination and was cleared as a suspect.

Nonetheless police received a number of tips about Cotton early in the case.

One said:

"Ref: Tim Cotton

"5/24

"F/W called advise that M/W first name either Tim or Tom is possibly responsible for the murder of the three 8 year old youths in Arkansas. Called advised that m/w is into self mutilation and has broken bottles and cut himself in the presence of his sister. His sister advised the called that her brother had killed animals before and that when she heard about the boys she suspect her brothers involvement. Suspect's sister name is Tamara and she works as a cocktail waitress at the Gulfstream lounge. Caller stated that the reason she believes he is involved is that he works at the Blue Beacon Car Wash (The three youths were found behind the Blue Beacon) Caller advised that Tim has been in an institution and like to play around with 5-8 year old boys."

Charlie Dabbs took another tip on May 27: "Received a call from Sally Brady and Gina Riccio about the nite the boys were missing Wednesday nite and they were out driving around trying to assist in locating the missing boy. They advised they saw Tim Cotten from Lakeshore riding a bicycle that was green and yellow go into Robin Hood Woods at dead end of McCauley and as they were driving around … about 45 minutes to 1 hour later they saw him again coming from the other end of Robin Hood and was wet & muddy all over and they heard him tell some of the Search & Rescue people he had fallen in the bayou was going home and change clothes. They said he was a weird acting guy and just wanted to check him out. he was seen going in woods around 10 p.m. and coming out around 11 p.m."

Cotton on May 8 told investigators that he did not know anything about the homicides but had helped in the search. He had just started working at the Blue Beacon and lived in the same neighborhood as the victims, not at Lakeshore.

He said he first learned the boys were dead around 3 p.m. Thursday when he overheard Gitchell. He passed a polygraph test on May 8. Cotton eventually passed along his own tip.

His note from March 4, 1994, pointed to L.G. Hollingsworth as the "4th Suspect."

The note, as preserved on callahan.8k.com, is difficult to read: "L.G. Hollyingworth have told me, as Tim R. Cotton Sr., I state that L.G. had told me that was the 4th suspeck in the three 8 yr old killing on or on May of 93, He was getting cooke cane from Mr. Byers, & he, that is L.G. told me that a drug deal went bad & he & the three young men, to get even with Mr. Byers. By put a hit on his family & he told me, that he and Damien made a deal, just to get the Byers boy & hurt him real bad, and he went on for about a week. Telling me, Tim Cotten Sr. I wanted to no if he could trust me & I told him yes, & he said the two other boys was not part of the hit on the Byers family but they were all together that day. Oh yes there are two other people that helped the killers." Cotton offered to testify in exchange for getting out of jail.

Sudbury and Durham interviewed Cotton on March 8:

"Timothy Cotton stated that around May the 5th or 6th he had left his house on Wilson Street and was going to job interview. Along the way he learned of the three boys missing. That someone in the rescue squad asked him to help look for the boys at which time he borrowed a 4 wheeler and helped look, but did not find anything.

"On the 13th of Jan. 1994 he was locked up in the CCSO. That later in February L.G. Hollingsworth was locked up. That he and L.G. had received a subpoena to court in Jonesboro. …"

Their link was that they both were potential (though minor) witnesses in the Echols/Baldwin trial in Jonesboro.

The report continued:

"That they talking about the subpoenas and L.G. told him: That he and Damien went to cult meeting together and that he and Damien drank beer together at the meetings and killed animals at the meetings. That the meetings were at Lakeshore then moved to the old RR bridge like you are going to Memphis. That L.G. told him, at one of the meeting a older man was there and appeared to the leader. ...

"That later that week something came on the news about a 4th suspect in the killing of the three boys. At this time L.G. stated to him that they were talking about him that he was the 4th suspect. L.G. said he had the knife that belonged to the boys meaning Damien and his friends. ...

"That L.G. has stated a contract was out on John Byers for a dope debt owed to him, but who ever was going to beat him up count get to Byers so L.G. decided to get Damien to beat up Byers son. That later Damien told L.G. that he had got him real good and two others boys that were there. ...

"That L.G. said Damien told him that after the killing he had someone pick him up and that person was driving a green and white van and that they lived in Lakeshore on the back side near the sewer plant."

The report repeatedly noted that Hollingsworth denied making these statements and denied that he knew Byers.

The report added: "It is the opinion of this investigator that Timothy Cotton is under the impression he will receive some type help or his case be dismissed if he can be a witness for the Prosecutors Office. There is nothing to substantiate the statement given by Mr. Cotton."

Police brought L.G. in yet again on March 8 while the Echols/Baldwin trial was under way.

Sudbury noted, at 11:25 a.m.: "The interview consisted of allegations made by Timothy Cotton whereas L.G. Hollingsworth had told him of his knowledge of the killing of the three boys.

"Mr. Hollingsworth denied having made any statements to Timothy Cotton. " It seems unlikely that L.G. never said anything to Cotton while they were locked up in a cell together for days. Police, reluctant to believe anything from L.G. to that point, took his all-coverage denial at face value.

Police then tape-recorded a portion of the interview, starting at 12:02 p.m. and ending nine minutes later, at 12:11. The interview did not delve into Cotton's allegations. Instead, L.G. told about a conversation he had with Echols about two months, "maybe not that long," before the murders.

L.G.: "We was coming back from my house, I believe. We was walking, I do know that..... We was going to Belvedere …. To meet up with my girlfriend and his girlfriend. … OK. Damien asked me could I kill somebody and I says, 'I don't think I could kill them unless they did something really bad to me.' I said, 'I'd probably hurt them bad first.' And then I says, 'Why you ask?' He says, 'Cause I'm thinking of killing somebody.' I says, 'Why you thinking about killing somebody?' He says, 'They're fucking with me.' That's what he told me. I says, 'If there's some man, then you just go and you break his ass or you get your ass whooped. If it's some little teenager, you tell his parents or you call the police.' I say, 'You don't need to do that, because that's not cool, you know. You'll go to jail for that.' And we keep walking and stuff and he says, 'Just say that you would kill somebody.' I says, 'OK, say I would kill somebody.' He says, 'How would you do it?' I says, 'Well it depends.' He says, 'What do you mean it depends?' I said, 'It depends on what they did to me to make me kill them.' I says, 'I'd probably put a bullet in their head, and if not I'd probably break both of their arms and make them wish they was dead.' And um I says, 'Well, What's up?' or you know, 'Would you kill somebody?' And he says, 'Yeah.' He says, 'I'm thinking of killing somebody' is what he told me. I said, 'OK,' I says, 'you don't need to do that. That's gonna fuck your life up.' I says, 'it will mess you up altogether.' He says, 'Well' like that, and we left it at that and we kept walking for a little ways more. And he says, 'If I was gonna kill somebody I would tie 'em up, beat 'em and fuck 'em. That way they would know that I'm not fucking with nobody. You know, I'm a straight up kind of guy. …

"And alright so I said, 'Well look, you don't need to do that, you know.' Alright. So we walked on. Alright. And then May the 6th, I think it was May the 6th, when I did talk to Damien he was just kind of like sitting there. He was kind of nervous. …. At Domini's house in Lakeshore."

L.G. said he remembered the date because he had been riding with Narlene when she was in a car accident the day before.

"That day we sat and I talked to him for a minute and then I left. And I came over there like three times and they were still whatever they was doing, you know, sitting and talking. So I didn't say too much and I left again. Anyway, he was on the corner, sitting on the corner and my cousin had run away. " L.G. said Domini ran away from Damien during an argument.

Sudbury: "This is on the 6th?" L.G. had described a similar scene on the 5th.

L.G. "This is on the 6th. … I said, 'Are you still thinking of killing somebody,' like that. He says, 'No I ain't. It's kind of tooken care of. Don't worry about it, you know it's OK.' He said you know kind of fast, you know, I didn't catch it at first. I thought about what he said and then that's when I realized that's what he said, you know. He said it's tooken care of."

L..G believed he knew that three 8-year-olds were missing at that time, but not that they were dead. "I don't watch a lot of the news," L.G. explained. "My aunt told me either on the 6th or the 5th there was kids missing. You know I didn't even know where they was missing from."

L.G. had not mentioned these conversations in his many other interviews with police. Police also found little corroboration from others questioned about L.G.'s activities on May 5 and 6.

Rumors have continued concerning the deaths of the boys as payback for a drug deal gone wrong. Mark Byers was a longtime smalltime drug dealer as well as a police informant. Greg Day's authorized biography of Byers, "Untying the Knot," detailed a number of Byers drug deals gone wrong, violent threats and retribution and Byers' knack for bad decisions.

Also, the Crittenden County Drug Task Force was under investigation in 1993 by the Arkansas State Police over missing confiscated items including $200, a small amount of drugs and firearms claimed by officers for personal use. The Drug Task Force had been spectacularly successful in a number of drug busts, as local forces cracked down on drug traffic moving through Interstate 55 and Interstate 40. Critics have seized upon involvement of Drug Task Force members in the murder investigation to suggest that police work was tainted, particularly in dealings with Byers.

Still, there was no evidence beyond Cotton's statement that the killers or L.G. had dealings with Byers.

Given the looming size of Byers, it's hard to imagine a couple of relatively small teenagers planning to beat him up, which would explain why they might target his son.

The mysterious "leader" of the Lakeshore witch cult was described as an older man. Other statements have located "Lucifer," "Lusserfer" or "Lucifier," with widely varying descriptions, as living on a back lot in Lakeshore or somewhere in Marion. Did this fabled creature actually exist, and did he drive a green and white van?

Cotton did not testify. Police apparently did not give his statement a great deal of credence. Similarly, police treated all statements from L.G. with justifiable skepticism, except for denials about Cotton's story.

The many contradictions in L.G.'s stories ultimately only confused matters as L.G. never emerged as a clear suspect.

In a case filled with unreliable potential witnesses, L.G. Hollingsworth was just another kid who seemed to be making up much of the story as he went along.

L.G. Hollingsworth Jr. was killed in a vehicle accident on Oct. 26, 2001.

Questions about the "fourth suspect" remain.

"WE SAW DAMIEN AND DOMINI .... "

Those who depended on the "Paradise Lost" movies for information about the West Memphis 3 killers heard little about eyewitnesses who placed Damien Echols near the scene of the murders.

The jury who heard testimony from Narlene Hollingsworth and her son, Anthony Hollingsworth, in the Echols/Baldwin trial labeled their stories "honest" in jury notes.

Narlene called the police on May 9, 1993. According to a handwritten note, she saw "Dominique" and "Damion" "walking from Blue Beacon toward Lakeshore Estates. They looked dirty. L. G. Hollingsworth (age 17) was at the laundromat at 9:30 p.m., it was noted.

"According to Mrs. Hollingsworth, her nephew L.G. made the statement on Thursday that he knew about what happened before anyone else.

"L.G. has 666 on the side of his boots.

"Damion is mean & evil, according to Mrs. Hollingsworth."

The next day at 4:05 p.m., Mike Allen took an anonymous tip from "an old white female who stated she had overheard that a Dominick + Damion killed the three little boys + that L.G. last name unknown took and laudered there clothing. Caller stated that Damion had body parts in a box from the children. The called ... didn't give her name + (stated) that she heard that L.G.'s mother was going to lie about L.G.'s where abouts."

At 4:20 p.m. that afternoon, Detective Charlie Dabbs and Lt. Diane Hester took a statement from Narlene Virginia Hollingsworth, a 42-year-old Lakeshore resident.

Ricky Sr., 37, and Narlene had four children who figured also in the narrative: Anthony Hollingsworth, 21, Ricky Hollingsworth Jr., 14, Tabitha Hollingsworth, 16, and Mary Hollingsworth, 10.

Narlene told police: "What happened was Dixie Hollingsworth had asked me to pick her up at where she works at a laundry mat, she said, will you pick me up, I get off at 10, I said yes I will ... OK, I got ready to go, and my husband went with me and my children were too. And, on our way, coming down like you're going to Love's, I saw Dominic and Damian coming down the street ... This was exactly 20 minutes till 10, exactly, cause we had our watches and we knew what time it was. OK they had dark clothing on and they were not cleaned."

Dabbs: "You said at one time that they were muddy all over."

Narlene: "They did have dirt on them, yes they did, now. ... They was coming back towards Lakeshore, this way .... They were, it was a yellow uh, sign thing up in, some stick standing up and then they were just before they got to there, where they was. ... OK, as we were driving by, she pointed the stick ... to us, and it's right there on the off ramp, where ... as you go east down the interstate ... the off ramp to the South Service Road ... is where the yellow stick or marker was."

She had turned her brights on "so that I could get a good look at them ... to see who they were, yes I did. And I said, that's Dominic and Damien, no look like, it is and I got a good close look and said, it sure is. ... I really don't know Damien, cause I don't go around him from all the bad things I hear about him, but therefore, I don't let my children go around him and Dominic, I've known her all of her life. Cause I use to hold her on my hip when she was six months baby. ...

"... I was upset about it, for them being out that late and around that area, but you know I was wondering what they were doing out at that time of night. My husband told me to quit worrying about it, cause they are out all the time. He said that he sees them all the time. So, he told me to quit worrying about it. ...

"... I don't know what L.G. is capable of, and I am not saying that he would do it, and I am not saying that he wouldn't, but I know Damien. Everybody said that Damien, I know that he's suppose to have 666 on his shoes. …"

Hester: "And your husband and your children saw him and Dominic both."

Narlene: "Yes, ain't no way they missed that."

She repeated the information on May 20: "… I left home about 9:30 I was going down the south service road and I looked to the right and I saw Daymeion Dominique walking they were dirty and muddy go to the laundrymat Dixie said LG just left and I said I just saw Daymeion and she asked was Dominique with him and I said yes."

Narlene testified in the Baldwin/Echols trial on March 3, 1994: "Well see, we spent most of our day together, Dixie and I did. And we had lunch together. And she asked me that day, would I come back and pick her … Well, she got off at 10, but we got there a little early."

She said she left home at exactly 9:30 p.m. and had all her children, along with a young friend, packed into a red 1982 Ford Escort.

John Fogleman asked: "… As you were approaching Love's and Blue Beacon, uh - did you see anybody there on the service road?"

Narlenc: "Yes, we did. … We saw Damien and Domini. … Damien had on a pair of black pants and a dark shirt. Domini had on a pair of tight pants - you know, fit tight. And she had flowers, looked like white flowers to me on her pants. … Which I know they were her clothes because 2 or 3 days before that, I saw her with those same clothes on."

Fogleman: "Alright. Uh -- in fact, Domini's tried to get you to say something different, hasn't she?"

Val Price, Echols' attorney, interjected: "Judge, objection! Totally inappropriate, your Honor."

Narlene was willing to talk: "I'll answer."

Judge David Burnett said "Wait just a minute." This was followed by laughter in the courtroom and a bench conference.

Price said the testimony would be a hearsay response. The Court agreed. Fogleman said he might call Domini on the matter but "she might lie." They moved on.

Fogleman: "Narlene, when you saw these uh -- Damien and Domini on the service road, did you do anything with your lights? ..."

Narlene: "... I put the bright lights on to be sure ... That it was them. ... Because I didn't realize there for a second how many I really had in the car with me and it was getting late and Domini was only 14. ... So I wanted to give them a ride back home. See, I knew I had a few minutes to get to the laundrymat. ... I looked back and my ex-husband said, 'Where are you gonna put 'em?' I said, 'Well, I'd put Mary in Domini's lap.' And I looked over, he said, 'Where you gonna put the other one, in Damien's lap?' and I looked at Damien and said, 'No, I don't think so.'"

Under questioning by Echols defense attorney Scott Davidson, she said, " ... I wanted to stop and pick 'em up ... Give 'em a ride so - so Domini wouldn't be on the street. I'm a real funny person about that and I don't think young children ought to be on the street after dark."

She also wanted to stop because "I just started feeling like all of a sudden I wanted to throw up. ... I stopped for a second and then went on 'cause they kept hollering -- the kids kept hollering 'Let's go on, let's go, you can get sick when we get there.'"

Laughter broke out in the courtroom again.

Baldwin attorney Paul Ford correctly predicted that the prosecution ultimately would argue that she had mistaken Baldwin for Domini that evening.

On May 25, 1993, Anthony Hollingsworth gave a handwritten statement to police: "Wensday night I was at my mom dads house when the phone rig at 9:15 pm and it was my grandmother she told us to come and get her from wroke. We walk out and get mom car Anthony Ricky Tabitha Matt Narlene Sombra Little Ricky and left to go pick up Dixie we get service road were going just west of Seventh Street. We saw Damaion and Dominque and they were on south side of the south service road. They were wearing black clothes that were muddy It was about 9:30 pm We went to Flash Market and pick up Dixie and took her home and then we went back to our house and didn't see Damion and Domique on the road."

Anthony also testified on March 3, immediately preceding his mother.

He testified he, his brother, his two sisters, his mom and dad and his little brother's girlfriend Sombra had gone to pick up his grandmother at a laundromat near Southland Park dog track, next to a Flash Market. He recalled the time as 10:30 but wasn't sure -- "that was a year ago."

He said they saw Damien and "Dominique, his girlfriend" by the side of the road wearing black, dirty clothes.

Anthony: "She had black pants on with sort of a black shirt -- the shirt was black but the pants had white flowers on 'em."

With the May 25 statement as reference under questioning by John Fogleman, he agreed that he had given the time as 9:30 and had stated that the clothes were not merely dirty but muddy.

Other members of the Hollingsworth family did not testify in the trial but gave statements to police.

Tabitha, 16, told Dabbs on May 20: "Well, first that night, we were going to get my aunt from work, and L.G. seen Damian nem walking, walking back from over there by that place where them kids got killed at. ... They were coming down by Love's, they right beside the place, cause they were walking back this way, walking back toward Love's. ... Well, Damien, had, uh, Dominic had black pants on with holes in the knees, and she had on a long black shirt and he was wearing all black, he had black boots on black shirt, black pants on, and they were muddy. ... No doubt n my mind, I seen them, they were all muddy."

She said they were going to pick up her grandmother at the laundromat at about 9 or 9:30, going down the south service road toward Ingram Boulevard to Flash Market.

She said she and Domini "use to hang around a lot when we were in school" and that she had been introduced to Damien at Domini's house ("he just live right around behind us").

"I think he's a devil worshiper, I don't like him ... He makes signs on the street and all of that, and he go back under the bridge and makes of the devil."

She said Domini knew Echols was a devil worshipper. "She doesn't say nothing about, I guess she don't care."

She also knew Jason. "I don't know his last name, I know where he lives though ... Yep, very good friends, they walk around with each other all the time. ... They act strange all the time."

On Dec. 7, Ricky Sr. gave this statement: "On 5-5-93, I Rick Hollingsworth was in a 1982 Ford Escort Stationwagon with my ex-wife Narlene, Anthony, Tabita, Mary and Little Rick at between 9:00 and 10:00 PM. We were going to get Dixie from where she works on Ingram. We were on the South Service Road between Blue Beacon and Love's truck stop when Narlene saw two people that she said were Damien and Domini. I did see the two people but I didn't look close enough to say who they were but I did see that they had long hair. Narlene thought it was strange and asked if she ought to turn around to give them a ride. I told her no that I had seen them walking all over the place and that they are always walking."

On May 20, Dixie Hufford, 50, said Narlene and Ricky Hollingsworth had picked her up from work at a few minutes before 10 p.m. that night and taken her home.

As predicted, prosecutors did try to use the sighting to place Baldwin at the scene.

Fogleman worked it into his closing argument: "Let's talk about Damien Echols or an accomplice, Jason Baldwin or an accomplice, causing the deaths of these boys. As the court instructs you, some of this evidence is only as to one, some of it as to both. In this case, you've got evidence that at about nine thirty -- sometime between nine thirty and ten on May the fifth, this is the area of the crime scene, and somewhere in this area Damien Echols -- who by his own admission dresses very distinctively and stands out in a crowd -- he is seen by somebody who's seen him hundreds of time, Narlene and Anthony Hollingsworth. And he's seen with somebody they identify as Damien's girlfriend. They're muddy, dirty, and they're here about nine thirty or ten, which Damien denies. Now, all of y'all -- I don't think any one of you could forget Anthony and Narlene's testimony. I got to thinking about it later, and you know -- we laughed, we all laughed. You laughed, we laughed, the defense attorneys laughed, everybody laughed -- they were dead serious. And, you don't pick your witnesses -- and because they're simple, and they're not highly educated, that should be no reason to discount anything they said. Think about what they said and really how they said it. I submit to you, you'll find that they were highly credible. And that they did see Damien Echols on this service road between nine thirty and 10 on May the fifth, 1993. Now, who he was with -- draw your own conclusions. Says his girlfriend and they describe her as having red hair and long. You got a picture of Jason Baldwin at the time of his arrest. Nothing wrong with having long hair and the picture in there is not shown to show that he's a bad person because he got long hair. But think about that. Think about who Damien was with on May the fifth."

Brent Davis didn't mention Baldwin in his portion of the closing statement, focusing instead on the credibility of the Hollingsworths' testimony: "And it's kindly funny, you know at one point they wanna believe Narlene but they don't wanna believe Narlene. … I don't think Narlene lied to you when she said she saw Damien out there. And once you accept that, and why in the world is Damien and the rest of his group lying to cover him -- where he was on the fifth. What difference does it make? Why don't he get up here and level with us? 'Why, heck, I was going down to Love's truck stop on the fifth.' Put Domini up here, let her tell you what they were doing. But if Anthony and Narlene are telling you the truth, and you know -- you heard her say about getting them in the car but she wasn't gonna have them in the car, she wouldn't let her kids sit on his lap. She know who was out there, I mean --- Damien himself admits what a distinctive looking character he is, and you wouldn't drive by and miss with your bright lights on at night if you knew who he was. And she knew who was out there. And if he's out there then he's lying to you. And if he's lying to you --- his whole family is lying to you, and the question I got for you is, if they're lying to you about all that, why? Why? Do they got something to hide? I put to you, they do."

It's unlikely that the Hollingsworths would be mistaken in identifying Echols, but how likely is it that they were mistaken about Domini? Baldwin and Domini were close enough in size, hair color and dress to be mistaken for each other at a glance in poor lighting. But according to Dennis 'Dink' Dent, Baldwin showed up at home around 9 or 9:30, which means he couldn't have been walking along the service road between 9:30 and 10.

Domini's alibi wasn't particularly strong because it was not corroborated by anyone other than her mother. But the story from the Teers was consistent. No one other than the Hollingsworths placed Domini anywhere but at home that evening, though Damien at one point claimed she had been over at his parents' trailer that evening.

The only evidence of Domini's possible involvement on any level is in the statements from the Hollingsworths, who clearly bore her no ill will. Narlene in particular seemed oblivious to possible implications of the sighting.

Police also talked to Dixie Hufford, 50, on May 20, after a tipster called into the West Memphis Police Department.

The note on the tip said: "-Boone- called stated the woman that works at the Laundromat on Ingram. Her name is Dixie, Dixie told someone? that 2 boys and a girl came into the laundromat about 10:00P.M.-10:30P.M. on Wednesday to clean up. They had mud and blood on their clothes. Dixie is supposed to be related to one of them, only name Boone new was Hollingsworth."

Ridge and Gitchell conducted the interview that evening at Hufford's apartment. The official record gives no indication that the tip was discussed, though perhaps it was cleared up informally.

Hufford did have much to say about Domini and Damien:

"Dixie stated that she feels that Damien does control Domini and that she is fearful for her.

"Dixie stated that she believed Domini was at home sick that day and that Domini's mom was home.

"Dixie stated that she does not like Damien ...

"Dixie knows Jason Baldwin and knows that Damien and Jason are very close friends.

"Dixie feels that Domini's mom knows some things but won't tell because of her fear for Domini. ...

"Damien controls Domini."

In a phone interview in March 2013, Narlene Hollingsworth revisited her story as told in 1993-1994, sticking adamantly to the fact that she had seen Domini walking with Damien. New details or twists had not been added over time.

"I'VE HEARD FROM A LOT OF PEOPLE THAT HE HAS BEEN POSSESSED"

Stories originating from Baldwin buddy Garrett Schwarting had almost as much credibility as the "Hobbs family secret" or the later imaginings of Aaron Hutcheson.

During his many interviews with investigators, the 15-year-old Schwarting was a font of information, some of it clearly misinformation, some possibly disinformation, often not only at great odds with statements from others but with himself.

While attempting to help Echols and Baldwin, Schwarting tended to confirm suspicions about them. He didn't help out Misskelley either. For instance, he said that his sister's best friend, Tiffany Allen, had been going out with Jessie, "and she would come to school telling me stories like he beat her and all kind of stuff like that. She had black eyes, busted lip."

Bryn Ridge, acting on a tip that Schwarting knew Echols and Baldwin and might have information on the murders, talked to Schwarting on May 19. Schwarting told Ridge that he had not seen Baldwin in over three weeks.

On May 25, Schwarting told juvenile officer Steve Jones that Echols was not involved in the murders.

Then, on June 7, the Monday after the arrests, Schwarting ran into Jones at Barfield's, a local store. Schwarting was looking for a copy of the Commercial

Appeal so he could read about the arrests. He explained that Baldwin could not have been a part of the murders. Schwarting claimed that he had gone to the Baldwin residence on May 5 on three occasions, first at 7 p.m., then at 7:30 and finally a third time.

Schwarting had wanted to borrow a long white Ozzy Osbourne T-shirt that the Baldwins could not find at first. So Schwarting returned twice more, bringing along his friend, 13-year-old Kevin Lawrence, the final time. Schwarting claimed he stayed and played Nintendo at Baldwin's home until 9 or 9:30, when he went to spend the night at Kevin's.

At first Schwarting's alibi for Baldwin seemed to have backing (sort of) from Kevin Lawrence.

Even so, Lawrence's version raised a question about Baldwin's school attendance that day.

Jones compiled his information from Schwarting in a handwritten report dated June 7 and filed on June 10.

On June 11, just before Ridge held an extensive interview with Schwarting, Lawrence told police that his mother had checked him out of school on May 5 at 12:45 p.m., and that Schwarting dropped by his home.

Lawrence said that around 2 p.m. they went to Jason's home to retrieve a shirt he had loaned to Jason (over four hours earlier than Schwarting had described). After Mrs. Grinnell opened the door, Jason told them that "he couldn't find the shirt or that he had to go get it from his friend," according to Lawrence's statement, handwritten by Ridge at the boy's request.

The boys returned to Kevin's house. About 20 minutes later Schwarting went back over to Jason's, returned about 15 minutes later without the shirt, and left again for Jason's about 30 minutes later. That trip took about 30 minutes. Schwarting returned again without a shirt.

Schwarting stayed at Lawrence's until about 7 or 8, playing Nintendo, before going home, said Lawrence.

No one else had claimed that Jason and his mother were both home at around 2 p.m. that afternoon. Jason's attendance at school was documented. Schwarting claimed he was hanging around the Baldwin home until 9:30 while Lawrence claimed Schwarting had been at his home that evening. The timeline from Lawrence provided no alibi for Baldwin.

Ridge then questioned Schwarting, who claimed he had gotten out of school at the usual time on May 5 and that Kevin showed up around 5 or 5:30 and they had gone to Kevin's home in Lakeshore, arriving about 6 or 6:30. Schwarting said he called his mother to get permission to spend the night with Lawrence.

He claimed he had gone to Baldwin's home three times, at roughly 30-minute intervals, starting around 6:45, the last time staying and playing Super Nintendo with Matt, little Terry and Ken while Jason looked for the shirt. He said Ken left around 7:30 to 8:30. They began playing Street Fighter around 8.

Schwarting also told Ridge that, after Jason cut his uncle's lawn, Jason had gone to Wal-Mart and played Street Fighter while a youth named Don Nam watched. (Nam initially gave a statement saying he had seen Baldwin at Walmart around 6 p.m. on May 5. He retracted the statement the next day.)

Schwarting —- who didn't see Baldwin cutting grass or at Wal-Mart — said Baldwin left Wal-Mart at about 7 p.m. for home. Schwarting claimed that he had run into Nam at Wal-Mart later,. Nam told him about seeing Baldwin. Schwarting said he had learned details about Jason's lawn mowing earlier on June 11 from the newspaper.

Ridge asked him: "… How do you know that's the night that occurred?"

Schwarting: "It said in the paper that they came up missing May 5th."

Ridge then asked him what else he did that afternoon. Schwarting first replied that he shot pool at the Lakeshore store. Ridge pointed out that just prior to the interview that Schwarting told him they went on a picnic. He claimed "we went to little picnic at Hernando Lake. …. somewhere in Tennessee, I think."

Pressed about the date, Schwarting was sure of May 5.

Ridge told him: "What I'm at is that two weeks after the murders occurred you don't remember going at Jason's house, now here it's a month and a half later and you remember that is the exact date and the exact times and everything exact about."

Schwarting: "Sir … I have talked to Matthew Baldwin couple of times since then … and I know he said that I was over there that one night. Then it started to come to me slower and slower."

Ridge pointed out that his story and Kevin's story "are no where near alike." Ridge added: "You made a statement a little while ago that Jason didn't do this and that you're going to do anything you can to get him out of it."

Schwarting also gave a handwritten statement: "The night of the murders, I stayed the night with Kevin. I went to Jason's house 3 times that night. Once at 7:00 (he said he hasn't had time to find my shirt) again at 7:30 (he said come back in 30 min.) the third time, I brought my friend Kevin. We stayed at Jason's house until 9:00 p.m. then left. When we was at Jason's the last time, we played Street Fight II on SuperNintendo. At about 8:30 Ken's mom came to pick him up."

Schwarting agreed to take a polygraph test.

On June 15, Schwarting changed his story: "On Wednesday, May 5th, I was at home because my mom won't let me stay anywhere unless it's at Kevin's house. I didn't stay at Kevin's that night but the next night I did. I stayed home, watched TV, played Nintendo and went to sleep at about 10 p.m. I didn't see Jason Baldwin at all that day or I didn't talk to him."

Police noted that Schwarting's version of going to Baldwin's home on May 5 actually occurred May 6.

So much for that alibi.

Schwarting had a wealth of other unreliable information to share.

Schwarting passed along stories that Echols allegedly told him and Murray Farris, a leader of a local Wicca coven, while they were cleaning the pool at Farris' home in mid-May. Schwarting said he didn't know Farris well. Echols apparently was just hanging out.

"We were trying to trick him," said Schwarting on June 11, "not really tricking but trying to get him to confess. Just say he did it cause me and Murray both were tired of being questioned and we wanted to find out who had done it."

Echols didn't confess but he did boast about how he had poured gasoline on a cat, stuck a bottle rocket up its rear and lit the fuse. Echols told them he once choked a small boy with a noose until he turned blue and passed out.

Earlier, on May 25, Schwarting told Jones that Baldwin and Misskelley were involved in a Satanic cult, along with Jerry Nearns, but that Echols was not involved in any type of cult or Satanic worship.

Schwarting claimed Baldwin had once invited him to a meeting of Satan worshippers in a building behind Lakeshore. Schwarting refused Baldwin's invitation but Schwarting told acquaintances that he was studying witchcraft.

Later, on June 7, he told Jones that Echols had a demon placed inside him by a man called Lucifer, and that Echols had lived with Lucifer prior to living with his parents. Schwarting said the demon possessing Echols must kill nine people before it becomes a God, with Baldwin being the first person to be killed (Echols would have been doing a poor job of fulfilling the demon's commands). Schwarting told police that Lucifer was involved in the murders.

Now, he said, Echols' former girlfriend, Deanna Holcomb, was dating Lucifer, further claiming that she was "very much involved" in Satanic worship. He claimed that "Damien broke up with Deanna and then she met Lucifer and started learning black magic." (Deanna had renounced her involvement in black magic and said that Echols practiced black magic).

Schwarting said that Echols was bisexual and that he and Baldwin often argued when Echols spent time with Domini (Schwarting was an "ex, ex, ex-boyfriend" of Echols' girlfriend).

Among the weird details: Lucifer at one time had a purple streak in his blond hair.

Later, Schwarting claimed that Misskelley was afraid of Lucifer, who made Misskelley turn himself in, and that Misskelley had implicated Echols and Baldwin because he knew they were suspects.

Schwarting said he did not believe that Echols had committed the murders, and named two other possible suspects, Jerry Allen Nearns and Frankie Knight, both of whom were interrogated by police.

Then Schwarting talked further about Nearns, who had lived at Little's Trailer Park at the same time as Schwarting. Schwarting said Nearns belonged to a cult where they were sacrificing cats and that Misskelley and Baldwin were members. Schwarting said Nearns nailed a cat to a tree with a railroad spike and would stuff cats into jars, throw them into the air and hit them with a board.

On June 11, he gave a statement to Ridge that included another mention of "Lusserfur," though he had no details about the alleged magickal mastermind and had never seen "Lusserfur," helpfully adding that "Damien I've heard from a lot of people that he has been possessed."

Schwarting denied his earlier assertion that Baldwin was in the cult.

Jason Frazier was a 16-year-old acquaintance of Schwarting's who told police on June 11 that he had talked with Schwarting about two weeks after the murders. A mutual acquaintance, Laura Maxwell, who had dated Echols, said that Schwarting had told Frazier that Echols and Baldwin held their devil worshipping meetings "in that park" — Robin Hood. Schwarting supposedly had heard from Baldwin that Damien had killed the boys because they saw something they weren't supposed to see.

Frazier told Allen and Ridge about Schwarting: "He said ... I know who did it, and all of that ... He told me Jason Baldwin and Damien Echols. ....

"He said ... that he was studying to be a psychic .... and him and this guy was studying it, and that ... Damien and uh Jason did it, but Jessie's names was involved, so uh they was practicing their witch craft and, he didn't say how the boys got there, or anything, he just said, they did it and that's where they practiced their witch, their Satan stuff."

Frazier later in the interview gave a confused account of how Schwarting told him that Baldwin had nothing to do with the killings. Frazier said Schwarting told him "it was just Damien" but "he said that Damien didn't do it."

Frazier said his cousin, Jeff Hood, 15, had overheard the earlier conversation with Schwarting. Hood gave a handwritten statement June 15: "It had to been on a Saturday it was after the murders, me & my cousin Jason Fraizer were in front of the old belvedere apartments, it was in the morning time about 11 or 12 and Garrett Swarting was on a bike & he pulled up on his bike & asked for a cigeretes & started talking about White Which Craft & said the Jason Baldwin & Damien Echols did the murders. He studied which craft & said it came to him. When he told me I didn't believe him."

If there was truth in Schwarting's stories, it was difficult to discern.

"WE NEVER WALKED ON THE SERVICE ROAD. EVER."

Domini Alia Teer, pregnant girlfriend of Damien Echols, gave an account of May 5 that placed her safely off the scene from the horror at moonrise.

Domini, a slender redhead, first was questioned by police with Jason Baldwin and Echols the Sunday after the killings in the front yard of the Baldwin trailer at 245 W. Lake Drive South.

Domini told Shane Griffin and Bill Durham "that on 5/5/93 she, Damien and Jason Baldwin were at Jason's uncle's house somewhere around Dover Road mowing the lawn in the early afternoon. Then stated that she got home around 6:00 pm and was there the rest of the night (verified by mother)."

Durham reported: " … Damien phoned his father to pick them up at the laundrymat at Missouri and N. Worthington. They said they were picked up at 6:00PM and Damien's father took Jason and Dominic home and Damien went home."

Bryn Ridge interviewed Domini at West Memphis Police Department headquarters on May 10, with Mary Margaret Kesterson of the Arkansas State Police sitting in..

Ridge reported: "Domini claimed that on Wednesday 5-5-93 that she went with Damien, Jason, and Ken to Jason's uncle's house to watch as Jason mowed his yard. Domini and Damien went to the laundry where they called for Damien's mother to pick them up. Domini stated that the time was about dark or just before it got dark. Domini stated that she was dropped off at her house and Damien went home. Domini stated that (she) called Damien and that he told her he was tired and was going to sleep. Domini's mother stated that Domini came in when Time Trax was on TV on Wednesday evening.

"Domini stated that on Thursday she and Damien had an argument and took out stress on each other. Domini claimed that the conflict was to do with Jason Baldwin & his girl friend."

Notes indicated the mowing was around 5:45 and that Damien's mother picked them up around 7:45 to 8 p.m. Also mentioned were teenagers in the local witch cult, Chris (Littrell), Murray (Farris) and Deanna Holcomb.

Discrepancies quickly grew in various accounts of the day. For example, police first were told that Damien's father picked them up, then Damien's mother, and finally the whole Echols family was in the car. "Time Trax" started at 7 p.m., well before dark. Sunset was at 7:49 p.m. In a later statement, Domini said she got home even earlier, perhaps as early as 5:30. In later statements, she made no mention of a phone call in which Echols claimed he was tired and going to sleep; her description of that conversation is the single instance in which one of the four girls Damien claims he was talking to on the phone actually said they had a phone conversation with Damien in the late afternoon/early evening. Echols and his family also claimed to have gone to the home of family friends at varying times that evening and afternoon, but well before 8 p.m.

Domini took a nap not long after she got home, and then argued with Damien starting around 10 about Baldwin's supposed girlfriend calling Echols.

Police confiscated a notebook from Domini that contained dark-themed poems with themes of death and suicide. Full of typical teenage angst, they were much of a piece with her boyfriend's morbid musings in his "Book of Shadows."

Teer gave an extensive statement to John Fogleman on Sept. 10 under a subpoena. Also in the room were her appointed attorney, Gerald Coleman; her mother, Dian Teer, and Gary Gitchell of the WMPD.

She explained she dropped out in the 10th grade because she was pregnant and described how she had moved around among various local addresses, her father's home in Illinois and California.

Fogleman asked Domini about Jennifer's relationship with Damien. Domini explained: "Jason was going out with a girl named Holly and Holly was Jennifer's best friend."

Fogleman: "Uh huh. Is that what Damien told you?"

Domini: "Yeah."

Fogleman asked: "Do you know Heather?"

Domini: "Yeah, that was another one of Jason's girlfriends."

Fogleman: "How many girlfriends does Jason have?"

Domini: "Jason started going out with the Holly girl, and then him and her didn't get along or whatever and they broke up and then he started going out with Heather."

Holly George had no interest in Baldwin and had never been his girlfriend.

Echols, 18-year-old prospective father of Domini's child, was talking on the phone to his "other" girlfriend, 12-year-old Jennifer Bearden, every day, and was using supposed phone calls from Holly as cover.

Domini described her day on May 5 for Fogleman, saying Echols had not spent the night previously, and that "a friend of his, Ken," had skipped school and come over at about 7 a.m. They "sat around and waited for Jason and Damien ... Damien got there around 1, and then me and him and Ken just kind of sat around waiting for Jason to get out of school."

Fogleman asked: "Alright. Is this something that y'all had planned before, about getting together?"

Domini: "Yeah, we had planned it a day before."

Fogleman: "Alright, what had y'all planned on doing?"

Domini: "Well, we planned on Jason skipping school, and just us hanging around, like at the mall and stuff. ... And Jason went to school that day so we had to wait for him."

She said school got out at 3:15, Baldwin arrived about 3:25.

Though Damien went to Lakeshore virtually every day to see Jason and Domini, that particular day was somehow different. They had a plan for May 5, just as Damien, Jason and Jessie had a plan.

Fogleman: " ... And after he got there, what did y'all do?"

Domini: "We walked back to Jason's house ..."

She said Jason stopped off at his home before coming to her trailer. His little brothers, Matthew and Terry, were home. "... And he called his mom, and his mom told him he needed to go over to his uncle's and mow the lawn. ... So, we all got up and we all walked over to his uncle's."

Fogleman: "Okay. About what time did y'all get to his uncle's?"

Domini: "Um ... 4 o'clock ... Something like that. .... We walked, you know on the highway, not the service road, but the highway ... We walked over the interstate, through the Wal-Mart parking lot. ... We walked around the side of the building towards the back ... and straight down to his uncle's house on those back streets. ... It didn't take us very long, about 10 or 15 minutes."

Fogleman: "... You got there about 4 or 4:15, then what did you do?"

Domini: "... Jason mowed the lawn ... We sat there for a while watching him mow the lawn, and then me and Damien got up and walked to the laundromat. ... Damien said he had to call his mom. ... To come pick him up. I don't know, he just called his mom."

When they left, Baldwin was still mowing, having circled the yard about three times. They left Ken there as well. They sat on the back porch while Baldwin's uncle got the lawnmower out of the shed.

They called Echols' mother "about 5 or 5:30, something like that," and his mother and his sister picked them up. After seeming uncertainty about whether Joe Hutchison was there, she said he was driving.

Domini: "They took me home ... around like 5:45, 6:00. In between there."

Fogleman: "Do you remember what was on TV when you came in?"

Domini: "I didn't look at the TV. I walked the dog. ... I just came in and I sat at the kitchen table just for a couple of minutes, and then I got bored, and then I got up, got the dog's leash and walked to the store with the dog." The walk was "probably about 10 minutes."

When she got back, "'TimeTrax' was fixin' to come on. ... And I took a shower, cause Mom had told me what happened while 'TimeTrax' ended. Til the end of 'TimeTrax' she had told me what happened. ... Then I got out of the shower, and I laid in bed for a while, and Damien called, and me and him bickered back and forth for almost an hour, and then she made me get off the phone."

Fogleman: "What time did he call?"

Domini: "About 10." Domini couldn't account for Echols' whereabouts from about 6 to about 10 p.m.

Fogleman: "What were y'all bickering about?"

Domini: "Jason, you know, Jason's girlfriend Holly, called uh, kept calling Damien, crying about Jason and I didn't like her calling Damien crying to him about Jason."

Fogleman followed up: "OK, I thought that Jason and Holly had already broken up and he was dating Heather."

Domini: "Uh uh. He'd ... No. He was going out with Holly, and just a little bit before y'all arrested him, he had started going out with Heather. But, him and Holly were still ... They weren't going out, but they were just seeing each other .... Cause she was supposed to be breaking up with some other boyfriend while they was trying to go out."

Fogleman: "Uh huh. OK. And y'all argue about that?"

Domini: "Uh huh."

Fogleman: "OK, why?"

Domini: "Because she was crying to him, and ... and he was just like, all poor Holly, and then I come crying to him, it wasn't all poor Holly. It was, he would get mad because I was having mood swings all the time, and I would just (inaudible) ... and he got mad about it, because he didn't understand. We kept trying to explain to him that I was (inaudible) to do that. ... And I got mad because he was sympathizing with Holly, and I didn't want Holly calling him at all."

Gitchell asked: "How come you weren't together that afternoon? You're usually together all the time."

Domini: "He was just at home. He had to go to the doctor that morning." That did not explain why they were not together longer that afternoon.

Fogleman: "Did he spend the night that night at your house?"

Domini: "That Wednesday."

Fogleman: "Uh huh. Did he?"

Domini: "No. He didn't spend the night that Wednesday."

Fogleman: "How about Tuesday?"

Domini: "Now, Tuesday, yes. Thursday. Thursday he spent the night because we got into another argument because of the same people and I wanted him to spend the night with me that night cause ..."

Fogleman: "Cause you were mad at him?"

Domini: "No, we weren't mad at each other. We got back. ... We were OK after that. But I still wanted him to stay with me."

Asked again about Tuesday, she said, "Yeah, he did spend the night Tuesday, cause he went home Wednesday morning ... cause he had a doctor's appointment." She said he did not spend the night

Friday. Other accounts placed Damien at home on Tuesday.

Domini said Damien spent the night on Thursday. Damien has said he did not spend the night at Domini's on May 6.

Fogleman backtracked, attempting to clear up confusion about Tuesday night and Wednesday morning: "Now what about Tuesday night, I wasn't clear on that. I thought you said he did, and then I thought you said he didn't and so I wasn't clear on Tuesday night."

Domini: "On Tuesday? Um … yeah, he did spend the night Tuesday, because he went home Wednesday morning … cause he had a doctor's appointment."

Damien would have to have left very early on Wednesday, as Ken showed up around 7 a.m.

She said Echols did not spend the night Friday. Instead, "I spent the night with him Friday."

Asked about being seen by the Hollingsworth family on the service road, she said, "We never walked on the service road. Ever."

Fogleman: "Y'all walk on the interstate?"

Domini: "Yeah."

Fogleman: "Alright, you were not with him. Has he told you that he was with Jason walking around that night?"

Domini fudged again: "I don't know. Number one he doesn't walk on the service road, whether he's with Jason or he's with me. He just doesn't walk on the service road because it's quicker to go over the interstate."

Fogleman: "OK. Did he tell you that he went walking with Jason anywhere that night?"

Domini paused.

Fogleman: "You quit looking at me. He didn't tell you that?"

Domini: "No. ... He didn't tell me he was walking with Jason anywhere at night, cause usually Jason has to be in the house. Cause Jason's mom is strict. ... Strict about Jason coming in. Because usually she's at work and she wants him to take care of his little brothers ... So, he usually doesn't go anywhere at night."

Fogleman also talked to Dian Teer, Domini's mother, on Sept. 10. Dian, disabled from a stroke then, has since died.

Age 44 and legally separated from her husband, Dian had lived in Lakeshore since February with her daughter, six cats and a dog in a filthy trailer.

She had known Echols "about two years" and met him "when he started going out with Domini." He lived with them for several weeks "waiting for his parents to come back from Oregon."

Fogleman: "Did Damien ever say anything about why he had left Oregon?"

Dian: "No."

Fogleman: "He never did tell you anything about that?"

Dian: "He came back to be with Domini."

Fogleman: "That's what he said?"

Dian: "Yes."

Fogleman: "OK. Did he tell you that?"

Dian: "Yeah."

Echols left Oregon after being thrown into a mental institution.

Fogleman: " ... After they came back, has he lived with y'all any?"

Dian: "No. Sometimes he would come over, and they would stay the night, and sometimes she would go over to his parents and stay the night with them."

Fogleman: "Now, in May, first week in May. Do you remember Damien coming over any?"

Dian: "Yes, just about every day."

Fogleman: "OK. Was it during that first week in May, would it be morning, afternoon, or would it vary?"

Dian: "It would vary."

Fogleman: "OK. Uh ... Did Jason ever come over?"

Dian: "Yes, usually he would be with Damien."

Fogleman: "Alright on the first Wednesday in May, it was May the 5th, uh, did Damien come over that day?"

Dian: "Yes."

She said he came over about 1 o'clock and stayed "until Jason got out of school."

Fogleman: " ... Damien didn't go get him or anything, Jason just came on over?"

Dian: "Yeah. They had already made plans the day before."

Fogleman: "OK. So Jason and Damien had already made plans to get together?"

Dian: "Yeah."

Fogleman: "OK. Did Damien tell you that?"

Dian: "I was there usually when they made the plans ... cause they came over a lot in the afternoon."

Again, the "plans" came up, but it was not clear how a day with "plans" differed from "just about every day."

Dian said the teenagers spent 15 or 20 minutes at her trailer after Jason arrived before they left.

Dian: "Later Domini came home ... It was still light, and I think it was around 5:30 or 6:00." She thought she was watching "A Different World."

Fogleman: "OK. Earlier, do you remember one of the officers talking to you earlier? Oh, like a few days after this happened. Do you remember that?

Dian: "Yes."

Fogleman: "Officer Ridge. Do you remember him?"

Dian: "Yes."

Fogleman: "Um, let's see ... OK. Do you remember telling him that 'Time Trax' was on TV?"

Dian: "Well, that was later. That was around 7. Because Domini took the dog for a walk down to the store, and when she came back, it was around 7, because 'Time Trax' had just come on. And she took her shower, and I had to tell her the ending of it ... cause I always watch 'Time Trax' and 'Kung Fu.'"

"And then what did she do?"

Dian: "She laid down on the bed by me and went to sleep."

Fogleman: "OK, did she talk to anybody on the telephone that night?"

Dian: "Yeah, Damien. ..."

She said Domini did not talk to anyone else.

Fogleman: "You do remember her talking to Damien?"

Dian: "Yes."

Fogleman: "What time was that?"

Dian: "He called around 10. And they talked for an hour. Cause I had to make her get off the phone. Cause they were just arguing back and forth anyway. ..." According to Dian, Domini had no contact with Damien from 5:30-6 to around 10.

Fogleman: "... What were they arguing about, do you know?"

Dian: "Jason's girlfriend had called Damien up crying to Damien about Jason. ... They weren't getting along, or had had an argument or something ... so she called Damien up trying to get Damien to talk to Jason for her. ..."

Fogleman: " ... Why would they argue about that, do you know?"

Dian: "Domini didn't want Jason's girlfriend calling Damien ... Kids get very possessive with each other ... and those two were very possessive about each other."

Fogleman: "OK. Did you know that Damien had a bunch of other girlfriends?"

Dian: "Not to my knowledge."

Fogleman: "You didn't know that?"

Dian: "No."

Fogleman: "How about Jennifer? A girl named Jennifer. You don't know anything about her?"

Dian: "Jennifer was Jason's girlfriend."

Fogleman: "Heather Cliett was Jason's girlfriend, or Jason had more than one."

Dian: "I think he had two at the time, I'm not sure. But, I remember hearing both their names."

She didn't know who Holly George was and only heard about Vicki Hutcheson after the case broke.

Dian said Echols' mother had brought Domini home in a blue car. She only saw Pam, Damien and Domini in the car, not Michelle or Joe as described by others, and not Jason.

Fogleman asked: " ... You'd mentioned that Damien and Jason had made plans. What kind of plans had they made?"

Dian: "Just that they were going to get together and do something that evening. Usually they would go over to Wal-Mart and play video games, or over to Jason's and play video games."

They had "plans" to "do something that evening" but Dian gave no specifics.

Fogleman: "What did you do on May the 4th? What did Domini do on May 4th?"

Dian: "Well, she was with Damien and Jason. I think they went to play video games that day?"

Fogleman: "OK. What time did they leave?"

Dian: "I don't remember."

Fogleman: "OK, was it morning or afternoon?"

Dian: "It was usually afternoon when they left."

Fogleman: "Do you know what time Domini go home that day?"

Dian: "No I don't remember, but it was usually later."

Fogleman: "How about May the 6th, on Thursday. What did Domini do that day?"

Dian: "She was with Damien. Damien came over that day, and he spent the night with us that night."

Fogleman: "He spent the night that Thursday night?"

Dian: "Yes."

Fogleman: "OK. And how long was he over there that day? Was it all day, or did he come at 1 o'clock or 4 o'clock?"

Dian: "Most of the day, I believe."

Fogleman: "OK. Was he there at lunch time?"

Dian: "Yeah."

Later, Gitchell asked: "How did Damian and your daughter leave on the 5th? How did they ... did they go anywhere together on the 5th?"

Dian: "That Wednesday?"

Gitchell: "Yeah."

Dian: "Yeah, they all went over to cut Jason's uncle's yard."

Fogleman: "And they walked."

Dian: "Yeah."

Gitchell: "Do you know what time they got back?"

Dian: "Around 5:30 or 6."

Fogleman: "Now did ... that night, did Damien call Domini or did Domini call Damien?"

Dian: "Damien called Domini ..."

In an affidavit dated May 27, 2008, Domini Teer Ferris, then living in Phoenix, Ariz., stated:

"On the morning of May 5th, I was at my home in Lakeshore. A friend named Ken came over. Damien, who had a doctor's appointment that morning, arrived at about 1 p.m. Damien, Ken, and I then waited for Jason Baldwin to come over after Jason finished school.

"Jason arrived at about 3:25 p.m. We then walked over to Jason's home, which was also in the Lakeshore area.

"Jason's two little brothers, Matthew and Terry, were at his home. Jason called his mother and was told that he had to go to his uncle's to mow the lawn. We then walked over to the home of Jason's uncle. We arrived there about 4 p.m.

"We watched Jason mow his uncle's lawn. Later Damien and I walked to the nearby laundromat and called Damien's mother. His father, mother, and sisters then arrived in the car to pick us up. They then dropped me off at my home.

"I walked the dog and took a shower. After I laid down for a while, Damien called at about 10 p.m., and we bickered back and forth on the phone for nearly an hour. I was upset because Holly, an ex-girlfriend of Jason, kept calling Damien to discuss her problems with Jason, and I didn't like that."

The 2008 statement offered no alibi for Echols and threw his "sisters" into the family car (Echols had only one sister, Michelle); Domini's story otherwise varied little from 1993.

Domini was available to testify for the defense but was not called. While roughly consistent, her statements offered discrepancies such as times and who picked them up at the laundromat.

In a phone interview in October of 2016, Domini Ferris said she was agreeing to talk because "It's all over now … It was a long time ago." She was polite and friendly and quick to answer questions, with no hesitation in a voice still high-pitched and soft.

Domini deliberately had withdrawn from any public presence in the case "because it just seemed like it interfered in my life; just because it had put itself in the middle of my life, I did not want to put my life in the middle of it."

She last talked to Echols "two days after he got out. 'Hope to see you. I'm fine.' That's about all that was."

Domini said she took their son, Seth, to visit his father in prison from time to time until Lorri Davis moved to Arkansas. The visits stopped because of Davis, who eventually married Damien. "I don't trust her. She just shows up from out of the blue from New York or wherever she came from."

Seth still does not talk with Damien. "My son tried to like talk to him. Damien just, you know, kind of blew him off so we just let sleeping dogs lie there."

Domini acknowledged about Echols: "He's weird. He's all into this weird magical BS stuff. I never had any interest in that."

She saw little interest from Jason in magick but she had not known him well. "Not really. We didn't get along. I didn't like him and he didn't like me. He came over to my house sometimes with Damien or I went over to his with Damien. But I didn't have too much to do with Jason."

She remembered Jessie as "weird."

Looking back on the investigation, trial and incarceration of her child's father, she said, "We would never want anyone to go through that situation. I wouldn't want to go through it again. Ever. I wouldn't wish it on my worst enemy. I wouldn't want it on my now-16-year-old girl. I keep trying to keep them sheltered because of all that happened then. It changed the way I look at cops and how I view detectives and everything. It just wasn't right.

"It's botched, every bit of it. Every bit. They probably handled that about as bad as they handled Jon-Benet."

Asked if she had any ideas on who committed the crimes, she said, "I guess I do have a lot of them … from just some random bum to maybe the parents were involved in a bad drug deal to just somebody that nobody knows anything about."

She had no doubts about the innocence of the West Memphis 3. "No matter how weird Damien is, no matter how weird Jessie is, they would never do this. No way. They were the scapegoats no matter what."

"WE'VE BEEN WANTING TO GET A BUM FROM UNDERNEATH ONE OF THE OVERPASSES AND TORTURE THEM"

A close friend offered disturbing details about Damien Echols and Jason Baldwin, not only suggesting that they did the crimes but that they had been joking about torture for some time.

Jason Lance Crosby, who lived in Shady Lake Trailer Park, just north of Lakeshore, first appeared in the record after talking to Marion Junior High principal John Heath shortly after the arrests. Like many acquaintances of Echols and Baldwin, he offered strangely contrasting and sometimes contradictory insights on the two.

According to the statement Heath furnished police, Crosby "stated he knew the boys that had just been announced on t.v. as the killers, were guilty of killing the three boys. He said a lot of people thought he was involved in the killings but he told them he wasn't, but he knew who did it." Like L.G. Hollingsworth, Deanna Holcomb and others familiar with Echols and Baldwin, he had no trouble believing they killed the boys.

Crosby had been afraid to talk because he feared Misskelley would kill him, describing violent confrontations with the thuggish Little Jessie.

According to Heath, Crosby told of an incident in which, after he retrieved a bicycle that Misskelley had stolen from him, Misskelley had beaten him up. Crosby also claimed "that he knew Michael Echols was into satin worship because he would kill animals and eat the meat." Crosby said he overheard a conversation a few weeks prior to the killings in which Echols and Misskelley discussed catching a bum at an interstate overpass and killing him.

Crosby expressed concern about a knife that supposedly just appeared in his backpack a few days before school got out for the year. He retrieved the knife, a 3- to 4-inch boot knife in a black leather sheath, from where he had hidden it, behind a counter, and gave it to Heath. He told Heath that someone might be trying to get him into trouble.

The next day, June 8, Crosby told police a differing story.

Crosby described an ongoing friendship with Echols and Baldwin, including Echols spending the night at his home several times and Baldwin staying over at least one night along with Echols. Crosby said Echols told him that a lot of people thought he was a devil worshipper but that he wasn't; Crosby had told Heath that Echols was into Satan worship. He would give other confused information on Echols' occult beliefs in subsequent interviews.

Crosby said that in 1992 Echols "told him that he and Jason Baldwin wanted to catch a bum under the overpass and torture him just to see what it was like," according to the handwritten police report. After Crosby told Echols he was crazy, Echols said he was just kidding. Heath's note had attributed the statement to Misskelley; Crosby later would say that Baldwin came up with the idea.

Echols also told Crosby that Baldwin "was about the only person he could run around with because he was the only one he never got into it with."

Crosby said he had been "pretty good friends" with Misskelley until Jessie's cousin had become interested in Crosby the previous year. Misskelley jumped him at school, hitting him in the face.

Before that incident, Crosby's bicycle had gone missing, prompting another conflict with Misskelley. Crosby saw a girl riding the bicycle and confronted her. She told him that Misskelley had given the bicycle to her brother, David "Dino" Perfetti, a close friend of Misskelley's. Misskelley then tried to pick another fight, Crosby told police.

Crosby again described how a knife appeared in his backpack.

After the statement, Crosby passed a polygraph test on June 8.

The 15-year-old Crosby gave a much longer statement to John Fogleman on Sept. 2, after the knife was found to have fiber evidence possibly linked to Baldwin's house and to Echols' clothing. Crosby was reluctant to say where the knife came from but said he had not received it from Echols or Baldwin.

Finally he said a youth named Rick Appling had brought the knife to school to defend himself against a group of bullies. Crosby took the knife from Appling. Crosby didn't know of any links between Appling and Echols or Baldwin. He was reluctant to take a polygraph concerning the knife; he didn't want to get Appling into trouble.

The knife, with no clear links to either Echols or Baldwin, was the source of fibers microscopically similar to fibers from one of Echols' shirts and to a toilet seat cover from the Baldwin home.

On Sept. 22, Carl Richard Appling Jr., 14, and his mother, Cynthia L. Appling, cleared up a few things.

Young Rick told Ridge that he brought the knife to school because he feared he would be attacked, the knife was reported to the office, and he and Crosby threw the knife behind a radiator.

Appling had gotten the knife for Christmas. It stayed in his bedroom unless he used it for hunting or fishing. Appling had met Baldwin and Echols once each and had a nodding acquaintance with Misskelley.

Crosby told police that he had a second knife that Echols left in his truck in February. The knife, which sat on the dashboard until June or July, had ended up in the possession of TV reporter Paul Morrison. After talking with Crosby, Morrison kept the knife, with the intention of photographing it. Crosby got that knife, a fixed blade with a bronze-colored handle and a black leather sheath, back from Morrison and turned it over to police on Sept. 16.

There were multiple knives confiscated by police, with none clearly linked to the murders. Like many of the knives, the "lake knife" and the knives linked to Crosby were fixed blade, not folding knives. Misskelley in his confessions said Baldwin used a folding knife.

In his Sept. 2 interview with Fogleman, Crosby again described the conversation about killing bums: "I was walking home with Damien and Jason. This is when they lived in Lakeshore. ... And it was either Damien or Jason who brought up the subject of torture. ... I think it was Jason that said that ... we've been wanting to get a bum from underneath one of the overpasses and torture them .... I think it was Jason, I'm not sure ... I don't know how good this will hold up or anything but them guys are notorious for joking around like that."

Crosby had little good to say about Misskelley: "... I don't talk to that boy. If I see him, I get on the other side of the sidewalk and walk." Crosby explained that Misskelley no longer went to school; "What I had heard is that he had dropped out of school and either Steve Jones whoever it was that the policeman over the little people told him that if he didn't go back to school they would put him in a reform school or something so he went back to school. ... Then he got the wild idea that he looked wild enough they wouldn't let him go to school." Others noted Misskelley's marked changes in appearance from the time of the killings, particularly his "wild enough" hairstyle.

Concerning Echols' beliefs, Crosby told Fogleman: "I heard him talk about once that he could be a Christian and everything else. He says that he doesn't criticize them about what they are. He was talking one time he was in a wicca or what that was. It was supposed to be about the same thing." Crosby said Echols never mentioned black magic.

As for May 5, Crosby told Fogleman: "I had come home from school and found that there was a lady's car in my driveway. I went across the street to tell her to move it, found out that my neighbor's kid had been attacked by a pit bull had 60 something stitches and then I heard that when he got out," he joined in the search for the dog, which continued all evening. There was daily drama in the trailer parks.

Both Baldwin and Echols were fascinated with knives, with a number of witnesses describing them carrying knives and their knife collections. Echols' practice of carrying a knife was among factors cited by jurors who found him guilty.

While Gail Grinnell claimed her boys did not have knives, Jason was trading knives around the time of the killings.

For instance, Billy Newell, a 17-year-old who lived in Lakeshore not far from the Baldwins, told police on May 11: "I had three T-shirts that I had traded a pick and a knife for, to Jason Baldwin. ... When I got home yesterday I found the pick and knife where Jason had brought it back. I made the statement to some kids that 'I wonder if these were the weapons used to kill the boys.' Then I said maybe I'd better call up to the police and tell them. I guess word got around to the police and they came to my house today. I know Damien and I think he's one of his own along with his sidekick, Jason." Baldwin made the trade for the ice pick and a curved throwing knife the day before the murders, and had Matthew return them May 8, the Saturday after the murders, after storing them under his bed.

Billy's brother Kenny Newell told police: "Jason was over at our house and Billy wanted to trade something for some shirts. And the only thing Billy has good enough to trade is the weapons. Billy picked the shirts he wanted and they traded. And 3 or 4 days later Jason's little brother brought the pick and knife back and got the shirts but we didn't find the Testament shirt so he still has it. ... The first trade took place at the early part of last week. The second trade took place at the last part of the same week." The weapons recovered were the ice pickax and a large curved machete-like knife. Testament was a thrash metal band who put out albums with occult themes.

On Sept. 23, Matt Baldwin told Fogleman that he returned the items because Jason was babysitting and could not leave the house. "... I took that over to Ken's, Billy Newell's house because, uh, Jason told me to, because there were trying to blame him for using it or something." Jason had stored the weapons "up under his bed for about a week or so."

"WE HURT A COUPLE OF BOYS, THAT JASON AND DAMIEN KILLED"

Little Jessie started talking the day after the killings.

Buddy Sidney Lucas was a 19-year-old working at a landscape company when he entered the case.

Relatives Amy and Eddie Wilson of Heth, Ark., told police that Lucas was talking as if he knew something about the homicides and Lucas had shoes with blood on them.

Detective Bryn Ridge went to Lakeshore on June 10 to meet with Lucas and his mother, Mary Hudson. Lucas said he received a pair of blue and white Adidas sneakers from Misskelley in February when he and Misskelley were riding a four-wheeler with Billy McGee. Lucas's shoes had gotten muddy in the beanfield next to Highland Trailer Park.

In his initial confession on June 3, Misskelley said he loaned his Adidas to Lucas after the killings.

Lucas told Ridge that he was friends with Misskelley and had gone camping with him but had not seen him for "a long time." He described Misskelley as "very strong" and said he liked to fight. He told Ridge that he "was not very friendly with Damien Echols" but knew him from school.

He surrendered the shoes to Ridge.

He said that, if Misskelley was hanging around Echols, the older teen could have talked Misskelley into doing almost anything. Lucas said Misskelley, known to huff gasoline and smoke marijuana, was very suggestible when high.

In a Sept. 8 interview with Durham, Lucas described a violent incident involving Misskelley: "I saw some people going down to the railroad tracks, behind Lake Shore. I don't remember when it was. (date) I saw Jessie Misskelley holding a knife to John Perschke's throat. I heard Jessie say to John 'If you mess with Jessica again, I am going to hurt you.' I didn't see anyone hit John and I don't remember who all was there but there were six or seven people there." Other witnesses described the incident similarly. Perschke named Lucas as one of the assailants and said Echols and Baldwin were among those who approached him.

On Oct. 14, Ridge and Durham traveled to Earle to tape another interview with Lucas. Lucas told officers that his family had a barbecue May 5. "We decided to take Jessie and them some chicken ... and everything, so me and my cousin Rex went over there, took them some chicken and everything. I ask them where's Little Jessie and everything. He, Big Jessie said that um, he went walking that way and everything, and we looked out the door and he was walking off with somebody else" toward West Memphis. Lucas said he ate "around 9" after visiting with Misskelley Sr.

"So turn around that next day I went over there I figured he would be home by now. ... I knock on the door about 3 or 4 times he was still in bed, so I got ready to leave and he opened the door and everything."

Jessie Jr. asked him to stay on the porch and talk. They talked about friends. Then "he started breaking out in sweat and everything and at that time I didn't know he had anything to do with these kids."

After the boys talked, they went over to a neighbor's house where Lucas got a haircut. Meanwhile, Misskelley "played Nintendo with her little boys."

After the teens left, "I told him, man ... I going to howler (holler) at you later, he said no man I got to tell you something, and everything and he was breaking out in a sweat."

Ridge asked: "You said something about his eyes when we talked earlier what was it about his eye?"

Lucas: "They ... they had water dropping from them. ...

"So we sit there, sit there, and I said, he said man me Jason and Damien we went walking in the town last night in the town of West Memphis, I said why didn't you all come by and get me? We will we uh, we were in a hurry and everything go up there and come back home. I said alright I understand ...

"He told me that uh, that he got in a fight, that's what he told me at first ....

"I said Damien and Jason they helped you? He said um-yea and everything so I said well did you all hurt anybody? And he said yea, I didn't think it was those 8 year old kids or anything, so I turn around and come to found out that Jason he was with Jason and Damien when they sacrificed them little kids ...

"He said um, we hurt, uh .... uh we hurt a couple of boys, that Jason and Damien killed. ...

"I finally got it talked out of him what did he do, he said I hit uh, a couple in the back of the head ... and everything to keep them from running and everything." This jibes with Misskelley's description of his role in the "fight" as hitting Michael in the head after chasing him down.

Lucas described how Misskelley gave him a pair of shoes that Thursday: "He picked up and started to hand them to me. All the suddenly he dropped them, and broke out in sweat, crying everything else, he said man take those shoes I don't want to see them no more, I said your sure? ... He said take them I don't want to see them no more. ...

"So there wasn't nothing on the shoes and everything so turn around he going, I got the shoes I went home and everything."

Lucas told Ridge that another pair of shoes, not the Adidas but white, black-soled Converses, were at his home in Earle, that he had worn them a couple of times, and "Well Robert he got them on now ... He ask me this morning could he wear them and told him yea."

Lucas didn't go to the police after first hearing Misskelley's story because "I was afraid that you all would lock me up for it, I didn't have nothing to do with it."

Lucas knew Misskelley was telling him the truth: "I could, could see it in his eyes."

Near the end of the interview, Lucas said, "I feel so good, I told you ... hundred percent better," adding "The reason I didn't come uh, then before he told you all everything, because I was afraid if I did that he would have somebody hurt me." Lucas not only feared the police but Misskelley's trailer park associates.

Lucas knew Echols and Baldwin were in a Satanic cult "because they look like the type of person that would," but Misskelley's involvement shocked him.

"I ain't got nothing to hold back," he told the officers. "... I just don't want to be brought up in the middle of this."

Lucas said Misskelley had told him that he was going to tell the police what happened.

Lucas took a polygraph test that included nine questions, four bearing upon his story.

Asked: "Did you tell the truth in the statement you gave us today?" He answered no. The examination indicated deception.

He answered no to "On Thursday May 6, 1993 did Jessie Misskelley give you a pair of tennis shoes?" The examination indicated deception.

He answered no to "Did Jessie Misskelley tell you that Damien and Jason killed those boys?" The examination indicated deception.

"Were you there when those three young boys were killed?" The examination indicated that when he answered no he told the truth.

Lucas explained he did not answer three questions truthfully because he was afraid of what might happen to his family. The readings indicated he was telling the truth when he said that Jessie gave him a pair of tennis shoes the day after the killings and that Jessie told him that Damien and Jason killed the boys.

Lucas agreed to trade the black and white Converse tennis shoes for new boots.

In a signed statement, Lucas said the shoes were given to him by Misskelley on May 6, the day after the murders.

On Oct. 13, Charlotte Ann Bly Bolois of Parkin, Ark., gave a statement to Ridge and Durham concerning Lucas and his relatives, Greg Wilson, Chris Wilson, Irene Wilson and Amy Wilson.

She had seen Buddy Lucas, her cousin, about a month before at the home of Amy Wilson, Lucas' aunt.

She described him living in fear of being pulled further into the investigation. "Buddy was out there and said that the cops was looking for him and that's why he was staying out at Amy's … and um, he said that the other reason was that he was working in Earle, but the main reason was because the cops was suppose to be looking for him, cause his mom found that shoes that Jessie Misskelley supposedly wear, and said they had blood all over them, and his mom was suppose to call the cops on him."

She described another encounter with Lucas: "He came up to my grandpa's house, where I'm staying at now and ask my grandpa to give him a ride to Earle and he had slept under the bay bridge. ... He had mud all over him. .... like he was running from the cops or something like he was trying to hide from them. ... the only reason I can think of."

Bolois recounted a conversation with Irene Wilson concerning the day of the murders: "Buddy um, left a few minutes before the kids got killed and she said, he didn't come back until the next day ... later that afternoon. ... He was suppose to go meet Jessie Misskelley out at Lakeshore." If Buddy had needed an alibi, he wasn't going to get one from Aunt Irene.

During the lead-up to Misskelley's trial, Ridge followed up on a report that Lucas told Amy and Eddie Wilson that Buddy received shoes with blood on them from Misskelley.

The Wilsons said Lucas had been staying with them after the killings. A co-worker told them that Lucas had been talking about the homicides as if he knew something about them. When Eddie confronted him, Lucas told him that he had not been directly involved but had traded shoes with Misskelley on which he had seen traces of blood.

The shoes were not used as evidence in the Misskelley trial. Lucas did not testify, in keeping with a pattern of potential witnesses scared off the case after a visit from Ron Lax, an investigator for the Echols defense.

Lucas described Lax as "a real nice man" who "just told me he wanted to help me and he said that he's the one that I could tell the truth to."

In February 1994, after the Misskelley trial, Fogleman called Lucas' mother, Mary Hudson, at her home in Earle to find out what transpired between Lucas and Lax.

Buddy answered the phone. Lucas told Fogleman that he became scared after Durham interrogated him.

Lucas said Durham threw down his notebook and yelled at him right before the polygraph. "I tried to tell him the truth before it happened, before he give it to me." Lucas gave extremely incriminating statements about Misskelley well before the exam.

Misskelley's lawyers later claimed they considered calling Lucas for the defense to build a case that Misskelley had been similarly intimidated, according to "Devil's Knot." Misskelley consistently told police that he was not scared of them.

Besides Lucas being "low-functioning" and "nervous," Dan Stidham and Greg Crow rightly were concerned that the prosecution would use Lucas' statement to impeach mitigating testimony.

Mrs. Hudson came to the phone and let Fogleman know she was unhappy with how her son was treated.

Fogleman, staying conciliatory, told her, "He told me that the reason he had never told them what he ended up telling them was because that he was afraid of Jessie's friends, Dennis Carter and Dino Perfetti."

Fogleman explained that police talked to Lucas based on information from Buddy's relatives.

Lucas interrupted to tell Fogleman that he was working the day of the murders — that he had an alibi. Fogleman said no one was saying Lucas was involved in the murders. Lucas told him: "I didn't want to be brought up in it and I don't -- Mr. John, I won't go to court on Damien and Jason."

Lucas said Eddie Wilson contacted the police because he thought Lucas had something to do with the killings. "They kept on jumping down my throat and I told them look just get off my back cause I don't know nothing about it. And I left. They kept jumping down my throat. I told them look I don't know nothing about it."

Fogleman tried to reassure Lucas. "We're not going to bother you, Buddy. We just want to know the truth about it because you know these people are telling us things and this investigator this Lax guy is going around getting all kinds of witnesses to change their stories. And I never had -- I've been doing this for over ten years and I've never had one witness change their story. Once they tell the police, I've never had them do it and we've had at least three in this case do it. And I'm just trying to find out what in the world is going on." Two acquaintances of Echols similarly backed out on testifying about incriminating statements.

Fogleman reminded Lucas that Misskelley told police that the shoes he was wearing at the time of the murders were blue and white Adidas that he had given to Lucas.

The phone call ended with mutual assurances of good will but Lucas' role in the initial investigation and trial ended there. Along with other potential witnesses for the prosecution, Buddy Lucas did not testify.

Lucas' name popped up again almost 20 years later in new allegations from a pair of convicted rapists that he, Terry Hobbs, David Jacoby and L.G. Hollingsworth killed the three boys. At that point, Hollingsworth was dead, Hobbs was the new "alternative suspect," and Jacoby and Lucas were notable as the most skittish witnesses in the case. There was no credible evidence supporting that story, though it received widespread media play for a few days.

"DAMIEN TOLD HIM THAT HE KILLED THOSE BOYS"

As the investigation continued, more fingers pointed toward Damien Echols. Then police heard about a confession from Echols.

DeQuita Dunham told West Memphis police that her son, William Winford Jones, "heard Damien stating that he pulled a fast one of the police and has been telling kids at Lakeshore that if they messed with him, he would do the same thing to them that he did to the 3 little boys."

William Jones, a tattooed ninth-grader from Marion whose father lived at Lakeshore, told police "that Damien told him that he killed those boys and the police could not catch him that we the police will end up like those boys. He later told him he didn't kill them. He stated Damien is a devil worshiper and he is dangerous and that he William Jones is afraid of Damien."

On May 26, police interviewed Jones, who told of a conversation with Echols on either Friday night or early Saturday morning, May 22. Jones' mother was present at the Crittenden County Drug Task Force offices. Ridge interrogated Jones in an aggressive style that pushed along the story from the laconic teenager. Jones gave no indication that he was intimidated.

Jones said he, Echols and Domini Teer were hanging out at Lakeshore when Echols, who was drunk, began talking about the homicides.

Jones had known Echols since the seventh grade. Jones said, "First he wasn't weird or nothing, but now he's got into that satanic cult stuff," further describing Echols as a devil worshipper.

According to the police report: "Damien stated to William that he killed the boys and that he had sex with them in the butt. He further stated that Damien told him that used a knife and described the knife used as being about 8 to 10 inches long."

Jones described the scene of the conversation: "On a Store street in Lakeshore, where we were talking in that little park up there, and it was like, everybody in Lakeshore heard it. Damien had did it and he got questioned and everything, so when I was his friend, or use to be his friend, so I asked him, everybody want me to ask him, so I asked him, and he said, that he cut them and that, you know, had sex with them, molested them And, he was real drunk, real drunk."

The conversation occurred around midnight, "probably after 12:30."

He, Domini and Echols were walking when the question came up. "He said that he had sex with them, that he molested them and had sex in the rear with them."

Echols told Jones he used "a little knife" and made a gesture as if the knife was 10 to 12 inches long.

"He stopped there and after he told me that, I freaked out. … I talked to him a few more minutes and I left, and went back to my aunt's house and told her."

Jones also described threats to "my cousin's girlfriend": "In Lakeshore, they went down to Damien's house, rode there and they were saying something to them and Michael Hutchison, well Damien, said that, he was going to cut their vaginas off, or something like that. That's what they told me."

Jones said, "When he was sober he came back to me, as a matter of fact, it was the next day and said, that, what was we talking about last night, and I told him what he said and he said, none of that was true, that he was just real drunk."

Jones believed Echols' story of cutting the boys and having sex with them. He said he could tell when Echols was lying because "he stole from me." He didn't believe the story was a lie. "I mean when you get drunk, that's how it does, make you spill your guts."

Echols showed no remorse and talked about the killings "like he was excited or something."

As for Domini, Jones said, "If you know Domini, you know how she is, she's real weird man, she just talks to herself, that's all she's in, is just talking to herself."

Jones said if anyone would have been with Echols, "I think that it would be Jason Baldwin, cause you know, they are always together. … Every since this has happened, they kinda staying away from each other."

Jones said he, like "everybody," had asked Baldwin if he committed the crimes. Baldwin told him no.

Jones assured police: "This is the God's honest truth."

Jones did not want to go to the police department to sign the transcript because "I've been in trouble before and I just try to stay away I guess, not really you all, you know but Crittenden County, I try to stay away. They don't like me."

The interview ran from 12:36 to 12:47 p.m.

Jones continued to talk with police detectives and prosecutors after the arrests.

He was scheduled to testify as a prosecution witness in Misskelley's trial. Then Jones met with Ron Lax. Jones recanted his story, saying he had been lying, starting with his mother and then to police.

Jones refused to testify despite threats of charges for giving false statements.

The prosecutors were notified at virtually the last minute that Jones recanted.

Jones' refusal to testify prompted a court hearing on Jan. 31.

Fogleman told the court: "We have now had the second witness that has told us one thing about incriminating information against one of the other defendants — the second one that has now after the investigator talks to them all of a sudden they see things in a whole new light and recant everything they have told the police. This particular witness that was to be called next has maintained since before the arrests that Damien Echols told him that he did it."

Kenneth Watkins also recanted a statement describing how Echols confessed to him.

Fogleman told the court that "there's some information to indicate that this Lax may be intimidating witnesses and, frankly, I have never had this come up in a trial.

"In the other case we have a videotape statement of a guy who after giving his statement .... after he came out the only concern he expressed to me was a fear of Jessie and his friends and then when I seek to talk to him further, all of a sudden the police department gets a telephone call from Ron Lax saying this guy will not be coming in at that time, that his witness decided he needs a lawyer and then recants his statement that he's given the police."

Fogleman told the court: "I have never had a case where I have had the kind of stuff happen with witnesses that I have with this."

Cheryl Aycock, who worked for Lax's firm Inquisitor Incorporated, told the court that Jones requested she be in the room when prosecutors talked with him.

She and Lax contacted Jones and set up a meeting at the store at Lakeshore. Lax told Jones he didn't think the Echols story was true because the dates don't match. It is unclear why Lax believed there was a problem with dates. Jones said he would have to talk to his mother before talking to Lax.

Then on Feb. 15, 1994, with the Echols-Baldwin trial looming, Jones' mother told Fogleman how Lax and other investigators approached Jones, "more or less talking to him like a teacher would ... he was understanding." Lax warned of consequences if his story turned out not to be true.

In a meeting in Heafer, a small Crittenden community, Aycock testified, Jones told Lax "that he had lied to his mother and that he had told her that he knew something that he didn't know. When he didn't think she would call the police but she did because she felt like it was the right thing to do. And he -- well, she accompanied him to give the statement and he didn't want to lie in front of her."

At that time, the court first learned that Lax not only had volunteered his services but that his fee would be submitted to the court as an expert witness. The judge warned that he had not approved any private investigator "so when you submit the bill for that, I'm going to sure look at it very carefully."

Jones testified and denied he had the conversation with Echols. "Nothing happened," he told Fogleman. He claimed to not remember many details of what he told police. He told Fogleman he didn't remember their having a phone conversation. Finally the testimony was stopped so Jones could talk to a lawyer. He was warned he could be subject to felony charges for submitting a false statement to police.

The judge said about Jones' original statement: "I don't know what kind of impression the Court has from listening to it. It could be a false statement from the beginning or it could be one that he's been coerced to recant. I can't tell."

Jones said he was going to tell "the truth" — that he had been lying — once he was sworn in.

Jones never testified about a story he first described as "God's honest truth."

"HE SAID, I WAS THERE WHEN THE THREE LITTLE KIDS GOT KILLED. ... THAT'S WHAT HE TOLD ME."

One major witness on the whereabouts of Jason Baldwin and Damien Echols spent much of May 5 hanging around, tagging along and missing out on all the major action.

Months later, he tried to provide an alibi for Baldwin that was so poorly constructed that no one took it seriously.

After failing a polygraph exam, he told police about Echols confessing to being present at the murders. Ultimately he backed out as a prosecution witness.

Kenneth Clyde Watkins had transferred to Marion schools in February, skipped school May 5, attended May 6, missed school on Friday, May 7, and never went back, withdrawing on May 12.

Nicknamed "Little Bit," sometimes called "Little Ken," the 16-year-old was just 5-5 and weighed only 100 pounds.

After many attempts to get a bead on his identity and location, investigators tracked him down and Ridge took several statements on Sept. 16, 1993.

In the first statement, starting at 11:12 a.m., in the presence of his mother, Shirley Greenwood, his sister,

Alice Dawson, and Detective Durham, who would later administer a polygraph exam, Watkins recalled May 5:

"I skipped school with Domini to meet Damien to go to his counselor with him, but Damien didn't show up, so me, Domini and Domini's mom watched TV until about 3:30 when Damien finally showed up. Then after that we stayed there for a few minutes, and went to Jason's house to get Jason. ..." Dian and Domini Teer both said Damien showed up at their home earlier in the afternoon and that Jason came over instead of the group going over to Jason's.

"Then I went home to check in, and tell them that I was going to leave and go to Wal-Mart with Damien and Jason. We went to Wal-Mart to play some video games, and L.G. came to Wal-Mart then we went back inside Wal-Mart to get away from him. Then, I left at about 5:30 to go home to babysit and eat. And then they came back around 7 and I went over early and played Nintendo."

Asked to clarify, he said they went back to Jason's house. Watkins' story bore little relation to statements from others.

Ridge asked who had planned to skip school. Watkins: "Just me, cause Jason, he was scared about his probation office, or something like that."

Ridge: "OK, now what time did you go to Domini's?"

Watkins first said 7, then about 7:15. Only Domini and her mother were home.

Ridge: "And how long did you stay there before you received a phone call from Damien?"

Watkins: "Let's see, he called about … I think Domini called about 12 to see what was going on, because he was supposed to come get us, and then we were supposed to leave. And Damien said his thing's been canceled or something like that, and that he wasn't going to be able to make it. Then, Domini got real mad. Well, she didn't get mad, but she was kind of upset. Then he came back around 3:30. He came over."

Echols kept his appointment but did not see his usual counselor. Neither Domini nor her mother mentioned plans for Damien to pick up Domini and Watkins.

Watkins volunteered that "L.G. came over earlier that morning to talk. …" to Domini, sometime before noon.

When they went to Jason's trailer, only "Dink," "his mom's ex-boyfriend," was there.

Watkins: "We was sitting on the car, and then Damien sent Domini to the store to get some ice cream and some chips."

Ridge: "OK, did you go into Jason's that day and play any Nintendo games or anything like that?"

Watkins: "OK, we went, first I went home, and checked in, and then went in, then I was playing Damien on it, and I was beating Damien … on Jason's Nintendo in his room. … Jason was there. I was just me, Jason, Damien and Domini. Then we left and went to Wal-Mart." He said the four walked across the expressway. "We started playing game, then L.G. came up. We went inside and looked around at some tapes ..."

Ridge: "You said L.G. came up and y'all went inside to look at some tapes. Is there a conflict between L.G. and somebody?"

Watkins: "I think Damien said he didn't like L.G. They're always talking about him."

Ridge: "So, when L.G. came up, it was Damien's idea to go in and go somewhere else?"

Watkins: "Yeah, he didn't want to talk to him. ..." Kenneth spent about 30 minutes inside Wal-Mart. "... We went out and played some more video games. Then we went out there and we were watching some other guys play then I left ... about 5:30."

Other accounts of May 5 had Jason cutting a lawn that afternoon.

Ridge: "OK, now you mentioned that you know of Jason mowing a yard."

Watkins: "Yeah, that following Saturday or Sunday, his uncle Earl, let's see ... It was right before the fair got here I think ... Yeah, it was right before the fair because we went and mowed his lawn. ..." Kenneth accurately described the location of Hubert Bartoush's home, though he couldn't remember the correct name or address.

Ridge: "OK, what occurs next after you leave Wal-Mart and go home?"

Watkins: "They stayed."

Ridge: "OK, why did you go home?"

Watkins: "To babysit, because my uncle had to go get my aunt from work." Kenneth was staying temporarily with relatives in Lakeshore.

There were three preschoolers. "… Babysat them for about 45 minutes … Then, I sit there and we eat. Then I leave again. …

"… Then I went to Jason's house this time, I didn't go to Wal-Mart, I went to Jason's house."

Ridge: "OK, who was at Jason's house?"

Watkins: "No one yet, so I went back home, stayed a few minutes, then I went back to Jason's and they were all there playing Nintendo. … I left about 6:30 when I went over there."

Ridge: "OK, and then you go back home?"

Watkins: "Yeah, for about 15 or 20 minutes, then I went back over there and they were home … Just his mom's boyfriend, Dink, I think it was his name, I'm not sure. Then Damien, Jason, all of them were over there. Damien, Jason, Domini and me." No one else placed Damien, Jason, Domini, Dink and Kenneth at Jason's trailer at roughly 7 p.m.

Watkins left "about 9, about 10. … No wait, it was 9, cause Bonanza was on. I went home, watched a little Bonanza, then goofed off on the couch."

Watkins said that, after the murders, Jason said "that he didn't do it and he didn't know why he was a suspect." Kenneth did not know Misskelley, "never even heard of him."

Watkins took a polygraph test and stuck to his story.

Asked "Did you tell the truth in the statement you gave to Detective Ridge?," he answered "Yes." Durham detected significant indications of deception.

Watkins answered "No" when asked "Are you involved, in any way, in the murder of those three young boys?" Deception was indicated.

Deception was indicated when he answered "No" to "Has anyone told you that they were involved in the murder of those three young boys?"

The examination indicated he was truthful when he answered "No" to "Were you present when those three young boys were killed?"

Confronted about the results, Watkins said he felt involved because he didn't tell police what Echols told him.

Watkins said that on Friday, May 7, Echols told him he was there, with two others, when the boys were killed.

Watkins told Ridge: "Friday, we was walking ... me and Damien ... About 4. To get Domini."

Ridge: "OK. You were walking from ..."

Watkins: "... Lakeshore cause we had to go get ... yeah."

Ridge: "And where were you going?"

Watkins: "Wal-Mart ... then we walked on the overpass, which Damien, and Damien said that he was there, and a couple of other friends. A few people."

Ridge: "Now what's he talking about when he says he was there?"

Watkins: "He said that he knows who killed the little kids, cause he was there, with a couple of people. ... And I started talking about something else."

Ridge: "You mentioned a few minutes ago that Damien said he wanted to be part of a group or had been being picked on. When did that conversation come up?"

Watkins: "It was before that conversation came up. Cause, everybody was picking on him and laughing at him and all that. And talked about him, and he said he wanted to do something that no one would pick on him or talk about him or anything. He wanted to do something."

Ridge: "You used the word drastic while ago."

Watkins: "Yeah, drastic."

Ridge: "What were his words?"

Watkins: "He wanted to do something drastic, so no one would talk about, or, you know, tease him ... Then we got in that conversation, where he said that he was there, and he know who done it."

Ridge: "OK. The conversation where he says, people were talking about him. People were picking on him, and he wanted to do something drastic so that they wouldn't do that anymore. ... Where were you at when that conversation took place?"

Watkins: "On the bridge. On the overpass, going to Wal-Mart."

Ridge: "OK ... he said he wanted to belong to a cult?"

Watkins: "He said he wanted to belong to something."

Ridge: "Wanted to belong to something. Alright, was something said about a cult?"

Watkins: "Nuh uh. Then a few days later, I was talking to a girlfriend of mine. She said that he used to be in a cult, but he got out of it. I guess he wanted to join, again."

Ridge: "OK. About what time was it, you were on the overpass and he told you he was there when the boys were killed?"

Watkins: "About 4 .... We went to Wal-Mart and got Domini and came back...."

Ridge: " ... Friday, you're walking from Lakeshore to Wal-Mart with Damien and he tells you that he's tired of being picked on ... And that he had done something drastic, and then a few minutes later he tells you that he was there with a couple of buddies when ..."

Watkins: " ... When it happened."

Ridge: "When it happened. He's talking about the murders."

Watkins: "The murders."

Ridge: "Is that what he said?"

Watkins: "He said, I was there when the three little kids got killed. ... That's what he told me."

Watkins underwent a second polygraph on Oct. 12, conducted by Durham.

The nine-question test included four questions relevant to the case:

"Did Damien tell you how any of those three young boys were killed?" Watkins answered "No," and the examiner saw no deception.

"Did Damien tell you that he was there when those three young boys were killed?" Watkins said "Yes," no deception, backing up his story about Echols' confession.

Deception was indicated in "No" answers to: "Did Damien tell you who all were present when those boys were killed?" and "Did Damien tell you who killed those three young boys?"

According to Watkins, Echols was not specific about how the boys were killed or who else was involved.

Prosecutors were prepared to have Watkins testify about this confession, but he retracted the statement shortly before the trial after a visit from investigators for the defense.

Echols has described different versions of how he heard about the killings.

Watkins described Echols' response, or lack of it, during the second interview with Ridge:

Ridge: "… On Thursday, the following day. What happened on that day?"

Watkins: "I went to school, Jason went to school. All day until we got home from school. Then we all, we was all sitting over at Damien's waiting for Jason, at his house. Then, me … then, uh, Carl came over …"

Ridge: "You say Carl. Carl who?"

Watkins: "Smith. Right across the road."

Ridge: "From Jason."

Watkins: "Yeah. And we were sitting there listening to some music and playing Nintendo, some of it. Then Jason's mom calls and says that three kids have been murdered, and uh, behind the, uh, woods back there. Behind the trailer park. Then, none of us believed it. Well, I did, and Carl didn't. …"

Ridge: "What did Damien have to say about that?"

Watkins: "Damien didn't say nothing. He was just sitting there being quiet."

Ridge: "So when his mother called … when Jason's mother called and Damien heard the news that three boys had been killed, did he react at all?"

Watkins: "He just sat back there and just did nothing."

Watkins said Jason took the call and told everyone the news.

As for Baldwin, said Watkins, "He was going crazy. Like, oh my God and all that. Like he couldn't believe it."

Ridge: "Or was scared?"

Watkins: "Well, I don't know if he was scared. Either one. He just got scared."

Ridge: "Now, you mentioned when a tape was brought into the house. When does that occur?"

Watkins: "Carl bought, next door to his house, they got a tape, and he came back and me and him went in there to put it in, and Damien and Jason went in the living room to talk."

Ridge: "OK, and when you came out of the bedroom …"

Watkins: "They stopped talking and started talking about something else."

Ridge: "So they were obviously talking about something they didn't want you to hear."

Watkins: "Yeah."

Watkins repeated his version of May 5 for Ridge, saying that when he left Walmart about 5:30 or 5:45, "They said they was going to the bowling alley. … I told them I had to go, because I had to go home and babysit."

He said he went back over to Jason's at about 6:45 and only Jason's mother's boyfriend was there. "Dink" Dent did describe Watkins dropping by about that time, when Dent was the only one home.

Watkins returned home. "I watched Full House, then watched something else, and I went over there. … I went back over there and we stayed about 2 hours and I came home, and was watching Bonanza, and I watched part of it, and I went to sleep on the couch."

Watkins' story was fairly consistent, though at odds on many details with virtually everyone else.

Watkins took two polygraph exams that both indicated Echols told him of involvement in the murders.

But, much like Buddy Lucas and William Jones, Kenneth Watkins recanted his story after a visit from Ron Lax. Watkins was not called to testify at trial.

"STATED HE WAS A WHITE WITCH WHO WORSHIPPED THE DEVIL"

Many residents of Crittenden County regard witchcraft as the Devil's work; many think sorcery and witchcraft oppose God and serve Satan. Those are not the beliefs of a tiny fundamentalist fringe; opposition to witchcraft is in the mainstream of American thought and belief.

Despite an increasingly pluralistic society tolerant of deviant behavior, opposition to witchcraft has deep cultural and religious roots that exert a powerful influence.

Exodus 22:18 in the King James Version of the Bible states: "Thou shalt not suffer a witch to live." That admonition was carried out in the Salem witch trials, to a point; those who confessed were considered to have repented and no longer in service to the devil; they lived; many who refused to confess died. Other Biblical passages, such as Leviticus 20:27 and Deuteronomy 18:9-12, admonish believers to not participate in magic.

While Crittenden County was and is conservative and overwhelmingly Christian, like much of the rest of the South, like much of the rest of America, its religiosity has been overstated. Its proximity to the urban influences of Memphis, history as a showcase for urban blues and early rock and roll, and longstanding embrace of gambling, drinking and other vices mean that West Memphis is less strict in religious practice than areas less tolerant of everyday sin.

One of the bulwarks of the local economy, the Southland dog track, was nearly in sight of the murder scene. In 1993, the track was rapidly fading, as locals with a yen for gambling headed to newly opened casinos in nearby Tunica County, Miss.

Today, as one of only two establishments in Arkansas with gaming machines, blackjack tables, roulette wheels and poker games, the reformulated and vastly expanded Southland Park Gaming and Racing has become Crittenden's most notable economic success.

As one of the few local buildings large enough for public gatherings, Southland has become a kind of community gathering place, though many shun the casino floor.

Truck stops, restaurants and motels along the interstates locally bring in a great variety of people from all walks of life. Marion and West Memphis are inward-looking small towns run by local elites, but they are not occupied by totally unsophisticated, culturally isolated rubes.

The percentage of the Crittenden population affiliated with a religious congregation runs well below the national average, according to recent statistical profiles, only 41.7 percent compared to 50.2 percent in the nation as a whole. The largest religious affiliations in Crittenden County are Southern Baptists at 58.4

percent, then Methodists at 12.1 percent and Church of Christ, 7.7 percent.

Many residents regard any form of occult practice as suspect, and particularly regard witches as in league with the Devil, and thus Satanists. In the trailer parks, however, witchcraft, occultism and Satanism have been longstanding practices, according to those familiar with residents there.

The San Francisco-based Church of Satan, founded by Echols hero Anton LaVey, has claimed a strange sort of intellectual property right on Satanist belief. The Church of Satan Web site says, "To us, Satan is the symbol that best suits the nature of we who are carnal at birth. ... He represents pride, liberty and individualism — qualities often defined as Evil by those who worship external deities, who feel there is a war between their minds and bodies." The Church of Satan doesn't believe in Satan as a literal entity, but instead as an archetype of individualism. "Satanism is not Devil worship," asserted Magus Peter H. Gilmore, High Priest of the Church of Satan, in "The Satanic Scriptures."

Many Christians would disagree.

Wicca and its defenders tend to define a Satanist as a follower of the Church of Satan or similar group. Like the Church of Satan, Wiccans generally do not acknowledge the literal existence of Satan and do not readily acknowledge that some Satanists are worshippers of an evil, wicked Satan at war with God. Wiccans worship a horned god (but not the Devil!, they are quick to add) and a goddess; once he came under suspicion in the murders, Echols consistently told police, psychiatric workers and others that he was a Wiccan who believed in a god and a goddess, but that he was not a Satanist.

Social workers the previous year had reported that Echols "said he's a devil worshipping vampire," "stated he was a white witch who worshipped the devil" and "believes that he is a vampire and does worship the devil."

West Memphis was not a lynch mob clamoring to sink their pitchforks into the occultists who had dared set foot on Delta gumbo; its citizens were terrified and furious over the deaths of three little boys and sought justice through proper legal channels. Teenage boys in black T-shirts were not found hanging from trees. No crosses were burned in the trailer parks. Not a single scruffy little Druid was tarred and feathered.

Juries formed in other counties found the three killers guilty. The convictions held up on appeal. Residents were satisfied that justice was served. These were not the Salem witch trials.

"DAMIEN ALWAYS SAID HE WAS INTO THE OCCULT"

Far from just imagining that witchcraft might be involved in the killings, local police had a very good source who loved to talk about his involvement in the occult, a very good source who early in the investigation suggested that "Satanists" were to blame.

That source, Damien Echols, was among the first to point to occultists as likely culprits. Police notes also indicated: "Damien had an opinion for who could have done the murders as being someone sick and that it was some kind of thrill kill. ... Damien felt that the homicide may have been for the purpose of trying to scare someone."

Echols had been sending out signals about the possibility of something bad happening for some time.

Almost a year before the murders, after his arrest in 1992, Echols had confirmed to juvenile officers their suspicions about occult groups in Crittenden County. Echols became a constant source of information on local occult activities during regular visits with Juvenile Court probation officer Jerry Driver.

Local authorities, concerned about occult graffiti and camp sites littered with animal carcasses, also communicated with Steve Nawojcxyk, a cult and gang consultant from Little Rock who was the coroner for Pulaski County.

According to a story in the Commercial Appeal on June 13, 1993, Nawojcxyk discovered "some disturbing things" around Crittenden County. Nawojcxyk found a room in the old Dabbs School decorated with occult symbols. Remnants of a bonfire were found, and the school had burned down since the investigation. Nawojcxyk found several other sites where ritual meetings apparently had taken place, including an old farmhouse (destroyed in the year prior to the arrests) and the remnants of an old cotton gin east of Marion known as Stonehenge.

Local officials first contacted Dr. Dale Griffis, a retired police captain in Tiffin, Ohio, who had been advising police departments about occult crime for many years, in 1992.

Police later send reports on the murders to Griffis, who sought out details on possible occult activity. Much of the information supplied to Griffis consisted of the highly suspect statements of Aaron Hutcheson about five strange men speaking "Spanish" in rituals at Robin Hood Hills.

Bryn Ridge acknowledged to Griffis that strange activities had been rumored there but never reported to police, that no drawings or other graphic symbols were found at the murder scene and that no items were laid out in a systemic manner nor were the bodies placed in a pattern.

As Echols told police, occultists likely would leave objects such as knives, candles or stones if they held a ritual. There were no egregious signs of cult activity but investigators nonetheless suspected Satanic links, largely based on the ritualized disposition of the bodies. A remnant of blue wax on a shirt, similar to blue candle wax linked to Echols, heightened suspicions.

Police had materials at hand to reinforce that opinion. For example, an issue of Missouri Police Chief magazine obtained by the WMPD contained a lengthy article on how Satanism was peculiarly well-suited to sociopaths.

Among the examples given were Charles Manson, Henry Lucas and Ottis Toole, Richard "Night Stalker" Ramirez, Robin Gecht and the Chicago Rippers and David "Son of Sam" Berkowitz. The author, Steve Daniels, cited Aleister Crowley, Anton LaVey and the Process Church of the Final Judgement as prime influences for the "self-styled Satanist" who found those philosophies highly compatible with the self-indulgent solipsism of the sociopath.

As the article put it: "A frightening picture emerges: an evil, drug-lubricated butchering machine who justifies his behavior by exalting Satan." The resulting crimes were often brutally violent, with mutilated victims and body parts used in rituals.

Daniels, a self-educated expert on occult crime, supplied the department with several other articles, including a paper he wrote on "Occultic/Fanatic Cults: A Profile." Daniels, a probation officer in Green Bay,

Wis., described how small, self-styled religious/political groups often coalesced around a charismatic leader with sociopathic tendencies. The followers were described as often being rootless "castoffs" from dysfunctional, abusive backgrounds. Group identity was often encouraged through distinctive haircuts, dress, jewelry and tattoos and reinforced through the use of drugs, forced nudity and other forms of ritualized sex. Rituals were marked by increased violence, often marked by self-mutilation and blood drinking.

Among the many correspondences with the Arkansas killers were: " —- condones chronic involvement with fantasy enhancing mediums: destructive music, watching slasher/violent movies, builds on a fascination with occultism ... through books by Crowley, LaVey, Regardie. ..."

Daniels also supplied an article he had written for the Training Key, published by the International Association of Chiefs of Police, which gave a brief overview of Crowley and LaVey, along with the Process Church, as the chief modern proponents of satanism, noting "Crowley advocated perverse sexual rituals and human sacrifices. ..."

The article described "experimentalist" Satanists as youths dabbling in drugs, heavy metal music and horror videos. "These young satanists read books by the aforementioned Crowley and LaVey ... and either alone or in loose-knit 'covens' mix and match rituals, spells and ceremonies. Often, sessions include drugs, sex, animal mutilations, and vile exercises such as drinking blood or urine. …

"As these youth spend more time immersed in heavy metal music … and drugs, they tend to pull away from reality. Grades plummet, parental hatred grows, the quest for dominance over others is paramount and a hateful, bone-piercing stare often develops. Also noticeable is isolation, adoption of a satanic nickname, and alienation from the family. Self-mutilation may begin in a type of cryptic gouging of tattoos. … Many of these youths compile a book of 'shadows,' a simple notebook decorated with satanic symbols, rock groups, and song titles. …

"With experimentalists, secrecy is minimal, as they brag to peers of their involvement with the devil and often attempt to recruit others into their schemes and criminal activities. Most commonly these include trespass, burglary, criminal damage and drugs, but suicide and homicide may also result for their satanic involvement."

The article cited a 1987 Satanic murder in a small Missouri town; Jim Hardy, Pete Roland and Ron Clements beat fellow student Steven Newberry to death with baseball bats as a sacrifice to Satan. The killers, into drugs and heavy metal, tortured a kitten to death prior to the attack on Newberry.

The article reported: "Estimates are that 30 to 40 percent of all serial killers are involved in satanism to some degree."

In "Juveniles, Satanism and Murder," Daniels cited the Missouri case again, along with self-described Satanic murderer Sean Sellers of Oklahoma and the team of Terry "Lucifer" Belcher and Bobby McIntyre, as well as the notorious cases involving Ricky Kasso, Scott Waterhouse, Tommy Sullivan and Lloyd Gamble.

Daniels observed a uniform profile of the killers: white, "intelligent, creative, artistic, verbal and sophisticated beyond their years, often underachievers," "bored, isolated and withdrawn from their families, often hold their families in terror," "deeply involved in drugs," history of cruelty to animals, sexual promiscuity, often compiled a "Book of Shadows" filled with morbid poems, song lyrics and magical spells. Blood drinking, animal mutilations, poor grades, fire setting and fascination with death were other signs of an unhealthy involvement in the occult, said the article.

Echols fit these profiles so consistently that they seemed to have been written about him.

In his testimony at the Baldwin/Echols trial, Bryn Ridge explained how evidence suggested that the killings were cult related: "Several indications at the crime scene convinced me that it is a cult related killing. One of these being the fact that it was an overkill. The fact there was way more injuries than was necessary to actually kill the children. There was torture involved. The removal of the penis, a penis is a symbol of power according to Damien's own statement: Placement in the water. Water is — has satanic symbolism according to Damien's own statement. … Items are to be returned three-fold, three as a satanic importance and symbolism. Crossroads area meaning neither in the middle of a community but not in the extremes of nature. It's sort of a neither in the city or out of the city. Neither public nor completely private. Cult meeting —- most cult meetings or rituals are held in deserted isolated areas, wooded areas away from people. In blood rituals, many times parts of the victim are removed, possibly eaten, or kept for use in other way. The notation being that the penis was not found. The bodies were in the nude, the satanic term for that would be 'skyclad.' Stab wounds, patterns, may have been done for the purpose of bloodletting. Incisions to the sex organs or mutilations, cut and bruises. Being a clean site, satanic or occult symbolism would mean that a clean site would have been noted. Injury patterns —- most sites would be on private property, this is private property, it's not public property, not normally travelled. The mutilation. Sex organs will be mutilated or removed. Their victims will be males, penis or testicle will be removed. The eyes will be gouged …. These are some notes I've taken from some research I've done in the occult."

Ridge's testimony was cited among the factors weighing heavily in the jury's conclusion of guilt. Ridge came to the belief that the murders may have been cult related early in the investigation based on continuing research. Ridge consulted with Dr. Griffis, who reinforced his opinion. Ridge said, however, that he had not used materials from Dr. Griffis.

Ridge particularly relied on a book popular in law enforcement. "Occult Crime: Detection, Investigation and Verification" gave an exhaustive look into the subject, with author William Edward Lee Dubois hitting upon themes common to the West Memphis case.

For instance, Dubois wrote, "For the occultist, blood contains the life force — the magickal power — of any living thing. A blood sacrifice serves a practical purpose to the criminal occultist. A killing during a ceremony pays homage to powerful entities and gives all the participants power. As the blood spilled, the power in the blood transfers to any living object that comes into contact with it."

Dubois wrote that while many Satanists smear blood over themselves, some drink blood. Echols was a blood drinker and similarly described blood as the source of magickal power.

Dubois also wrote: "Animal sacrifices associated with criminal Satanism are relatively common and are well documented in the United States. On the other hand, of the literally thousands of human sacrifices that have been reported to law enforcement, most do not stand up to close scrutiny. Since 1985, only about a dozen verifiable cases of human sacrifice have been reported in the United States.

"In short, human sacrifices are rare, but they do occur." Contrasting with Dubois' view is the official FBI stance that Satanic murders do not occur. Since it is not difficult to discover isolated incidents of occult human sacrifice nor difficult to determine that someone somewhere at some time killed someone as a ritual sacrifice, Dubois' bare facts negate FBI dogma.

Much of Ridge's testimony about the setting of the crime drew directly from Dubois, such as: "The ultimate magickal place, according to occultists, is a location that is 'neither here nor there.'"

Dubois cited a beach as a classic example, being neither land nor sea, but gave other examples of "a place between" that would roughly fit Robin Hood Hills: "forest clearings, where meadows and trees meet; river banks, where water and land meet; hilltops, where earth and sky meet. ... Such borderlands are called crossroads. These places are traditionally seen not only as borderlines in the physical world, but as borderlines between the physical world and the magickal world."

Dubois noted that "Sunsets and sunrises are also crossroads," and "The phase of the moon often dictates when a magickal operation should take place at a crossroads. Constructive magick is done when the moon is waxing — headed from new toward full." The moon over West Memphis on May 5, 1993, is often described as a full moon; the moon was 99 percent illuminated, still waxing gibbous while rising, at the time of the killings, turning full at around 10:30 that evening.

Sunset was at 7:49. Moonrise was at 7:51 p.m. The brief interval between would have been a "time between time," a suspension of powers between the crossroads with the closeness of the celestial events making it a particularly auspicious magickal evening.

Some investigators believed the killings were related to the pagan holiday of Beltane, celebrated by Wiccans on May 1 or, alternatively, under the closest full moon. May 5 was also close to Walpurgis Night, or Walpurgisnacht, the night of April 30, the night of a major witches meeting in German lore. Walpurgisnacht is a major holiday in the Church of Satan, representing the anniversary of the cult's founding by LaVey. May 1, of course, is a folk holiday with deep pagan roots.

Materials from Rev. Michael Rokos of Baltimore received by police stated that "Beltane is the time of year when the power passes from the god to the goddess," another form of crossroads.

Soon after the arrests, on June 8, Jerry Driver received a call from another juvenile probation officer, Steve Jones, who asked to meet him under the I-55 overpass crossing the railroad tracks near Lakeshore.

Jones told Driver that he had an informant involved with individuals practicing ritualistic animal sacrifices.

On the north end of the overpass they found the carcass of a cat and the bones of another animal along with 10-15 dead pigeons in a pile. Some small bonfires had been set.

They found graffiti along the railroad tracks. Jones found a knife with a serrated edge, like the one used in the killings, on the south side of the tracks south of the retaining wall. They called in the Crittenden County Sheriff's Office. Arkansas State Police Investigator Bobby Stabbs, WMPD Assistant Chief Don Bray and Lt. Gary Kelley of the Marion Police Department also responded. The areas were photographed and videotaped; the knife was bagged and removed by Kelley.

Law enforcement officials had been finding similar sites from time to time. Even before the killings, there was news coverage on witchcraft sites, sparking concerns from the public.

In an interview with Bill Durham on Dec. 3, Driver explained the background of his dealings with Echols, dating back to May 1992, when Echols was arrested after running away with Deanna Holcomb.

Echols told Driver and Det. John Murray that he was involved in the occult, but as a gray witch, not a devil worshipper. Echols told them that a number of people, including Jason Baldwin, were involved in occult practices.

Asked about cult activities in Crittenden County, Echols said it was fairly extensive, with three or four active groups in West Memphis.

Echols said these groups were further along in the practice of magick than perhaps he was and that they had reached the end of practices regarding animal sacrifice. The next step would be human sacrifice. Echols refused to give names or details but said that one cult was awaiting the return of seven members in the summer of 1992 to participate in a sacrifice.

Echols gave great detail about his occult activities, saying that he worshipped Hecate and Dianna. Echols told Driver that he had been brought into the group by an older woman, but he never gave Driver, over the course of some 20 conversations, her name.

Indications were that the woman was around age 30.

Echols told Driver that Deanna had been involved in occult activities prior to their involvement with each other.

Hecate, originally an ancient Thracian and then a Greek goddess who ruled over the realms of Earth and fertility rituals, has become a patron deity to Wiccans, the neopagan witchcraft religion that Echols claimed to practice. Hecate, sometimes spelled Hekate and having a variety of other names, was the Goddess of the

Witches, ruling magic, the moon, the night, ghosts and necromancy.

Hecate was another "three" linked to the case, having a tripartite nature of "Mother, Maiden and Crone."

She had power over three realms: the sky, the earth and water; the three young victims were exposed to the "three realms." Being stripped nude made them "skyclad," according to Wicca terminology; they were beaten and thrown into the mud, then immersed in water. The circumstances gave the appearance of a reenactment of a pagan ritual (such as the Druid threefold ritual murders that Echols likely had read about).

The nearby I-40-I-55 co-joined highway is one of the most significant crossroads in the nation; two smaller state highways also form a crossroads nearby.

Hecate was also the Goddess of the Crossroads and the guardian of the three paths in Wiccan lore; she was known, like Echols, for walking the roads at night as well as for visiting cemeteries during the dark phases of the moon. In the folklore of the South, the crossroads is where deals with the devil are made, as in the well-known legend of blues singer Robert Johnson.

According to Richard Cavendish's "The Black Arts," three is the number of creation in the occult sciences, indicating procreation and the male genitals. Ridge on May 10 noted that Echols "stated that the penis was a symbol of power in his religion known as

Wicca. He also stated that the number 3 was a sacred number in the belief."

"3 is a potent number, because it represents the generative sexual force of the male and the highest spiritually creative force, through its connection with the Trinity," wrote Cavendish. The author of the "The Black Arts" and Echols concurred on the potent significance of three.

Remains of dogs were routinely found at sacrificial sites in Crittenden County. Various witnesses told of Echols' involvement in cooking and eating dogs' flesh.

Necromancers, who called up the spirits of the dead to divine the future, traditionally ate dogs' flesh in preparation for those rites. Echols was comfortable enough with the term "necromancy" to participate in an "art" show called "Necromancy" in the fall of 2015 that included other notables from the horror genre.

Dogs were among the animals sacrificed to Hecate in the ancient world, holding a special significance, as most of the other animal sacrifices among the Greeks involved just four species, all related to food production: goats, sheep, cattle and swine. Dogs were considered sacred to Hecate. According to Cavendish, "The dog is the creature of Hecate, the goddess of ghosts and death and sterility, the terrible and inexorable one, the dweller in the void, who is invoked with averted head because no man can see her and remain sane."

Diana was the goddess of the hunt, the moon, water and birthing and was associated with wild animals and woodland. Considered the Queen of the Witches, she is another Wiccan Goddess who conforms to the three-part nature of "Maiden, Mother and Crone" and whose three-faced statues were found at crossroads in antiquity.

In the Wiccan mythology, the influence of the Goddess (whether Diana, Hecate or another) is balanced by her consort, the Horned One.

According to Margaret Murray's "The Witch-Cult in Western Europe," a dubious but influential survey of witchcraft and one of the primary sources of Wicca lore, the Horned God was worshipped by a pan-European witch cult from time immemorial and was demonized into the figure of the Devil by the Roman Catholic Church.

While the figure of the minor horned Greek god Pan was revived by the 18th Century Romantics as a largely positive figure celebrating the joys of nature and then incorporated into the Wiccan mythos in the middle of the 20th Century, there's little evidence that underground networks of European witches worshipped a Horned God over many centuries. As with much else in Wicca, the lore is based on romantic fantasy.

Among the other Horned Gods was Baphomet, the name of the pagan idol that the Knights Templar were accused of worshipping during the Inquisition in the early 14th Century. That charge brought about the destruction of the order, along with confiscation of their great accumulated wealth and the execution of many Templar leaders.

The occultist Eliphas Levi made the first use of the figure of "Baphomet" as a benevolent fertility god rather than the Devil, using such previous images as the Devil card in the Tarot of Marseilles.

The illustration of of Levi's Baphomet figure, also known as the Goat of the Witches' Sabbath and the Goat of Mendes, has been widely reproduced in such books as "The Black Arts." The figure is that of a winged, horned goat with human female breasts, masculine arms and shoulders and a wand-like phallus rising from the groin. The figure was intended to embody the reconciliation of such opposites as animal and human, male and female, black and white, etc. To the uninitiated eye, Baphomet looks like the Devil.

Aleister Crowley, whose name figured prominently in the murder case, believed himself to be the reincarnation of Levi. Crowley's mother had referred to her son as "the Beast," and he embraced the nickname as his own, adding others as his reputation grew. Among those assumed nicknames was Baphomet. The Beast, of course, referred to a sinister power in the Book of Revelation, and is a common metaphorical figure for the animalistic and the demonic.

So the Horned God is in many ways a rehabilitated and sanitized version of the Christian

Devil. Some argue that veneration of the Horned God is simply Satanic worship in skimpy disguise, and they would not be far wrong. The Horned God figure was devised during the invention of Wicca as a benign stand-in for the Satanic figures with whom witches had been associated.

Wicca is known for "white witchcraft" but Echols' "gray witch" status left him free to follow his impulses, however malevolent they might be, and invoke whatever gods, angels or demons that struck his fancy.

According to Driver, indications were that Jason Baldwin was involved in cult activities in 1992.

Driver also mentioned a Michael Beath, whom he had never been able to track down, a boy named Jared Clark and Sherry Bartoush, who lived at Lakeshore.

Driver saw the three future killers walking together on Nov. 15, 1992: "Damien, Jason and Jessie were walking together over in Lakeshore ... walking down the street all dressed in black, long black coats; Damien had ... had a black slouch hat on, and they all 3 had staffs, and .... I ask them what they were doing and they told me they were going ... going to watch, laugh, so I kept an eye on them pretty close after that, and I saw them on several other occasions" at Lakeshore and Highland.

"They use to go down to Wal-Mart to shoplift, he and Domini Teer and ... and I think Jason probably Jessie too, but I just never saw Jessie with anything at that location."

Driver had talked to Baldwin, who denied any involvement in the occult.

"The reason we got involved in looking at him at one time that night after we started dealing this uh, the Damien business, we had a report that there was a pentagram carved on the door post ... at ... Jason Baldwin's house and in fact there was ... And Damien had of course told us he was ... his main guy. ... Deanna Holcomb said that was the case, ... that Jason was .... his confidant."

Driver had "quite a few" dealings with Misskelley.

Asked if Misskelley had mentioned the occult, Driver said, "He always denied it ... but he always said he knew about it ... and he was always very evasive when we talked to him about it. Jessie -- the main reasons we would see Jessie was violence and criminal mischief complaints, he would be involved in breaking things, tearing things up, hitting someone, uh I think several occasions where he ... he hit girls and would get in difficulty over that ... just before, his appearance changed considerably, that spike hair and that stuff that you all saw, we hadn't seen until maybe a month or 2 before all this happened. That kid's attitude and his ... his demeanor probably turned around over maybe a 3 month period .... that uh, he looked like a different guy. ...

"Damien always said he was into the occult, just used to always deny being a devil worshipper, always said he knew who did it. He knew, he told me at one time, that he know of ... a book here in West Memphis called the Necronomicon I think it is -- and he didn't mean the one you could buy off the shelf. This was an old one ... that had been passed down for generations.

"So what he was telling me was that he thought that he was saying there was a generational Satanist here in town. He wouldn't tell me who it was but he was adamant that ... there was one.

"It always seem to me that ... he knew too much about it not to ... have had ... some great dealings in it. ....

"One of the things that occurred while this was going on is (he) told me he had joined the Catholic Church, so I went down and talked to the priest ... in the summer of 92."

Echols had attended St. Michael's Catholic Church in West Memphis.

Driver said, "I asked him .... if he remembered Damien. He did. He said that Damien came to church, I think he had came that previous ... winter or fall and had professed a great interest in the Catholic religion and had (converted) and has his name changed ... and then had quit coming and he related to me that right after he quit coming someone tried to break into the sacristy and he had always wondered if ... if he had anything to do with it..

"Of course, that's one of the things that those guys do that's kinda modus operandi. (They) go to the

Catholic church and find out as much as they can, break in to the sacristy, steal the host and the lunette and that's how some of them (operate). ... That's not to say he did that, but that would not be out of character with the things that they do. .... Every time I talked to him, um, said he knew who the other people were that were involved in it serious, never denied that he didn't know what was going on. He just said it's not him."

It is common in certain occult circles to feign interest in Catholicism to gain access to materials for a Black Mass.

Driver said Echols told him there was going to be a sacrifice in the summer of 1992. "We were on the roads and the back roads, and Dabbs School, and we went every where in the world that summer, every time there was a witches sabbath, we were out in force, and whether that did any good or not I don't know, but to my knowledge nothing happened that summer."

Driver said about Domini: "We've had her on uh, probation, in fact she got off it. ...

"She's told us uh, that they were witches and ... worship nature and Hecate and Diana and when I took her .... to Charter Hospital Little Rock -- she went over to the same place -- uh, she discussed with me the blood drinking and said that, the first thing she said was uh, why should I not drink blood, because my .... mother drinks blood, and I thought now thats a strange thing to say. But that's what she said and she and her mother got into a little discussion about this and um, the mother didn't deny it, and Domini said that when ... the mother ... was young, I guess in the 60s, that she was pretty heavily into this blood drinking stuff, uh and Domini also stated that blood drinking was ... was nothing wrong with it. ... We want to do it, we'll not be taking blood from anybody and it gives us strength." Driver said the "we" referred to Echols and Domini. She has consistently denied making these statements and has disavowed any interest in the occult or blood drinking.

"The original deal was she was Damien's girlfriend prior ... to Deanna Holcomb and when the Deanna Holcomb thing broke up, then he went back to Domini. Our concern all along was that we had (indications) back when he was going with Deanna that ... he and Deanna was trying to conceive a child and that child was to be sacrificed. ... We got that information from informants and from some drawings that we ... had confiscated ... from Damien at the time. ... One which had four tombstones and a baby's foot from behind it and a rattle and power emanating up to the moon or something, and they always denied that. They always said no, that's not (the) case, but several people very close to them, confidential informant people, said that's what was going on. ... And then Domini and Damien get back together ... What happens they have a baby uh, I'm very concerned about that, just I'm sure everyone else is. Domini is no longer on probation to us, so I don't have any ... further ... contact with her other than .... just telling DHS what I know about it, so they can take their action."

Durham asked if Echols had gotten into trouble when he was in Portland, Ore.

Driver said, "He got into trouble the time he fought with his dad and went to the emergency room at the psychiatric hospital and ... I got so much crap on him. ...

"The dad called me and .... he did not say anything about weapons. ... He said that ... Damien intended to kill him. ... He called me up and said that they had sent him home, he didn't ask if he could come home, he just said we've sent him home because he went crazy one night and threatened to kill me and we went (to) the hospital and he jump around and said he was going to eat me. He said come on I'm going to eat you up. ... He also had made ... threats previously, I think probably this would have been in 92 also, against a boy in school at Marion .... He threatened to claw his eyes out, and I don't know if you ever saw his nails but he had talons." Echols had attacked Shane Divilbiss in a jealous rage over Deanna.

"He had threatened to enucleate his eyes, and he has also made other (threats) to kill Deanna's mother. ... He threatened to kill numerous people ... in Marion. Most people didn't take him serious, because at the time he was ... just looked on as kind of a kook, you now, that wore black clothes and acted silly. But the more I got into it, you know, I found more and more people that said ... yea I know him, he did this, he did that, I've seen him kill dogs, I've seen him drink blood and (none) of these people will come forward.

"But it's my opinion that there's 10 or 15 that know what happened and could probably give you some excellent ... information if they ... just would. ...

"There was, to the best of my knowledge, there was about 7 or 8 of them in the group ... He always said there was between 7 and 10 people."

Durham added: "I suspect there's some people at Lakeshore that were involved with him that we don't even know and there's probably some still out that .... that were involved at the time, because we're still (finding) dogs and things you know that they cut up and (do) that kind of mess."

Investigators had asked Driver if he had seen Echols wearing a black leather studded belt, which they believed might be linked to bruising on the boys. Driver had seen Echols wearing such a belt "on several occasions, one of which was when I saw him at Wal-Mart ... and asked he and his group to leave Wal-Mart" on Nov. 12, 1992, when Driver had handled a complaint that Domini was shoplifting.

Driver added: "I have seen all 3 of them together, I have seen all 4 of them together, Domini was with (them) ... with other boys, too, all of them would be together walking along the interstate ... the grassy area of the interstate, Lakeshore to West Memphis, and I would say I saw them together probably 4 or 5 times in daylight that could tell ... that's who it was. There wasn't any doubt that's who it was, and ... when we talked to Jason Baldwin, he never denied that he and Damien were close, just said he wasn't a devil worshipper."

Driver testified in both trials.

In the Misskelley trial, he testified he first saw the three accused teens together around Nov. 15, 1992, at Lakeshore Trailer Park. "It was nighttime ... They all had on long black coats, and Damien had on a slouch hat and they all had staffs ... Long sticks that they were walking with."

He gave similar testimony in the Echols/Baldwin trial, with clarification that he had seen all three together "about three times," twice at Wal-Mart and once at the trailer park. He saw Echols and Baldwin together on other occasions, generally dressed in black.

"HIS ORIENTATION WASN'T RIGHT. I SHOOK HIS HAND ONCE AND I SHIVERED."

When Shane Griffin and Bill Durham interviewed Damien Echols on May 9, Echols readily told them that he "doesn't believe in God or devil. Used to be involved in Wiccan religion -- Covenant of Divine Light, which practices white witchcraft."

While many of the teenagers named as members of an occult group denied any affiliation, a few local youths admitted their interest in witchcraft.

There was a small but active group who had formed the Covenant of Divine Light. They followed the neo-pagan religion of Wicca, using a standard text, "Buckland's Complete Book of Witchcraft," as a guide at small gatherings in bedrooms and backyards.

Two members were questioned extensively by police early in the investigation and, months later, showed up at a public ritual at Audubon Park in Memphis organized by local Wiccans.

According to the Commercial Appeal story from Feb. 28, 1994, the witches wanted to organize the event to demonstrate that there was nothing to fear from Wicca.

Predictably, the event brought out Baptists with Bibles trying to win souls for Christ.

The story quoted Murray Farris, who watched from the sidelines: "Ever since the murders all of the covenant groups in West Memphis have sort of dried up." The West Memphis case became a cause for area Wiccans, prompting, for instance, the founding of the Southern Delta Chapter of Wicca as part of the Aquarian Tabernacle Church in January 1994, which has been active in the Jonesboro area ever since.

Farris, closely acquainted with Echols, told the reporter that Echols was not in a satanic cult but wasn't a member of his religion either. "Damien said he was a Wiccan but he wasn't. I asked him questions only a Wiccan would know and he didn't know any of them," explained Farris.

Echols told Farris and others that a female witch who followed him to Arkansas after his brief, disastrous stay in Oregon had engaged him in a psychic war. Farris termed Echols' fantasies of persecution by a Satanic cult "misconceptions of an ill mind."

Another Crittenden Wiccan, Christopher Littrell, attended the Audubon Park event, at which witches and pagans complained their religions were misunderstood — they were not devil worshippers. Both Littrell and Farris were subpoenaed as witnesses, though they did not testify, in the Misskelley trial, which had just concluded. They expected to be called in the Echols/Baldwin trial. Neither testified.

There was no evidence that the Divine Light coven's members, with perhaps a single highly significant exception, regarded themselves as involved in Satanism or demonic worship.

Echols claimed membership in the Covenant of the Divine Light. The cult leaders said he was not a member, though he had attended at least one ceremony. Echols was well-known to them, as statements to police indicated frequent contact between Echols and the self-described "white witches." The cult leaders were also well-acquainted with Deanna Holcomb. The former Echols girlfriend admitted practicing black magic but said she had not been a member of the coven, having practiced magic by herself.

According to Misskelley's confessions, Echols led ritualistic ceremonies in which he praised Satan; Misskelley said he, Domini Teer and Jason Baldwin attended these ceremonies, held around a fire behind Lakeshore.

A number of Lakeshore residents told investigators that Echols was a demon worshipper who walked around with "666" and "a sign of the devil" emblazoned on his boots.

Echols was a voracious reader who admired Anton LaVey, head of the Church of Satan. Echols' actual familiarity with LaVey is unclear, based on his own testimony: "I said I haven't read anything by him, but I am familiar with him." The world's best-known Satanist was familiar enough to Echols that a note in his psychiatric records listed the Church of Satan founder, still alive in 1993, as someone Echols would like to meet.

Contemporary pagans, modern practitioners of witchcraft and occultists have created some of the so-called misunderstandings concerning their beliefs and practices in their writings about ritual sacrifice, which was a part of the religion of many ancient pagans. Very few if any modern groups openly espouse the ritual sacrifice of humans but many flirt with hints of such diabolical practices.

The Crittenden County coven, also was referred to as the Order of the Divine Light, was around in 1993 at the time of the killings but apparently did not survive the arrests.

Still, as late as November 2014 at least, a group by the name of Covenant of Divine Light Church was active in Texarkana (on the other side of Arkansas from West Memphis) and planned a "merry meet" for Beltane 2015 called "Reclaiming Our Roots." There is no record of any of these witches or any other covens being rounded up in a good old-fashioned Arkansas "witch-hunt."

Police began questioning members of the Crittenden coven within days of the killings. An undated note from the police department showed a pentagram as a "Hex-Mark" and listed Chris Littrell, Murray J. Farris, "Michail" and Don Warwick. The note contained Hebraic characters transcribed as "yud-hey-vob-hey," which roughly corresponds to the spelling of the name of Yahweh in Hebrew: Yod-Hey-Vav-Hey.

They talked to Murray Jay Farris as early as May 9. Farris was, according to undated notes, heavyset with a big belly, and drove an off-white or cream-colored van (police received tips about a white van in the vicinity of the killings). The son of a former police officer, Farris lived in Lehi, near Earle, a small town west of Marion. The note said "leads an Evil cult." The original notes placed his age at around 37 but he was only 18, still in his last year of high school.

According to Ridge, "Farris came to the Police Department because his friend Damien had told him that the police had been talking to him. Farris stated that he was in a group of so-called White Witches and was wearing a star in a circle that he claimed he had just bought. He explained that the group believes in harming no one and gave a list of 4 members. He told of his necklace being a Hex Mark rather than a Penta-type medallion. He explained that the group studied the first 10 books of the bible and that they prepared the members for purity. ...

"He told of a Black Witch in Marion named Deanna Holcomb."

Farris said Echols was never initiated into his coven of white witches. "His orientation wasn't right," Farris later told the Commercial Appeal. "I shook his hand once and I shivered."

Farris readily agreed to a check of his fingerprints, photos and polygraph test.

On May 11, Farris passed the lie detector exam (unlike Echols and Misskelley). Unlike any of the WM3, he had a verifiable alibi. He was never a suspect.

Farris got out of school about 2:40 on May 5 and went home. Littrell came over about 3:30 p.m. They stayed at the Farris home until they went to a revival from 6:30 to 9:30 p.m. at First Baptist Church. Why were these young witches attending a Baptist revival? In a phone call on May 10, Jim Agee, a youth counselor, said the church had held a "youth night" featuring pizza and water balloon fights.

Agee said Littrell and Farris were "noted for being involved in cult — white witchcraft!" but they were with him from 6:45 to about 8:45. Agee said the boys had attended church there a few times about a year before but had not been back until that night and had returned the following Sunday. Agee said, "Chris is scared about something."

Police also talked to Christopher Douglas Littrell, 16, who, like Farris, was studying the printing crafts at West Memphis High School.

Littrell, like Farris, was a large youth, 6-2 and 270-plus pounds, according to police reports.

Littrell, an 11th-grader, first talked to police on May 10. Littrell gave Ridge a detailed account of his whereabouts, including Tuesday afternoon and evening and the school day on Wednesday.

Littrell said that on May 5, he attended school, dropped his books off at home after school and dropped by two friends' home before meeting Farris. They left his van at the Health Department, where his mother worked. He attended the revival until a little after 9 along with Farris and one of their friends, Karen Webb; he took Webb to her house and then went home about 9:45 to 10 p.m., where he was in the company of his mother and stepfather.

By the afternoon of May 6, he had heard that the three boys had been found behind the Blue Beacon, that they were tied up and at least one had been castrated.

The polygraph and a credible alibi cleared him of suspicion.

At the time, Littrell was a neighbor of the Echols/ Hutchison family in Broadway Trailer Park.

On May 27, Littrell told police how he, Farris, Don Warwick, and David McCarty and Rena Hallmark, students at West Memphis High School, formed the coven three or four months before the murders. Echols attended just one meeting.

Littrell said that on Friday, May 7, around 5 p.m., he had picked up Echols for a trip to the mall, returning around 6 p.m. He had not seen Echols since but talked to him on the phone the night before the interview. He had met Baldwin but didn't really know him, and had not talked to L.G. Hollingsworth, another acquaintance, in about a month.

He told police "whoever did it was sick." Littrell described Damien/Michael as being in a black magic cult and said Echols had been in the hospital. He identified the Priestess of the black magic cult as Deanna Jane Holcomb, aka Mary Jane Holcomb. The black magic cult had unspecified ties with Michigan.

Later, he said he had met Echols and "Dominique" at Walmart and asked Echols if he was involved in the killings. "Denial was stuttering & slow" with Echols being "very nervous" and careful about his answer.

Littrell said he was involved in a "Witchcraft religion," as part of the Order of the Divine Light, that it was a "religion of nature. " The notes list the religion as "Wicker," with the credo of "do whatever you want as long as it harms no one," a variation on Wicca's rede "An' it harm none, do what ye will" which in turn is a reworking of Crowley's "Do what thou wilt shall be the whole of the law." Littrell's version had a decidedly more self-serving meaning than Crowley's.

Littrell described the cult's initiation as taken from Buckland's "Complete Book of Magic," including being bound and "blindfolded," symbolizing a body in the womb as part of a "rebirth" ceremony, with the hands bound back to form a triangle. There were obvious parallels with the binding of Christopher, Michael and Stevie.

The cult's ceremonies had taken place in Farris' bedroom and backyard. Special note was taken of the moon's phases, particularly the new and full moon, with rituals denoting the solstices and four major "sabots."

Littrell first named Farris, Echols and David McCarty as participants. Later, on May 27, he listed

Rena Hallmark, Don Warwick, Farris and himself as members.

　With the permission of Littrell's mother, Durham interviewed Littrell further on May 27.

Littrell repeated his story about May 5.

Then Littrell told him that Damien, interviewed as a prospective member, told them that, while in reform school, he drank blood from a cut in a gang leader's arm so he could join the gang.

He described how Echols liked to torture frogs, how he had burned down his father's garage and chanted as he stood amid the flames and how he had claimed he had set his own foot on fire (fire setting and animal torture, along with bedwetting, form a triad as major predicators of violent criminal tendencies). Littrell said Echols planned to marry Domini so he could get a bigger government check when the baby came.

Durham added: "Chris said that Murray Farris said that Frankie Knight said his brother had said he helped kill the three boys."

The brother in question, David Wren, had already been interviewed and polygraphed on May 13. This sort of statement pops up often in police investigations and illustrates how rumors fly and possible suspects mount up in second- and third- and fourth-hand reports. Ridge's notes on his May 10 interview with Echols included this statement about the Wrens: "Damien knows Michael and David Wren who he considers to be like brothers."

Potential suspects were being routinely checked out but West Memphis police apparently did not even interview some known members of the coven, such as Hallmark and McCarty. It is not apparent that police interviewed a number of others named as occult practitioners.

"Satanically panicked" lawmen had better leads to follow.

"DAMIEN IS A CRAZY, MIXED UP WITH DRUGS AND THE CULT."

Deanna Jane Holcomb, former Echols girlfriend and self-admitted former black magician, was a crucial link in the local occult scene. At the time of the murders, she was a 16-year-old 10-grader at Marion High School, but she was already steeped in occult lore.

Holcomb told officers that she had performed magical ceremonies, but "only ceremonies I did, I did by myself."

On May 11, she answered 32 questions from James Sudbury and Bryn Ridge, including "Why would someone do this?" Her answer: "May have walked up on a drug deal, but the cult has a big deal in May."

The officers also took extensive notes on the interview. At no point did Deanna suggest that Echols might not be involved in the killings. She felt Echols was too big a coward to do the killing himself and would order a follower like Baldwin to carry it out. She also gave police a great deal of information on local occultists.

She mentioned such locations as "Stonehinge," the stark remains of a granary that had burned down, and Murphy's Bridge, a local landmark with a reputation for being haunted. She said ceremonies might include doing drugs in a wooded area, with participants asked to drink blood. New members would be stripped.

She told police she had been at Trinity Baptist Church on May 5 from 7 to 9 p.m.

Unlike Echols, Holcomb admitted she had practiced black magic, which traditionally refers to the use of ritual and other forms of practice to call upon supernatural powers for evil, malicious or selfish purposes. The invocation of demons or spirits does not necessarily involve explicit worship of Satan.

Holcomb said Echols also was involved in black magic but she had never attended ceremonies with him. Holcomb had renounced her involvement with the occult and regretted her foray into witchcraft.

Echols told Jerry Driver that he was a "grey witch," which also is how Holcomb described Echols. It's not clear what is involved in "grey witchcraft." For some occultists, the magical process is deemed morally neutral. For instance, for the Church of Satan, the exertion of true will with the aim of fulfilling desires through ritual and practice is magic, neither black nor white.

Holcomb said she had broken up with Echols when she learned he planned to sacrifice their firstborn if it was a girl. She said that Echols would not have been able to perform the sacrifice so she felt he would try to get her to sacrifice the baby.

Holcomb submitted to a polygraph test, which indicated no involvement in the murders. The May 11 test did indicate she was not telling the truth when she said "no" to "Do you know, for sure, who killed those boys?" After the exam, she explained she was convinced that Echols was involved in the killings. She had no special knowledge other than knowing Echols very, very well.

Deanna also made these comments:

"Damien is a crazy, mixed up with drugs and the cult."

"Damien has a skull and books on the cult in his room."

"I was a black witch, it was a game people got into for the power and stuff."

"Damien says he is into White Magic but that is a lie. He is into Black Magic and sometimes he says he is into Grey Magic."

"I hate I was stupid enough to get involved in this stuff."

"Damien could never hurt himself. He doesn't love anyone but himself. He loves himself too much."

"Damien once told me that he had never killed anyone but wondered what it would feel like."

The police asked, "Did you say that the death of these boys was ordered to a friend of yours at school?"

She answered: "I said that Damien would not have been there. He is a coward and would be afraid of going to jail, but he could have ordered it done and if so probably Jason Baldwin would have been the one. He is a follower."

They asked: "How are you and Damien connected?"

She said, "I ran away with Damien. I went to a hospital in Memphis and he went to one in Little Rock. I found out that he planned to kill our firstborn if it was a girl. Damien would not do it. He is a coward and would have tried to get me to do it. That's when I knew he was nuts and I had nothing else to do with him. I (met) Damien at school. I read some of his poems and felt sorry for him."

As for Domini: "She would lie for Damien. She has never been normal."

Domini apparently had her own fears about what Damien might do to a baby. On Oct. 7, 1993, Dr. Sheldon Korones called investigators, stating that during the delivery of Damian Seth Azariah Teer, Domini expressed fears about the possible sacrifice of the baby.

Deanna said Echols' special hiding place was in sewer manholes. He had tried to get her to hide in one when they ran away.

One fantasy popular with some WM3 "supporters" has been the Manhole Theory, speculation that Robin Hood Hills was a dump site, not a kill site.

The theory is that the killer or killers came upon the boys in the woods about 7 p.m. and beat them until they were unconscious. Then the killers supposedly deposited the boys down a manhole that ran to a drainage pipe, returned overnight and transferred the bodies to the ditch.

Deanna said the cult preferred knives or staffs as weapons (the weapons used) but would use what was on hand. Damien "always had on something black."

On Feb. 14, 1994, Holcomb told investigators that the "lake knife" found behind Baldwin's trailer reminded her of a knife with a "ridge edge" owned by Damien that he often carried in his trench coat.

Holcomb testified on March 7 in the Echols-Baldwin trial.

She told the court that she had gone out with Echols starting around September 1991, from the beginning to the end of that school year.

Asked about his acquaintances, she named Jason Baldwin, Jessie Misskelley, Joey Lancaster and others.

She identified the "lake knife" as similar to one Echols carried. Echols carried knives "because he said that he didn't feel safe."

Deanna has kept a low profile since 1994.

At one time she was going by the name "Deanna Blue" on Facebook, and her Facebook page indicated a deep interest in witchcraft and the "fairy faith." Her involvement in the occult began with casual use of an Ouija board. She still lives in Arkansas and did not respond to a Facebook query about her involvement in the case.

"I KNOW A LITTLE ABOUT WITCHCRAFT"

A lot of teens in Crittenden County knew a lot about witchcraft.

Domini Teer had family ties that brought up questions after a reporter found flyers from the Secret Order of the Undead in trash cleared out of the Teer home. "It's like a little club," said Domini about SOUND.

The vampire club newsletter published in California by Domini's 22-year-old cousin, Tammy Jo Teer, featured macabre topics appealing to fans of Gothic horror. "The Blood of Innocents," the first book on the case, written by Commercial Appeal staffers Guy Reel, Marc Perresquia and Bart Sullivan, described the newsletter as containing "an ink sketch of a winged demon molesting a woman, a list of thirteen songs 'suitable to accompany any ritualistic murder,' and a column instructing 'boys and girls' in the fine art of building a homemade 'landmine' from threaded pipe and shotgun shells."

Domini told John Fogleman that she had spent a lot of time with "T.J." in California and "T.J." had been involved in "just a group of friends" practicing witchcraft. "They just burnt candles. That's really about it," said Domini.

"It's something my cousin does just to take up time," Domini told Fogleman on Sept. 10.

T.J. "Pandora" Teer remains active in the goth and vampire subcultures, and considers herself a bohemian goth. Known as "Auntie Pan Pan," her Facebook profile photo for the 2016 holidays featured a skull in a Santa hat. She appeared to have had fang dental implants. Her bio on "WikiFur," the guide to the "furry" subculture, said her "fursona" is a "gothic vampire red panda," reflecting her interests in a variety of deviant subcultures.

Domini told Fogleman she had not participated in her cousin's witchcraft group and that Echols was no longer involved in witchcraft, "not when he was going with me."

Fogleman asked, "But he didn't meet with other witches while he was going with you?"

Domini told him, "The only person he met with while he was going with me was Jason." That ambiguous answer called for a followup question but was never clarified.

Fogleman asked about other girlfriends. Domini mentioned "Diana Holcomb."

Said Domini of Deanna: "She's a kook. ... She's the one that's obviously involved in witchcraft and stuff because of ... the way she talks about it. ... She come up with off the wall stuff."

Fogleman: "OK, what kind of stuff? Just to give me an example."

Domini: "Just like, him and her would be involved in witchcraft and stuff. They would go out and read books and crap about it."

Fogleman asked if she had been to an "es pot," a reference to an esbat, a meeting for Wiccans.

Domini: "I don't even know what an es pot is. ... "

Domini persisted in denying knowledge of occult practices as Fogleman continued: "... You went to the hospital in Little Rock one time, right, okay. ... You accused your mother of drinking blood in the past."

Domini: "No."

Fogleman: "You don't remember that?"

"No."

Fogleman: "Alright, so you know anything about blood drinking?"

Domini: "No."

Fogleman: "You know anything about Damien drinking blood?"

"No."

Fogleman: "You've never seen him do that"

"No."

Fogleman: "Do you remember discussing with Mr. Driver about witchcraft and vampirism?"

Domini: "He asked me about it."

Fogleman: "What did you tell him?"

Domini: "He asked me if Damien was involved in witchcraft. And I said I really have no idea. I mean, he was when he was going out with that one girl. And he said, well is he involved with vampires and all that? I said, no he reads books about them, but that's all I know."

Fogleman: "But you don't remember in Mr. Driver's presence talking about your mother drinking blood?"

Domini: "No."

Domini remain close-mouthed throughout the investigation, trial and afterward. As Domini Ferris, she has lived in the Phoenix, Arizona, area for a number of years.

The son of Domini and Damien, born while his father was awaiting trial, was named Damian Seth Azariah Echols and is known as Seth Echols or Damian Teer. The name "Seth" has Hebraic roots, with Seth being the name of Eve's third child, conceived as a replacement for the murdered Abel. The name means "anointed" or "compensation." The name is also an alternative spelling for Set, the Egyptian god of the desert, storms, chaos, war, disorder, deceit and violence who killed and dismembered his brother god Osiris. Azariah was the name of a number of Biblical figures, mostly notably as the Babylonian name of Abednego, one of Daniel's companions in the fiery pit.

Fogleman took a statement from Domini's mother, Dian Teer, on Sept. 10, in which he asked her if she was aware that Echols and her daughter "were involved in some of this witchcraft stuff."

Mrs. Teer said they weren't involved, adding, "I know a little about witchcraft, but they never did anything like that as far as I know."

Fogleman: "You didn't know anything about it."

Dian: "No."

Fogleman: "Well, you said that you knew something about witchcraft. Have you at some point been involved in the occult?"

Dian said "I used to read about a lot of it when I was in California" but denied participating in witchcraft.

She added: "... I've read a lot of books about different things. And I used to have a pack of tarot cards and rune stones."

Fogleman: "Uh huh. OK. What kind of stones?"

Dine: "Rune."

Fogleman: "OK." Clearly he had no idea of what this casual dabbler in the occult was talking about.

Dian: "R-U-N-E."

Fogleman: "What do you do with the rune stones?"

Dian: "You have somebody touch 'em and put them out on the table, and pick out ever how many you need to and tell them, um, like their fortune, or something that's ongoing in their life. I also have a deck of rune cards." Echols crafted a similar set of rune stones while incarcerated and has a continuing fascination with the Tarot.

Fogleman: "OK. But you say that you've never participated in any kind of group ..."

Dian: "No."

Fogleman: "... that practice this kind of stuff."

Dian: "No, the only kind of group that I was ever in like that was the 'Rocky Horror Picture Show.'"

Fogleman asked "OK. What kind of group is that? What do they do?" and she explained the activities involving the cult movie.

Dian said she was not aware that Echols had a pentagram tattooed to his chest, but volunteered that he wore a pentagram necklace.

Fogleman asked: "Were you aware that Damien claimed to be involved in witchcraft?"

Dian: "They never did around me. He liked to read some of the books, cause I had some books that I loaned him too."

Fogleman: "OK. Are these white magic or black magic?"

Dian: "White."

Fogleman: "OK. But you've never known Damien to participate in any of those activities?"

Dian: "Not that I know of."

To sum up, Echols' girlfriend's mother told the prosecutor that she owns rune stones, rune cards and Tarot cards, explained the use of rune stones for divination, volunteered that Echols wore an occult emblem around his neck and said he was an avid reader of the "white magic" books she lent him, but said she had no knowledge of Echols being involved in the occult.

Similarly, Echols' mother's complaints about his occult preoccupation and Satanic beliefs were cited repeatedly in the documents surrounding his three trips to mental institutions in 1992, when he was 17. Subsequently she claimed tolerant disapproval of his Wiccan beliefs. Echols told the Village Voice, according to a 2014 blog posting about his plans to move to New York City and hold Tarot workshops, "I got my first deck (of tarot cards) when I was seventeen years old. It was a gift from my mother."

"THEY WERE IN THE OCCULT"

On June 16, 1993, Ricky Don Climer, 16, described life in a gang of Satanists in lurid and unlikely detail.

Climer's statement was full of wild accusations about Baldwin, Misskelley, Echols and others involved in the Crittenden County witch cult. As with stories from Aaron and Vicki Hutcheson, Garrett Schwarting or the Echols family, the truth was difficult to determine. Climer had spent time in the Arkansas State Hospital. He was in state custody at the DeDe Wallace Wilderness Program in Shelbyville, Tenn., after he was taken from his parents due to behavioral problems. He had confessed his involvement in the occult to program counselors.

Climer also had been friends with a group of West Memphis youths who had come under scrutiny.

He described one exceedingly unlikely incident in which he and a group of boys had jumped a police officer or security guard and beaten him up, with Climer claiming he used a baseball bat while Misskelley used his fists. They supposedly left the officer unconscious.

Concerning Misskelley, Echols and Baldwin, Climer told Ridge that "they were in the occult ... I knew that they rape some people ... they always made barn fires uh in the woods. Uh, I know that they jumped a cop, they cut, you know, a pig's head off, you know put it on a porch ... Occult, a satanic type, it's pretty much the same thing."

He explained occult symbols, such as a pentagram: "With the symbol being all black, you know it suppose to be an updown cross look like somebody's hanging from it."

The pig's head was placed on the porch "to scare and show people that death is on its way ... to show people that we have power."

He said parts of cats and dogs were cooked and eaten at ceremonies and a variety of intoxicants used: marijuana, cocaine, alcohol, gasoline sniffing and acid. Climer said drug use sometimes would lead to fights or "you're be sitting there, you know, the next thing you'll start thinking of some cartoon character. Let's say, the little guys in blue ... Smurfs, things like that."

In contrast to others, Climer didn't seem to have any idea of special days or times for the Satanic meetings held around Lakeshore and the Marion area.

Climer, with some prodding and leading questions from Ridge, said they discussed plans on how to get away with murder.

He said if they killed someone, they would use "torture, you get a thrill out of torture."

He claimed that they had killed someone "in the projects" over "Bloods, you know that's a gang." He claimed "cult are Crips, you know, some cult people are Crips."

On June 18, Climer told police in a phone conversation that he had witnessed Baldwin and Echols torture a girl with a rope, hanging her from a tree with a slip knot around her neck. Climer said he didn't know the girl, who was from Marion and wasn't a girlfriend. He said he left the scene, which happened in woods toward Marion, after she dropped.

Climer said of the rapes: "I don't know if you want to call it talking her into it, by getting her doped up and everything, that she would say, yes. ... I don't know if you would call that talking." Climer repeated his claim that Baldwin and Misskelley had "jumped" a police officer and "did it because you just hated cops, you know."

Climer said he had been involved in the occult group since he was 8 or 9, which would have been around 1985, and had left it two years before.

According to Misskelley's confessions, Misskelley was a relatively recent recruit to the occult scene and only participated in a few ceremonies. There was little evidence to suggest that Baldwin was involved in the occult earlier than 1991. Even Echols may have gotten involved in witchcraft mostly as the result of his relationship with Deanna. Echols claims he first became interested in "magick" around age 12, which would have been around 1987.

Despite the many problems with Climer's story, his description of certain cult practices —- cooking and eating animal parts, drug abuse, the pentagram, sexual assaults — agreed with other descriptions of the local occult scene.

"ONE OF THE GUYS HAD A DEVIL WORSHIPING BOOK AND WE WOULD GO BY IT."

Self-confessed Satanists in trouble with the law became a prime source of information.

Alvis Clem Bly, 36, had been charged with sexual abuse, first degree in March 1993, and was still in the Crittenden County Jail when Detective Allen talked to him on June 29 about his involvement in the cult. Bly at times seemed almost incoherent while nonetheless giving details that concurred with others' statements.

Bly had lived on East Barton in West Memphis, in the neighborhood of the victims, and in Lakeshore prior to being arrested. He had been involved in the cult for about a year. About 20 people, never less than eight, were involved.

"We always had a certain time to meet out there during the week. ... We always go on Sunday" at 6 o'clock in the evening. "It was in the book that's what time you're suppose to start it." "Buckland's Complete Book of Witchcraft," the go-to text locally for witches, said, "Most covens meet once a week, but there really is no hard and fast rule." There was little agreement among professed occultists talking to police about meeting times.

Bly explained: "Well we just go out there and one of the guys had a devil worshiping book and we would go by it, which was sacrificing dogs or chicken. We would drain their blood. Then we would take and cut the heart out and put it in the center of the pentagram and set fire to it and worship the devil."

He described the pentagram as "a devil symbol" placed "on the floor."

"They had some chalk, some white powder chalk and some blue chalk like carpenters chalk and would draw it with it."

Bly, who had been following the case in the news, named Misskelley and Baldwin as participants.

He said cult members called Baldwin "Davien." Allen got out a newspaper with a story about the killings and photos of the three suspects.

Allen: "Okay is this the one they call Damien?"

Bly: "No sir."

Allen: "That's, I'm point to Jason Baldwin?"

Bly: "I see, that's ... that's not Davien, the other boy was Damien, I don't see him on th ... there he is, that's Davien there."

Allen: "Okay that's the one they call Damien there."

Bly: "Yes sir."

Allen: "Davien, what ever you know him as."

Bly: "Davien that's devil name."

Allen: "Okay, and this is the person you know as Baldwin?"

Bly: "Yes sir."

Allen: "Point to a picture of Jason Baldwin and this person here, do you recognize him?"

Bly: "He's the leader, Misskelley is." Clearly, Misskelley was not the leader.

Allen: "Okay, um."

Bly: "All I know is Jason or Jes or Jessie, something like that."

Bly named locations for cult activities, such as an old red barn behind Lakeshore, a huge, empty house out on Highway 50 North and a shed behind a house on Rich Road in West Memphis.

Bly claimed he had had a ski boat and had taken Misskelley down to Hernando Point in Mississippi the previous summer (though he was uncertain about Misskelley's first name).

Bly: "I don't know how we brought it up but I used to not believe in the Bible or the Lord, and he ask me if I was atheist and I told him yes and that's how I come about getting in it, he told me that devil would give me more than God ever would."

Allen asked about illegal activities within the group.

Bly: "Killing the dogs was illegal to start with because we would steal the dogs from people and um, that rape where they rape that girl out there I know that was illegal."

He said the rape of a girl who was a member of the cult occurred at Stonehenge. Ricky Climer had mentioned a rape as part of a hanging ritual.

Bly: "Well, Misskelley came up with the idea of it and then Baldwin went along with it. Baldwin was the first one that rape her, which she kinda went along with, but when the other guy started doing it, she had a fit about it, said she would tell."

He named a 16-year-old who lived in Lakeshore as the victim. She apparently was never interviewed.

Stonehenge, he said, was "the only place we sacrifice dogs at."

"How we do the dogs, we beat them to death first ... with sticks ... and they were alive when they we hung them up. We would beat them to death over the top of the pentagram. ...

"The pentagram would be drawn on the floor right under where we hung the dog up ... We would hang the dog up above that and then we would cut his throat his thing, and we would catch the blood in a pail. ... And then we drink a cup full apiece of the blood and then we would cut its head off, then we would cut him open and cut his heart out. ... We would put the heart in the middle of this and pour alcohol on it and mixed with baby oil ...

"We had a pie pan that we would set in the center of this, which is the same thing I'm talking you know we got the blood in it and then we would put the baby oil on the heart and you know burn it, it wouldn't burn it up but it would burn it, and then we would praise to the dev ... devil and stuff."

The dogs were tied up by the hind legs. "Everybody had to hit the dogs, everybody ... if you didn't hit him you had to leave."

Bly said he would have expected the boys to have been beaten to death with sticks. "They would have raped them, usually. Like I say, I won't know why they didn't cut their heads off cause you suppose to, if you've done that you're suppose to cut their heads off, we cut all the dogs' heads off. ... We would hand the head up and do away, throw the body down it, it big ditch there by Stonehenge." This was a rare mention of disposing bodies in a ditch.

Allen asked, "Any other body parts that they might cut off?"

Bly: "Their penis ... bite it off ... that's what it reads in the book to do ... devil circumcision."

Allen: "What did they, did they do this dog?"

Bly: "No sir ... wasn't nobody, wasn't nobody had the courage to do it to the dogs. ... We would cut, we would cut their penis off ... But they wouldn't bite off like you were suppose to."

Bly: "Misskelley always had the knife he carried on his side all the time, it's a hunter's knife. ... It uh, had a leather handle wrapped leather handle ... It had a can opener ... It come out and it was swivel down the top ... like a little saw deal." The blade had "ripples in it ... it called a gut knife." Bly said the knife was about 11 inches, total length. "It's called a bleeder, what it is, gut knife."

Bly couldn't remember what was said in the ceremony. "We read it out of book that we got from ... from the library here." He described the book as "the devil something," "black, shiny black," "about a 100 page book," "it's got like a dragon, like a dragon with like a goat's body" on the cover.

"It was St. Lucifer second son ... it was Satan on the front that's who it was."

Allen asked about Echols' role.

Bly: "Well we took turns, sometimes he would cut the heart out, sometimes I would, or Misskelley, or any of the other people, we all, we spread it out different times every who didn't do it the last time would have to do it that time."

Bly said that when he left the cult, they were discussing the sacrifice of children. "They were trying to pick out, you know wanting to know who we could pick out to do it to ... I was already leaving the cult anyway because they raped that girl. ... This was about a month before the boys got killed. ... They were planning on sacrificing them up here on 50 at that house and leave them there."

Another Bly, Charlotte Ann Bly Bolois of Parkin, met with Detective Ridge at the First Baptist Church in Parkin on Oct. 13 partially to describe to him the site of a Satanic ritual in Crittenden County.

She said that someone named Chris, from either Lehi in Crittenden County or Paris, Tenn., and Greg Wilson, from "somewhere in Alabama," had set up the ritual site close to Shell Lake, about a mile and and a half out in the woods, south of Earle. Ridge, who had been to the site, said it was east of 149 Highway.

"There's a bunch of tarpaulin up there now and then was just a old green rag tent," said Bolois.

She said they were staying with Amy and Eddie Wilson, relatives of Misskelley confidant Buddy Lucas.

She said she went to the site with Chris and Greg in September of 1992.

Ridge asked, "OK, what was taking place when you go there?"

"They were doing a bunch of devil worshiping talking silly," said Bolois.

Bolois: "They was huffing gas and glue and everything else they could find. ... They got the glue out Eddie's shop back there."

Ridge: "OK, you got upset I understand?"

Bolois: "Yes."

Ridge: "OK, did anything else occur or was there anything told to you that's what they were doing devil worshiping?"

Bolois: "I seen Greg turn into something silly, I don't know what it was but it was some kind of animal." Her reference was unclear and Ridge did nothing to clarify; a reasonable assumption would be that Greg imitated an animal.

Ridge: "OK, now Greg has told you he has did something with an animal out there is that correct?"

Bolois: "He killed one of Amy's dogs. ... It's suppose to have been a sacrifice."

Bolois, who was cousin to Buddy Lucas and knew Damien from school, said about Echols: "He's a weird person, I know he uses drugs and he's a devil worshiper I know that much. … He ask me if I was a devil worshiper and I said no, he said well you're hanging around one, that's exactly what he said."

Bolois, who had lived at Lakeshore, never heard of any devil worshipping there.

Bolois said devil worshiping had continued at Shell Lake since her visit, and that Buddy Lucas had gone to the site with Chris and Greg Wilson on Halloween of 1992.

As Ridge observed, "Halloween should be a big night for devil worshiping." In the Mid-South that time of year is a welcome respite from oppressive summer heat, when lots of community festivals take place, school football games are well-attended and nighttime becomes pleasantly cool. Echols has named Halloween as his favorite holiday.

Like October, May in the Mid-South is a distinctive time of year, being a relatively warm but pleasant climate before the summer heat arrives in June; along with the end of the school year, there are many outdoor activities and festivals. May is not a month easily mistaken for another in West Memphis and Marion.

Both months were prime time for witch cults.

The disjointed and otherwise suspect accounts of Alvis Bly and Ricky Climer, despite obvious problems, offered further evidence that witch cults were alive and thriving in Crittenden County in 1992-1993.

"IT WAS LIKE IT NEVER EVEN HAPPENED"

The Hutchesons, Vicki and son Aaron, were key to solution of the case, offering tantalizing evidence that resulted in the confession of Jessie Misskelley and subsequent arrests of Damien Echols and Jason Baldwin.

Their stories, though, never quite panned out, as mother and son both put their imaginations to work on colorful yarns that increasingly posed problems for the prosecution.

Tall, red-haired Vicki had a sketchy past, including charges for writing hot checks. In May 1993, she recently had separated from her husband, having moved April 19 from the West Memphis neighborhood adjacent to Weaver Elementary to Highland Trailer Park. There the 30-year-old had befriended Jessie Misskelley Jr.

Aaron, a sturdily built, dark-haired 8-year-old, was in the same grade as the dead boys and in the Cub Scout troop run by Michael's father, Todd. Aaron had played regularly with Michael and Christopher.

Aaron's description of their friendship grew over the course of police interviews into an ever-changing narrative in which he became a witness to the killings —- and ultimately an unwilling participant. But at first he was regarded as truthful in his tales of seeing five men participate in group sex in the woods and cooking a cat near the boys' "club house," near where the killings occurred.

In a report on May 28, Ridge found Aaron's claim to have seen cult activities from the "club house" to be credible. Ridge, though, was unable to find any sign of the "club house" —- apparently a tree stand that no longer existed by the time Aaron led officers into the woods.

Meanwhile, his mother, drinking heavily and consuming a variety of prescribed and illegal drugs, resolved to "play detective" by getting to know Jessie's friend Damien. She had heard rumors that Echols was responsible for the murders. She claimed she learned that he was involved with a group known as the Dragons, who supposedly worshipped dragons and whose meetings included a ritual in which they sacrificed genitals.

Victoria Hutcheson first heard about the murders while at the Marion Police Department on May 6, as news of the discovery of the bodies spread. She had taken a lie detector test about a $200 credit overcharge at the truck stop where she worked. She was checking on the results; she passed the polygraph and was cleared of potential charges but was fired nonetheless.

She brought Aaron with her to the station, after checking him out of school when she learned the boys were missing.

The boys were not known to be dead when the Hutchesons arrived at Marion PD.

When Assistant Chief of Police Donald Bray learned Aaron had been friends with Michael and Christopher, he called the WMPD to inform them that Aaron might be a source of information. Then he was told the bodies had been discovered.

Bray immediately began questioning Aaron and his mother.

Vicki said Chris and Michael had asked Aaron to come play with them Wednesday right after school but she had refused permission.

Aaron said he had been with his friends several times at Robin Hood Hills and that Michael had gone swimming in the ditch. His initial account contained none of the over-the-top details that marked later statements.

Bray was well-acquainted with Jerry Driver and Steve Jones, two juvenile officers who had extensive dealings with Echols and friends. Bray readily concurred with them about possible occult aspects to the killings and with their suspicions about Echols and Baldwin. Bray was quickly convinced that Aaron could be the source of vital clues. He pursued information from Aaron long past the point of credibility.

Aaron's first statement to West Memphis police on May 10 was full of vivid description that had little relation to reality — he said a black man with yellow teeth driving a maroon car had stopped to tell Michael that Michael's mother had sent him to pick up Michael and that Michael rode off with him. The Moore back yard literally backed up to the main entrance at Weaver Elementary; no one picked Michael up or would have had reason to pick him up; he walked home that day, as always.

On May 27, Aaron told another fantastic tale, though just credible enough to excite investigators. A snippet of that interview, with his childish voice eerily saying "Nobody knows what happened but me," was played back to Misskelley on June 3, one of several effective interrogation techniques used to elicit Misskelley's confession.

Aaron said he, Michael and Chris had a club house in Robin Hood and that "sometimes we watched these men. ... They were uh, doing nasty stuff. ... They, they do what men and woman do," going on to say that the five men gave each other oral sex while the boys watched from a hiding place.

He said all but one of the men wore black T-shirts, with one wearing a white T-shirt and having long hair. They all carried "big knives." He described them smoking rolled-up cigarettes that "stunk" and said they painted their faces black. "There was a skull commander he had on a necklace and there is a snake in its eye. ...'" The necklace was a pendant similar to a pendant or earring that Echols lost at the Hutcheson home. Aaron had become fascinated by the jewelry after discovering the earring.

Aaron said the men used a briefcase, a detail that agreed with later stories from Jessie Misskelley Jr. about the cult meetings. Aaron said the men had been "mean" to a dog but "they caught cat they cut his head off and ate it. ... They ate the whole cat but his head" after cooking him. Misskelley and others told about killing and eating pets.

Aaron thought the boys went to watch the men on Wednesday ... "They got caught, and then they never told the men, and the men sorta killed them."

On June 2, shortly before the arrest of his friend Jessie, Aaron elaborated with details about the men, saying they would dance around a fire and say "bad stuff" about "Jesus and God. I mean the Devil and God. ... That they said they like the Devil and they hate God." Aaron told Ridge and Allen: "They wore all white and they painted themselves black. ... They all talk in Spanish."

Aaron also had a strange story about Misskelley: "Little Jessie said that um, he seen Michael. .... He seen a police car. He was coming out from the um and he seen the police car and like he ran under ... back underneath the bridge. ... He didn't see Chris or Steve. ... Little Jessie said he seen a um he seen a cop ... cop car coming out from underneath the bridge close to my house ... It was close to my, I think there were coming to my house, and they ... they got lost to where I lived."

Ridge asked: "... You think Stevie and Michael were coming to your house?"

Aaron: "Because I think they all was, I told Michael before."

Ridge: "Where you lived, so you thought maybe they were going to ride over to your house? And Little Jessie said he thought he saw them that day. Is that right?"

Aaron: "He did see Michael."

Ridge repeated: "He did see Michael."

Aaron: "Michael has brown hair and he had on our Cub Scout T-shirt and his blue pants."

Ridge: "Oh, where did he see him at?"

Aaron: "He seen him — you know that bridge where that train going today um, he seen him underneath that one. … That's close to my house." If Misskelley actually told Aaron the details about the clothes, that would be highly incriminating, but Aaron's statements had little credibility; as for second-hand statements from Misskelley, even less so.

In his initial statements, Misskelley said he had seen a boy on a bicycle near Seventh Street — one of the routes between Highland and Robin Hood — who hid when he saw a police car. Apparently Misskelley also told Aaron this story —- to no clear purpose.

Ridge asked Aaron about Misskelley's friends, and Aaron mentioned Bubba (Ashley) and Dennis (Carter). Asked about someone named Damien, he said "Bubba's friend, Bubba's friend. … I never knew him, but Jessie … Jessie um, shown me him and I didn't get real close to him."

Ridge asked questions trying to connect possible suspects with the men in the woods, but Aaron had never seen any of them elsewhere, except once at a Flash Market convenience store. The one who wore a white tank top was paying for gas for "a nice car ... it was a convertible."

Asked if the men had seen the boys, Aaron replied, "Uh, I think so because that one man with the white tank top said 'Hi fellows, it was ... he said wasn't you guys watching us?' ... We got ... We got ... We got kind scared, we ran right out. ... he just said come back, and we didn't say a word because we knew we wasn't suppose to talk to strangers?"

Ridge pushed Aaron to be specific about the "nasty things" the men did. Aaron explained they would put a penis "in somebody's bottom."

After the June 3 arrests, Aaron gave statements on June 4, 7, 8 and 9 describing how he rode over to Robin Hood after going home with his mother to Highland on May 5. He began claiming he witnessed Damien, Jason and Jessie kill his three friends.

The June 4 statement to Don Bray had such unlikely details as Michael and Chris finding guns during the assault: "... They said on a count of three, we are gonna jump out and Michael said, one, two, and he jumped out, he pointed the gun at them ... he pulled the trigger and nothing came out cause it wasn't loaded."

He described Misskelley pursuing Stevie: "He chased him down, he caught him and ... he put his face in the water for about five seconds and pulled it out, and he said I don't want to kill you, yet, until what my boss says. … He went to his boss and he said that, you need to kill him, cause we already killed the other two." The "boss" was Damien.

He alleged Damien raped Michael and that Michael had died and turned blue after being cut in the neck. He claimed Chris also was cut in the neck and "they cut their private parts off" all the boys.

He claimed Baldwin had walked around the Hutcheson home, tapping on the window, while carrying a "policeman's gun."

The parts of the June 4 statement that could be checked out — such as injuries to the boys — bore little relation to reality, but police continued to set up interviews with the boy.

Aaron repeated much of the statement on June 7, including the description of the boys using guns and of Damien being "the boss." After being asked about contradictory statements concerning the roles of Jason and Jessie, he claimed that Jason asked to be called Jessie.

Aaron said on June 8: "Jessie told me that something was gonna happen. … Something was going to happen to Michael, Chris and Steve … He uh, he just said uh, you go and get your friends and I'll go and get my friends, we will do down to Robin Hood and do something. …

"I seen them Wednesday … I told them to let's go to Robin Hood, and then ask my mommy if I could go.

… Steve and Chris came up to my mommy's window and asked if I could go to Robin Hood. … They asked if I could go over to his house for two hours and stay. … She said, no. … Then I went there after I got finished doing … on my bike. … I went the Service Road, then I got to Luv's and turned ... I went to Blue Beacon." Then, Aaron told Bray, he went into the woods where he saw Michael and Chris hiding from "them men" behind a tree. The five included "Jessie Jason and Damien. I didn't know the other two."

Aaron said Michael told him that Stevie, who wasn't there, had gone with "the fifth man," Misskelley. "Steve got away, he got caught back and got killed. … Steve seen Jessie and started running. … Then he got away, and ... he got away again and got caught. … He uh ran and Jessie uh, was chasing him and he hit his face on the pipe. … the pipe that you walk across. It wasn't bleeding, he just uh, started crying and stuff. … It was just a little bruise."

He said Michael and Chris jumped out of the tree to help Stevie. "Then they got caught, and got killed."

Aaron said Jessie killed Stevie but then described Stevie running into Damien and being stabbed in the stomach —- not an area where Stevie was actually stabbed. Then, he said, Stevie was cut in the neck. Stevie was stripped and thrown into the water, and "they turned blue and died … all three of them." Later, he claimed Jessie raped Stevie.

At this point Aaron's story, with some credible —- or at least possible — aspects but wrong on the wounds and other details, veered again into sheer fantasy. "And then they caught me and got tied up and about 40 seconds I got untied and left and then I didn't remember nothing else about it."

Aaron then said Michael died first with a stab wound to the neck and another wound from Jessie.

Aaron said he saw all this from up in a tree: "I was trying to climb down, but I fell down and hit my, I hit my back ... I could hardly walk or get up ... I got up and I kicked. I kicked the knife and he, he tied me up and just left me there. ... They said that they might kill me."

He said Chris was killed after Steve, after being raped by Damien. The story grew increasingly confused with various claims about who died first, with a story of Michael falling down after trying to get up after being stabbed and then hitting his face on a rock and wrapping up with the claim that Michael was cut on his private parts.

The supposed plan for a meet-up in the woods to "do something" resonated with Misskelley's description of the teens' plans to go into West Memphis that day. But, coupled with a incoherent, error-filled fantasy, and coming after the arrest of Misskelley, Aaron's story only served to frustrate investigators.

Vicki originally said Aaron was with her as she ran errands on the afternoon of May 5.

By June 2, she was telling a different story to Bray. After initially refusing to let Aaron go over to Michael's house, "she thinks (4:00 p.m.) he rode his bike to his uncle Johnny Dedman's house, three streets over. He is supposed to check in with her every two hours. She has not asked Johnny if Aaron was there, on that day. She has not asked Aaron either. She doesn't remember if Aaron was back home by 6:00 p.m." With that lack of detail about her small son's whereabouts, it suddenly was possible, if unlikely, that Aaron had been at Robin Hood Hills on May 5.

Johnny Dedman also figured into Jessie Misskelley's alibi for May 5, with Misskelley and Aaron Hutcheson supposedly both being over at the Dedman home at roughly the same time. Despite being a potentially important witness both on the Aaron Hutcheson narrative and the Misskelley alibi, there is no available police interview with Dedman, though he did show up on the list of potential witnesses for the defense.

In his June 9 interview with Bray and Gitchell, in the presence of his mother, Aaron repeated the story about Misskelley arranging the meeting. Aaron told them: "Jessie told me that um, something was going to happen to my friends." Aaron said he was told this on Tuesday, with a meet-up between the groups set for Wednesday.

The story was similar to the previous day's tale, with added details such as Jessie was the one who caught him and tied him up again.

Gitchell pressed Aaron to tell the truth, with Aaron claiming that Jessie "abused" him.

Police interviewed Aaron again on Dec. 31, 1993, with John Fogleman, Bray and James Thompson, Vicki's boyfriend, at the East Arkansas Mental Health offices. Taping behind a two-way mirror were Ridge and Gitchell. Vicki Hutcheson was elsewhere in the building, with Judy Hicks, the Hutchesons' therapist.

Aaron told them that, before the killings, Jessie told him that he wanted to meet some of his friends. He said he had seen Jessie, Damien and Jason at Robin Hood when he had lived in the neighborhood. He saw them do "what men and women do." Looking down, avoiding eye contact, Aaron told his story in a quiet, hesitant voice, often difficult to hear.

Eventually he began crying. He said he did not want to talk about his story and had nightmares. "It makes me scared."

Pressed for details, he stopped talking and sat picking at his hands and then playing with a watch to keep his hands busy.

He admitted his fear of Misskelley: "They'll kill my mom if I talk."

He claimed he had been abused by Misskelley: "he put his private in my bottom." Aaron said he was afraid he would be taken from his mom because he had been abused by Jessie.

Aaron said Misskelley wanted him to "do something bad" to get into Misskelley's "club," and Michael and Chris were invited to join. Aaron did not know Stevie would show up.

Aaron again told of riding his bicycle from Highland Park to Robin Hood, traversing the routes of the interstate and service roads. Such a trip, particularly a route of about 3 miles over the 7th Street overpass, would be feasible though not bicycle-friendly.

He claimed he saw the attack from a hiding place, though Misskelley was aware of his presence. "He asked me if I wanted to kill them and I said no." When the attack was over, "he said don't tell anybody. Don't tell anybody or I'll kill your mom."

"It was almost dark" he returned home.

The next day, Aaron went over to Misskelley's home and "he only looked at me like I did something bad."

His description of Misskelley holding down Michael, Damien holding down Stevie and Jason holding down Chris was in accord with Misskelley's confessions generally. Aaron offered a number of contradictory statements about his own role.

Aaron heard Damien say "We tricked you" as the attacks started. Aaron claimed there were two others present, a male in a hat with a dragon T-shirt and another male. He could offer little description beyond that, though he consistently described five attackers.

He said the killers carried a duffel bag with equipment for the kill. They used canes in the beatings. Asked in which hand the teens held their canes, Aaron told Bray, "I get mixed up with right and left."

The Dec. 31 interview was in two parts, both roughly an hour. Aaron benefited from a break, returning in a confident and relaxed mood. Thompson was out of the room for the wrap-up session.

At times, Aaron seemed strangely lighthearted, smiling as he talked about being abused by Jessie or about his friends being killed, in contrast to the earlier session.

At one point, he stood up and playfully pulled a knife from his pocket that Thompson had given him. That prompted Aaron describing Jessie having a knife. Aaron played with the knife as the interview progressed, opening and closing the blade. Bray eventually took the knife from the boy.

As the conversation turned toward knives, Aaron identified Damien as having the knife found in the lake behind Baldwin's trailer.

Toward the end, Aaron got bored and restless. "I told everything two or three times. Can we leave?"

Aaron said he was not scared of anyone "unless they're witches. I hate witches" and oddly expressed concern about Damien's son Seth, an infant, being a witch.

Like many others, he said Damien possessed a cat's skull. He said "they ate the cat" after cooking it on a grill top. Then he drew a picture of the cat saying "help me."

While Aaron's story on Dec. 31 was less fantastic and more consistent than his earlier fantasies, the small, emotionally fragile boy clearly was not a reliable witness.

Bray conducted yet another interview with Aaron at the Marion Police Department on Jan. 30, 1994, prompted by Aaron volunteering details on "some other stuff that happened."

Aaron told an implausible story about how Misskelley forced him to participate in the castration of Christopher and then drink a glassful of blood. Among unlikely details, he told how a "a white guy and a black guy" arrived on the scene, with the "black guy" threatening Aaron with a gun "and he made me say I hate Jesus and I love the devil." Bray pressed for details until the boy lapsed into long silences.

Aaron did not testify at trial. In 2004, he told the Arkansas Times he was no longer sure if he saw the murders or if, shocked by the deaths, he imagined he had seen the murders. At that time, he was convinced the boys had been killed by Mark Byers.

In the same story, Aaron said his statements had been complete fabrications. He said the police tricked him into saying things that were not true. The statements clearly did contain elements of truth — he did know the dead boys, for example. As with his mother, who eventually claimed her Echols stories were wildly exaggerated, a blanket disclaimer raised questions that likely will never be answered.

His mother did testify in the Misskelley trial, though not the Echols/Baldwin trial, giving a fairly straightforward description of how Echols, with Misskelley, took her to a witches' meeting. She testified she and Echols left but Misskelley stayed. Jurors did not hear salacious details about incipient orgies and other bizarre goings-on.

In a 2004 story in the Arkansas Times, she said about the trip to the esbat: "Every word of it was a lie." Lie or not, her testimony played no role in the Echols/Baldwin case and was not crucial to the conviction of Misskelley. Jurors there were largely convinced by the confession, particularly where Misskelley described chasing down Michael. Some jurors told reporters that the occult trappings were not particularly convincing and were ultimately irrelevant to reaching a guilty verdict.

Though she later claimed coercion, police interviews indicated Vicki was eager to play a starring role in the investigation, perhaps with hopes of collecting a reward.

As Bray described her role in his notes on a June 2, 1993, interview: "She said she was trying to play detective because she had heard Damien was involved in devil worship and she thought it might be connected to the murders."

In 2004, Hutcheson told the Arkansas Times that she only testified as instructed by the West Memphis PD, under a threat that she would have her child taken from her and that she could be implicated in the murders. There was no evidence of a police threat.

She testified in 1994 that "West Memphis knew nothing" about her plan to "play detective" when she set up meetings with Echols. "I decided that on my own. Those boys I loved, and I wanted their killers caught." As for the $30,000 reward, "it had nothing to do with it."

She did receive help from law enforcement in checking out occult books from the library, in an effort to impress Echols, and in setting up a recording device under her bed. Police said the resulting tapes were of such poor quality as to be of no use; she claimed to hear high-quality recordings.

She testified she never met John Fogleman until a month or two before the trial.

Her statements were filled with largely unsolicited and unschooled details about interactions with Misskelley and Echols.

Aaron considered Michael and Christopher his best friends, dating from when he lived on East Barton. According to his mother, "those were his only friends."

In a May 28, 1993, interview with Ridge and Sudbury, she described picking up Aaron after school on May 5: "I was waiting in where the teachers park on the side of Weaver Elementary, and watching for Aaron. It was approximately 15 after 3, and Michael Moore came to one side of my truck and Christopher Byers to the other and Aaron you know close to them … and they were telling me Ms. Vicki there's a Cub Scout thing tonight, and Aaron needs to go, and Michael's father is their troop leader and … Michael was really incessant upon Aaron going, and uh, they just keep saying there's a Cub Scout thing. Ms. Vicki … he has to go, he has to go. And I said no this is Wednesday night. Cub Scouts are tomorrow Thursday night and they just kept on. Finally you know, they got it through he wasn't going to go, because I just thought they wanted to go and play, and um, he said well then can Aaron just come to my house, and you can pick him up in two hours. Which I had done frequently so he had assumed I would do it then, and I just said no because I had some errand to ran. Aaron did not go. … I went home."

She went to the grocery about 5:30 and stopped somewhere to eat, with Aaron in tow. "He was never alone." They got home "probably about eight or so."

Among her errands, she would tell prosecutors, was going to the liquor store to purchase two bottles of Evan Williams whiskey for Jessie Misskelley Jr. and Dennis Carter, who were both underage.

His mother's story on May 28 contradicted any stories Aaron told about his trip to Robin Hood that afternoon. She gave a different version of Aaron's activities for May 5 on June 2, abruptly becoming unable to account for him that afternoon while he was nominally under the care of a babysitter. The June 2 version gave Aaron time to go to the woods.

On May 6, after discovering his friends were missing, she pulled Aaron out of school and took him over to the Moore house. She said, "Todd asked Aaron if he might know did Chris or Michael say anything to him, to the effect where they might be. He said no, there, you know you can tell when your child is lying and it was like he knew something was up. And uh, he said after we had left the Moores coming out of their door he told me Mama let's to go the club house. We need to go to the club house."

She had been to the site before, the "clubhouse" being boards nailed up in a tree. She was not able to get there because the entry at the dead end of McCauley was cordoned off by police.

The question persists as to whether there was a "clubhouse." Jessie Misskelley in one confession mentioned the "clubhouse" and then corrected himself, saying he had been thinking of a clubhouse near Highland. Aaron gave little description of the clubhouse, which he repeatedly mentioned. It may have been formed largely by imagination —- whether by the boys or just Aaron. Boys commonly stake out territory as "clubhouses," treehouses and "forts" in play. Old boards at the scene could have been part of the "clubhouse."

"Aaron told me that um he and Michael and Chris visit their club house every day and they rode their bikes and they were spying on 5 men and ah I asked him who they were and he said I don't know Mom who they were I just you know we just spying on em. I said why would you be spying on 5 men, you know? And he said well they were there every day so we would watch them. I said what made you interested in them. He said because they paint themselves and they have dragon shirts and they talk in Spanish. And I say, Aaron, they talk in Spanish how do you know that's Spanish? I mean, you don't know Spanish. He said well I don't understand what they're saying, and they sing bad things, and I said like what kind of bad things. My father being a preacher, Aaron has been in my church quite often, you know, and …

"He said they sing about the Devil, and, you know, that we love the Devil and um he said, I think that they love the Devil more than God, Mom. And I told him … why didn't y'all leave why didn't you come home, were you scared? They said no we hid. They couldn't see us. … I said so y'all went there every day. He said we went there every day but wouldn't go on Friday. And I told him why how do you know Friday? And he said, well because that's the day before the weekend, you know, the last day of school and I know that it was Friday and they didn't come. And ah, I said okay what happened? What did they do? And he said well when they first saw them you know they sat around a fire in a circle by this tree ... they did this like several times and then they'd sing a song and they'd ... dance around the tree. Then he told me that these 5 men took their clothes off. And I said Aaron you know that they took their clothes off, why didn't you leave? And he said because we were scared. And they were scared, I guess, of getting caught then and ah he said Michael kept telling him that it was an Indian thing they were supposed to do and Chris said no they're getting ready to have sex. And I told Aaron, Aaron doesn't know about sex and we talked about it and all the books that you've seen um he said that they had their peters in each other's butts and said they watched. ... And I just got into detail with him. With the sex thing. ...

"I know he's telling the truth."

Vicki added: "Jessie Misskelley had told Aaron that um the boys killer had been found. And ah Aaron was ecstatic over it. He was very happy....

"He later found that that wasn't true ...

"... What's really weird is that he said you know exactly that it was a Satanistic group, namely the Dragons."

She also related that she had heard third-hand that Robert Burks — actually Robert Burch — had told a teen girl that he had killed the boys and would kill the girl if she talked. Burch, whose name came up repeatedly in the investigation, talked to police and offered no alibi, but there was nothing but rumor and an acquaintance with Baldwin and Misskelley linking him to the case.

Vicki also named some of Damien's friends in the Satan worshippers: Shawn "Spider" Webb, "Burks," "Snake," "Jason, some little boy named Jason, I don't know his name he lives in Lakeshore," and Misskelley.

"There's a guy he calls Lucy but everyone else calls Lucifer. … He's an older guy he's, he's probably closer to my age, thirty. … I haven't really been real up close with him you know I've seen him in a car, um, he's got brownish hair and he does have a big nose. … I believe he had glasses on." She said Lucifer drove an old beaten-up car "like an Impala or Caprice. … It looked like ah primer color. You know like they were gonna paint it."

The mysterious "Lucifer" popped up again and again in descriptions of the cult in Lakeshore, with varying characteristics, though consistently described as older than the teens.

In her May 28 interview, Vicki described how, shortly after the killings, she sent Aaron out of town for eight days to stay with her sister, meanwhile talking to people about the case, including "a Little Jessie, Jessie Misskelley, lives down the street from me and you know that I was really close to him … because he was always around. He doesn't go to school or anything. He like help you mow the lawn and stuff and I'd gotten really close with him. He made mention after this came out that um he had saw Chris Byers over by the Beacon

that morning on the morning that you know they were found and that Chris was in a pink shirt and even picked him out in the paper to me ... that was odd for him to say something like that so ... I just keep talking with Jessie cause ah Jessie's I means not a bad kid but you know you don't know who people know. So I just kept talking to Jessie about stuff and Jessie told me about a friend of his named Damien and this friend drank blood and stuff. He just keep going on and on on about how weird he was and stuff. So by the way you know the stuff that we knew the public knew that was coming out in the paper and stuff I just thought how they were killed was odd but you know maybe it was like a devil worshipping thing or you know something just hit me that might be it and I thought that this kid doing this you know maybe he knew something or ....
or maybe Jessie knew something so um Jessie had told me that Damien hang out at Lakeshore and so I went out of my way, you know, to try to go around Lakeshore and, you know, people around there and I told Jessie I had seen Damien and he asked me how did I know it was Damien? And I said that there was a little boy Adam who's a friend of mine's little boy ... and he had ... pointed him out to me and ... he said well you know he's kinda weird. I said no, I think he's hot. I really want to go out with him. Can you fix me up with him? And you know he was real surprised but he said yeah, if you want to go out with him I'll fix you up with him and he did."

So Hutcheson thought that "maybe Jessie knew something" based on strange things he had said and the fact that Misskelley was fascinated with Echols' weird practices and beliefs, such as drinking blood.

Jessie fixed up Vicki and Damien. It didn't take much persuasion; Misskelley drove Hutcheson's pickup over to Baldwin's home, told Echols that he knew a women who wanted to meet him and Echols went along for the ride. Eventually Echols would show up at her trailer about six times, apparently never spending much time, according to Hutcheson. She told police that she was not attracted to Echols and found him frightening. She said they never had sex. Based on her retraction statements years later, Echols actually showed up just once for a very brief, awkward visit.

Hutcheson told Ridge: "He came to my house, the very first time I met him. … We talked about um lots of different stuff. He's not real real talkative. You you kinda have to pull things out of him but he uh keep telling me about the boys murders and how he had been he said… questioned. He always said that I was accused for 8 hours I was accused of killing those 3 little boys and … I just acted like it was no big deal. … And I said well you know why would they pick you in West Memphis you know? There are bookoo's of people. Why would they just pick you out? And he just looked at me I mean just really weird. And said because I'm evil. …

"He called me um he told me that he would like to see me again and stuff like this and ah I said okay. So you know he just kept coming over and he never really um gave me times or when I'm coming but he would just drop in. ...

"And uh in the meantime communicating with Officer Bray I had gotten some Satanic books and witch books and all this and we were sitting on my couch and I had laid them out where he could see them right close to my table. He said, you know he picked one up, and asked me what I was doing. I got out a Cosmopolitan, and in the back there was a wicka thing that you write to, and you can become a witch or go to witch school or something like that. Anyway I told him not to worry you know this is what I'm wanting to be and he just looked at me really weird and he said you don't have to go like that. You don't have to go there to do that. ...

"No. It would all come in time is what he said. It'll happen in time. ...

"The next day after he finds out that I'm wanting to go do this he told me and asked me did I want to go to esbat. I didn't know what esbat was. I looked it up in the book and found out that it was a meeting and I thought immediately yeah this is where I want to go. I want to see what's going on. ...

"Then he took me, he picked me up and he took me in a red Escort. He drove us to Turrell, and ah ...."

She said Misskelley went along for the ride to Turrell, a small poor community of about 800 residents

about 12 miles north of Marion. The Wapanocca
National Wildlife Refuge, centered around Lake
Wapanocca, is adjacent to the township. The esbat
location sometimes is referred to as Turrell-Twist or
Twist, the name of a small farm-based community at the
Crittenden-Cross county line.

Misskelley told officers on June 3 that Damien
drove a red car owned by Jack Echols. Among the many
criticisms t about the esbat story are a) Damien didn't
drive and b) Damien didn't have access to a red car. It
seems unlikely that Misskelley mentioned the red car
just to corroborate Hutcheson's story.

Hutcheson described the trip "... He um took us
to —- I'm not really familiar, I'm from Springdale, so
I'm not familiar with this area even — but Turrell. I was
really lost. ...

"... I do know where kinda where he went you
know we turned off and hit a dirt road and about by
some kind of water and in woods in a field and by the
time we had gotten there ... it was dark. Um, it was
quite a drive. ...

"And we went out, got out of the car and ... it
was just really dark especially out you know in the
woods. It was just dark and I was scared a little bit in
fact but we held hands just like you would hold my
hand and keep trying to comfort me. He knew I was
scared. ...

"… He told me it would be okay you know not to be scared, don't worried and ah Jessie went to the crowd. Then you could see there was a crowd of kids."

There were about 10, none over age 18, with faces painted black.

"… What you could see of their bodies without … their clothes you know was painted their … arms were painted, you know, they had on jeans …."

"They stood around and it seemed like they were just talking and stuff and Damien and I stood back away from them. We never went to the crowd."

A teen she knew, Shawn Webb, stepped away to talk with them.

"… When he got close enough to me I could tell who he was. He talked with Damien um you know just what's up you know just bull crap and then walked back over and then these kids took their clothes off and began touching each other and I knew what was going to happen …."

"I looked at Damien and said I want to leave … He said okay. … Jessie stayed. …

"After he brought me home we went into my house and you know just sat there and talked and stuff and he never made comment about it or anything. It was like it never even happened. … He went, he left, and went home."

She said this occurred on Wednesday, May 19.

"… He called me on Thursday and he told me about this girl being pregnant … and you know he's

going to have to take care of her or make her think he's
that you know he's faithful to her. ... And so ah the
word has gotten out that I was seeing him because I'm a
you know an older woman and ... everything so he said
we're going to have to kinda cool it and keep it down ...
and so I kinda thought well God I've ruined it, you
know, she's ruined it for me and I'm not going to be
able to see him anymore. I thought he'd just quit calling.
...

"But he called all the time wanting me know you
know what men are at my house. ... And I do have a
boyfriend that I see all the time and ah so he you know
is there quite often.

"... My house was really quiet ... this last
Wednesday. Nobody came over or anything. Jim came
over after he got off work and it was about 1:30 when he
got off and we just sat and talked on the couch and
watched a movie. It was about 3:30 and we heard this
big when I mean it sounded really horrible, it scared me
to death. And ah so Jim got up, he and I both got up and
went to my door and we looked out front underneath
um my window where I keep plants. I have like a really
thick board that's been nailed up and has some bolts
underneath it and this thing was broke completely in
half. ... No one was around. ... I asked Damien. He
called me last night. I asked him um what did you do
Wednesday night, hung out. I said you didn't come to
my house did you? He said I know you were there with

Jim, that's all that matters and that's it. That was the end of it."

Ridge asked, "Did he say he was jealous of that?"

Vicki replied, "Are you kidding, I mean you could tell that he's mad. ... He was very calm but aggravated is what I would call it."

In a June 2 interview, Hutcheson repeated much of her story to Bray and said someone the night before had been looking into her windows.

She left 15-year-old roommate Christy Anderson babysitting Aaron while she went to Kroger. When she returned around 11 p.m., a 15-year-old friend visiting the trailer said she had seen someone looking into the living room window. Aaron reported someone had been looking into his bedroom window and had pulled on a wire leading into the bedroom hard enough to pull a console from under the bed.

Apparently no one called the police, and no suspect was found. The incident was similar to incidents in which Echols was seen stalking children and young girls.

The night before he was arrested, Misskelley spent the night at the Hutcheson trailer, reportedly sleeping on the couch, because she was concerned about a prowler.

Echols stopped talking to Vicki after May 28, when the FBI supposedly came out and took photos of his trailer. She had planned a party for Saturday, May 29, inviting Echols, Misskelley and Robert Burch. When nobody showed up, she phoned Echols around 8 or 9 p.m. He told her he had something important to do. When she asked if she could come along, he said no.

She tried to talk him again on June 1 around 7:30 p..m. Echols' sister Michelle told her Damien had gone to bed. Bray noted: "Vicki says she is scared now."

Hutcheson took a polygraph test June 2. No deception was indicated when she said that she had not met Echols prior to three weeks before, that she had not told Aaron what to tell police, that she had no foreknowledge of the murders and that no one told her they were involved in the killings.

A decade after the trial, on June 24, 2004, Hutcheson gave a sworn statement to the Misskelley defense team in which she claimed that Don Bray and Jerry Driver persuaded her that Echols was guilty.

She described her initial meeting with Echols as a fiasco, describing him as a normal teen.

Vicki claimed that the tapes of their conversation were of good quality but worked against the case the police were hoping to build.

She claimed Ridge suggested that, if she could not deliver evidence against Echols, she could be seen as the vital link between the killers and their victims, that she could be implicated in the homicide. "And they also told me it would be a shame if I lost Aaron over this whole thing."

She claimed Ridge schooled her over 12-and-a-half hours on a made-up story about the esbat trip.

"And then I just started making up stuff as I went because I didn't know what else to do and I did."

After their first meeting, she claimed she talked to Echols just once, when she called him and he said he was under FBI surveillance.

On the day of her court appearance, "I was kind of high. I couldn't even stand up. I even had somebody go get me some more pills."

She had taken four Prozac, at least 13 Valium and four pain pills prior to testifying.

She had been taking Prozac, Valium and a sleeping medication, Trazodene, during May, all from the East Arkansas Mental Health Center, as well as pain pills from Melissa Byers, Christopher's mother, and downers from another friend. She was seeing a therapist and a psychiatrist. She said she was bipolar, had been diagnosed with paranoid schizophrenia and had post-traumatic stress syndrome.

At the time of the trial, her part-time job as a bartender at the Ramada Inn allowed her to drink "as much as I wanted. I should say that when I left I felt pretty good every night."

In 1994, after the trials were over, she told defense investigators that she drank a bottle of Wild Turkey whiskey prior to the trip to the esbat and could not recall the circumstances or who accompanied her, only that she awoke the next morning lying on her front lawn. The drinking bout was spurred by a disagreement with her boyfriend.

She claimed Misskelley stayed overnight at her home, armed with a gun, because Mark Byers "was always bothering us."

Hutcheson said she became a methamphetamine addict while working at a strip club prior to going to prison around 1995. In 2004, she said she had recently gotten off meth.

The timeline on harassment by Byers in May 1993 seemed to make little sense as her role in the case wasn't public knowledge then. In 2004, she said "We kept it quiet until Ron Lax's big mouth and he opened up that whole can of worms you know. And everybody found out they had talked to Aaron and then they found out about me and all that deal."

She said Byers wanted to talk with Aaron "by himself with him to McDonald's." She refused. She complained Byers started buying Aaron gifts and brought a Christmas tree to their house. She would see "someone," "a really tall, big person" hanging around her back porch. "And I just knew it was Mark. I just had a feeling it was Mark." At the time she was telling the story, she and her son were on board with Byers being an "alternative suspect."

She said Misskelley was familiar with Michael through Michael's friendship with Aaron.

Vicki appeared for a Baldwin Rule 37 hearing on Aug. 14, 2009, and answered a few questions. Then the court, the prosecutors and her attorneys conferred on whether contradicting her testimony from 1994 would be perjury, finally determining that she could be open to prosecution. There was no offer of immunity. She did not testify.

While the Hutchesons provided a crucial link to the solution of the case through their friendship with Misskelley, Vicki's "investigation" yielded little of worth — Echols was an acknowledged witch so she would have provided "proof" only of what was already known if she had testified. He made no self-incriminating statements to her.

As for Aaron, childish fantasies aside, he provided a seemingly plausible link between the killers and their victims. Whether there was a pre-arranged meeting between the killers and their victims remains an open question.

"THEY WERE GOING TO GO OUT AND GET SOME BOYS AND HURT THEM."

The initial confessions on June 3, 1993, were the basis of the charges against Jessie Misskelley Jr., Jason Baldwin and Damien Echols.

The "Paradise Lost" films and many subsequent references to that confession frame it as the result of a 12-hour interrogation, with the implication that police browbeat the none-too-bright Misskelley into a false confession.

The times are on record. The facts vary greatly from the "Paradise Lost" timeframe.

At an 8 a.m. squad meeting that morning, West Memphis Police Department officers "discussed attempting to pick up Jessie Misskelley Jr. in reference to his being a member of cult that Damien Echols and Jason Baldwin are said to be members of. Check possibility of his being a witness to homicide or any statement he may have overheard from Damien or anyone concerning the homicide."

Mike Allen went to the Misskelley home and was told Jessie Jr. was not there but his father was at his job at Jim's Diesel Service. Allen talked to Jessie Sr. at 9:45.

Jessie Jr. was picked up at the home of Vicki Hutcheson. Allen and Jessie Jr. drove to the police station.

A subject description was filled out at 10 a.m., listing the 17-year-old's height as only 5-1, with his weight at 125. He had an "FTW" (Fuck The World) tattoo on his right arm, tattoos of a skull with a dagger, the initials of a former girlfriend (A.H.) and "N.W.A." on his left arm and a "Bitch" tattoo on his chest.

Allen interviewed Misskelley. Ridge observed. Allen and Ridge took separate notes.

According to those notes, Misskelley said Echols was "sick" and drinks blood, that Echols was always in the company of Baldwin and that Echols had a girlfriend, Domini, skinny, pregnant and red-haired. Misskelley said he had known Echols for about a year.

According to Allen's notes, Misskelley said he last saw Echols about three weeks before at Highland Trailer Park at the home of Vicki (Vicki Hutcheson). "I told her he's sick." Misskelley said he had never been in Robin Hood Hills.

Ridge's notes indicated Misskelley said he had not seen Damien in over two months and did not know anything about the murders. Misskelley denied any involvement in Satanism. He acknowledged introducing Hutcheson to Echols three weeks before (after saying he had not seen him in two months).

According to both sets of notes, Misskelley had heard rumors that Damien and Robert Burch had committed the crimes.

Misskelley said he was working with Ricky Deese along with Josh Darby on roofing the week of the murders; on May 5, he got off at 5 p.m. and went home and stayed home. There was no mention of wrestling, socializing or a police call.

Misskelley said he went to the skating rink a lot and saw Echols there nearly every time he went. He had seen Echols with Carl Smith and Baldwin.

Misskelley saw Baldwin get into a fight and get his nose busted at Lakeshore, and saw Echols stick his finger into the blood and lick it.

He agreed to take a polygraph.

Allen read Jessie Jr. his rights around 11 a.m. Misskelley signed the form. The police determined that Misskelley Sr. needed to sign a consent form.

Little Jessie had been read his Miranda rights and signed similar papers on at least four previous occasions: in 1988, twice in late October 1992, and again that March. He had been put on probation for stealing flags from school in 1988, part of a harebrained plan to build his own raceway. Thirteen-year-old Tiffany Allen filed a police report on March 12, 1993, accusing Misskelley of punching her in the mouth.

At 11:15 on June 3, Allen was driving with Jessie Jr. riding in the front seat when they spotted Jessie Sr. driving a tow truck on Missouri Street. The three met at the corner of Shoppingway at Chief's Auto Parts. Big Jessie, who had been to prison and was familiar with the legal system, signed a waiver allowing Jessie Jr. to undergo a polygraph exam.

Jessie Jr. was advised again of his rights by Bill Durham at around 11:30 a.m. in preparation for the exam. Jessie Jr. initialed and signed the form.

Three charts were completed, at 11:55 a.m., 12:03 and 12:11 p.m., with about 15 minutes spent on an interview after the tests.

After analysis, Durham announced around 12:30 p.m.: "He's lying his ass off."

Durham indicated Misskelley gave deceptive answers of "No" to these questions:

3. Have you ever been in Robin Hood Hills?

5. Have you ever took part in devil worship?

7. Have you ever attended a devil worship ceremony in the Turrell/Twist area?

9. Are you involved in the murder of those three boys?

10. Do you know who killed those three boys?

Misskelley broke down after being told he failed the test, and immediately began to confess, as officers took notes. From 12:40 to 2:20, Ridge and Gitchell continued interrogating Misskelley, who admitted he saw Echols and Baldwin kill the three boys.

Misskelley said he had received a call from Baldwin, with Damien on the line in the background, the night before the murders.

"They were going to go out and get some boys and hurt them." Baldwin and Echols wanted him to go with them; Misskelley heard Damien tell Jason that he ought to tell Misskelley that they were going to get girls or something but Jessie knew what was planned.

Misskelley had gotten three calls about the killings, one the day before, one the morning of the murders, one "after dark." In the last conversation, Baldwin was on the line but Misskelley could hear Echols in the background saying, "We did it. We did it. What are we going to do now? What if somebody saw us?"

He said it sounded as if Baldwin was at home on that call, since he heard Baldwin's brother in the background. Misskelley couldn't give more exact times on the calls.

Misskelley said he saw photos of the victims during a cult meeting. Misskelley was shown a photo of Christopher Byers. After he "looked hard" at the photo, Misskelley said it was the "Moore boy" and said the boy was in the Polaroid shown at cult meetings.

He said that a 15-year-old friend of Jason's named Ken, who wears a long coat, would bring a briefcase to the meetings, always held on Wednesdays. The briefcase contained guns, marijuana, cocaine and a picture of the three victims in front of a house. He did not know who had the briefcase, which was never found.

Misskelley said Echols had been in the woods watching the boys prior to the attacks. He said Echols had been watching the boys for a long time, that he was hanging out at the skating rink to find boys. He told officers that Echols and Baldwin had sex with each other. Baldwin had a folding knife and always carried a knife, while Echols did not.

Misskelley said he "didn't want to be a part of this," that Echols and Baldwin were killers while he was not.

Misskelley described meetings of a "Satanic cult" held in different places, including Robin Hood, at which they would build fires of paper, wood "and stuff." Misskelley said, "Someone brings a dog and they usually kill the dogs. They will skin the dog and eat part of it." The animal killing was part of the ritual; if a person ate the meat, he became part of the group. Misskelley named some attendees: Christina Jones, Dennis Carter, Jason, Damien, Adam, Ken, Tiffany Allen and Domini (he didn't know most of the last names). Jones and Carter were friends with Misskelley. Those subsequently interviewed by police denied any involvement in the occult.

Generally eight or nine people would attended, and had an orgy afterward (three on one, he said).

Ridge: "Jessie told of one occasion he had gone to the scene of the murders and sat down on the ground and cried about what had happened to the boys. He had tears in his eyes at this time telling about the incident. I felt this was a remorseful response about the occurrence and that he had more information than what he had revealed at this point."

Those close to Jessie had seen signs of guilt and remorse.

Misskelley's friend, Buddy Lucas, later told officers that on May 6, at about 9 a.m., a tearful Misskelley had confessed his involvement in the crimes from the night before.

Lee Rush, Jessie Sr.'s girlfriend, lived in the family trailer. After Jessie Jr.'s arrest, three police officers visited the Misskelley home and secured the scene until a search team could arrive.

Det. Charlie Dabbs wrote: "While sitting in their living room for approximately two hours, and during conversation Mr. and Mrs. Misskelley talked about different incidents. During the conversation, Mrs. Misskelley got to talking about how Jessie Jr. was waking her up at night crying and having nightmares. Every time she went into his room he would be crying hysterically and he would tell her it was because his girlfriend was moving away. She told us it happened a number of times, and that she could not believe his girlfriends' moving would cause that kind of hysterical behavior, but that little Jessie had been acting strange."

Det. Tony Anderson wrote: "During the course of this conversation Mrs. Misskelley made the statement, 'I knew that something was wrong, a few nights ago little Jessie was in his room and crying so loud and sobbing so hard that it woke me up, I went in and asked him what was wrong?, his reply was that his girl friend was moving to Florida.'

"Another short period of time passed and Mrs. Misskelley made the same identical remarks again about little Jessie crying and waking her up!"

Deputy Howard Tankersly wrote: "We sat there for 2 or 3 hours making casual conversation with each other and the Misskelleys. At one point Misskelley's wife stated that one night Little Jessie awoke her he was crying and screaming. He asked him the next date what was wrong and he stated that his girlfriend had him upset, as she was suppose to be moving to Florida."

Between 12:40 and 2:20 p.m., police broke down what little resistance Jessie Jr. had with a series of adept moves, such as showing him a picture of a victim.

Misskelley was already talking freely when Gitchell played a tape-recording of an eerie voice saying: "Nobody knows what happened but me."

The voice was Aaron Hutcheson. Misskelley told Gitchell and Ridge: "I want out of this! I want to tell you everything!"

He did just that.

Misskelley explained through tears what happened. Ridge, also brought to tears, said in his notes: "Jessie seemed to be very sorry for what had happened and told that he had been there when the boys were first coming into the woods and were called by Damien to come over to where they were." Preparations began for taping the confession.

At 2:44 p.m., Misskelley was officially arrested for murder after being informed of his Miranda rights.

From 2:44 p.m. to 3:18 p.m., he confessed again in a tape-recorded session.

Because of discrepancies (Misskelley later said he deliberately misrepresented key facts), Gitchell conducted a followup tape-recorded interrogation sometime between 3:45 and 5:05 p.m. Work started on obtaining search and arrest warrants for Echols and Baldwin.

The total time between Misskelley first being brought to the police station and the conclusion of taping that day was 7 hours and five minutes, with 2 hours and 19 minutes between the time the tape recorder was turned on and the last of the recording. Interrogations with Misskelley as a suspect began at 12:40 and ended at 5:05, a span of four hours and 25 minutes with intervals of down time. Misskelley had brought in around 10, much of the time between 11 and 12 was spent securing permission from his father for a polygraph. He was telling all after a mere two hours and 40 minutes. Claims in the second "Paradise Lost" movie that the interrogation lasted 12 hours were highly misleading.

Misskelley was offered food at 3:22 p.m. but "he refused saying that he couldn't eat anything."

He was given two cigarettes.

He drank a Coke about the time of the followup interview.

He was asked again if he wanted to eat at 5:05 p.m. He refused, but "did go ahead + get something to eat."

He was given a hamburger and a coke at 6:15 p.m. and was asked if he needed to go to the restroom at 6:33 p.m.

At 9:06 p.m., Ridge, Gitchell and Fogleman appeared for a probable cause hearing before Judge "Pal" Rainey. Warrants were issued allowing immediate searches.

At 10:28 p.m., police cars descended upon Highland Trailer Park, Lakeshore Estates and Broadway Trailer Park.

Baldwin and Echols were arrested at the Echols trailer while watching a horror film, "Leprechaun." Echols' parents were at Splash Casino in Tunica County, Mississippi, about 50 miles away. Damien, Michelle, Domini and Jason were celebrating the last day of school, although Jason was the only teen attending school.

Well into the prosecution of the case and after his conviction, Misskelley talked freely; at times he made claims of mistreatment and untoward coercion by police. He continued to swear he was innocent when talking to his father and family but talked of his guilt with police.

Various officers and attorneys, both for the prosecution and defense, heard his confessions in a variety of settings and circumstances. Misskelley consistently told them that Baldwin and Echols killed the three boys on May 5 in Robin Hood Hills in his presence and with his cooperation.

BIBLIOGRAPHY

In addition to the listed books, research relied heavily on the case records preserved at www.callahan.8k.com. Also frequently consulted was www.westmemphisthreefacts.com as well as the site's Facebook group, whose followers often inspired deeper levels of research. The YouTube account of "Abomination" author William Ramsey was a constant source of insight and inspiration. While they were not primary sources of information, the three "Paradise Lost" documentaries, the fictionalized feature film "Devil's Knot" and the "West of Memphis" documentary were viewed a number of times. The "supporter" Web site www.jivepuppi.com was also consulted several times to double-check facts.

Adams, W. H. Davenport; "Witch, Warlock, and Magician: Historical Sketches of Magic and Witchcraft in England and Scotland"; 1889; J. W. Bouton; New York.

Adler, Margot; "Drawing Down the Moon: Witches, Druids, Goddess-Worshippers and Other Pagans in America Today"; 1979; Beacon Press; Boston.

Ahmed, Rollo; "The Black Art"; 1994; Senate; London.

———; "The Complete Book of Witchcraft"; 1970; Paperback Library; New York.

Anderson, M.W. & Brett Alexander Savory, eds.; "The Last Pentacle of the Sun: Writings in Support of the West Memphis

Three"; 2004; Arsenal Pulp Press; Vancouver.

Athens, Lonnie; "The Creation of Dangerous Violent Criminals"; 1992; University of Illinois Press; Urbana.

———; "Violent criminal acts and actors: A symbolic interactionist study"; 1980; Rutledge & Keegan Paul; Boston.

————; "Violent Criminal Acts and Actors Revisited"; 1997; University of Illinois Press; Urbana.

Baddleley, Gavin; "Lucifer Rising: Sin, Devil Worship & Rock 'n' Roll"; 1999; Plexus; London.

Babiak, Paul and Robert D. Hare; "Snakes in Suits: The Disturbing World of the Psychopaths Among Us"; 2006; Harper Business.

Baron-Cohen, Smith. "The Science of Evil: On Empathy and the Origins of Cruelty"; 2011; Basic Books; New York.

Bebergal, Peter; "Season of the Witch: How the Occult Saved Rock and Roll"; 2014; Jeremy P. Tarcher/Penguin; New York.

Bouisson, Maurice; "Magic: Its History and Principal Rites"; 1961; E.P. Dutton; New York.

Brown, Sandra L., M.A.; "Women Who Love Psychopaths: Inside the Relationships of Inevitable Harm with Psychopaths, Sociopaths, and Narcissists"; 2009; Mask Publishing; Penrose,

N.C.

Buckland, Raymond: "Buckland's Complete Book of Witchcraft": second edition, revised and expanded, 2013; Llewellyn: Woodbury, MN.

Bugliosi, Vincent and Curt Gentry; "Helter Skelter: The True Story of the Manson Murders," 25th Anniversary Edition; 1994; W.W. Norton.

Capote, Truman; "In Cold Blood: A True Account of a Multiple Murder and Its Consequences"; 1965; Modern Library; New York.

Carlisle, Al, PhD; "I'm Not Guilty: The Case of Ted Bundy (The Development of the Violent Mind)': 2014; Genius Book Publishing; Encino, CA.

———; "The Mind of the Devil: The Cases of Arthur Gary Bishop and Wesley Allan Dodd (The Development of the Violent Mind)"; 2015; Genius Book Publishing; Encino, CA.

Cavendish, Richard; "The Black Arts"; 1967; Perigee Books; New York.

———; "A History of Magic"; 1987; Penguin Group; London.

Cheit, Ross E.; "The Witch-Hunt Narrative: Politics, Psychology, and the Sexual Abuse of Children"; 2014; Oxford University Press.

Christie, Ian; "Sound of the Beast: The Complete Headbanging History of Heavy Metal"; 2010; HarperEntertainment.

Clarkson, Wensley; "In the Name of Satan"; 1997; St. Martin's Paperbacks.

Cleckley, Hervey; "The Mask of Sanity"; 1982, revised edition; New American Library; New York.

Cohn, Norman; "Europe's Inner Demons"; 1993; University of Chicago Press; Chicago.

Crowley, Aleister; "The Book of the Law (Liber AL vel Legis)"; 2014; Enhanced Ebooks.

———; "Enochian Magick, Volume I (The Best of the Equinox)"; 2012; Red Wheel/Weiser LLC; San Francisco.

———: "Magick in Theory and Practice"; 1976; Dover; New York.

———; "Sex Magick, Volume III (The Best of the Equinox)"; 2013; Red Wheel/Weiser LLC; San Francisco.

Cullen, Dave; "Columbine"; 2009; Hachette Book Group; New York.

Cunningham, Scott; "Wicca: A Guide for the Solitary Practitioner"; 2005; Llewellyn Publications; Woodbury, MN.

Davies, Owen; "America Bewitched: The Story of Witchcraft after Salem"; 2013; Oxford University Press; Oxford.

———; "Paganism: A Very Short Introduction"; 2011; Oxford University Press; New York.

Dawkins, Vickie L. and Nina Downey Higgins; "Devil Child"; 1989; St. Martin's Press; New York.

Day, Greg; "Untying the Knot: John Mark Byers and the West Memphis Three"; 2005, 2012; iUniverse; Bloomington, Ind.

d'Este, Sorita, ed.; "Both Sides of Heaven: A Collection of Essays Exploring the Origins, History, Nature and Magical Practices of Angels, Fallen Angels and Demons"; 2014; Avalonia; London.

d'Este, Sorita and David Rankine; "Hekate Liminal Rites"; 2009; Avalonia; London.

———and ———; "Wicca Magical Beginnings: A study of the historical origins of the magical rituals, practices and beliefs of modern Initiatory and Pagan Witchcraft"; 2008; Avalonia; London.

Douglas, John, and Mark Olshaker; "Law & Disorder"; 2013; Kensington Books; New York.

———; "Mind Hunter: Inside the FBI's Elite Serial Crime Unit": 1995; Scribner; New York.

DuQuette, Lon Milo; "Enochian Vision Magick: An Introduction and Practical Guide to the Magick of Dr. John Dee and Edward Kelley"; 2008; RedWheel/Weiser, LLC; San Francisco.

Dubois, William Edward Lee; "Occult Crimes: Detection, Investigation, and Verification"; 1992; San Miguel Press.

Echols, Damien; "Life After Death"; 2012; Blue Rider Press; New York.

Echols, Damien and Lorri Davis; "Yours for Eternity: A Love Story on Death Row"; 2014; Blue Rider Press; New York.

Ellis, Bill; "Raising the Devil: Satanism, New Religions, and the Media"; 2000; The University Press of Kentucky; Lexington, KY.

Ewing, Charles Patrick; "Kids Who Kill"; 1990; Lexington Books; New York.

Farrar, Janet and Stewart; "A Witches' Bible: The Complete Witches' Handbook"; 2012; David & Charles; Cincinnati.

Fletcher, Jaye Slade; "Deadly Thrills"; 1995; Onyx; New York.

Flowers, Stephen E., PhD; "Lords of the Left-Hand Path: Forbidden Practices and Spiritual Heresies"; 2012; Inner Traditions; Rochester, Vermont.

Gardner, Gerald; "The Meaning of Witchcraft"; 2004; Red Wheel/Weiser, LLC; New York.

Gilmore, John and Ron Kenner; "Manson: The Unholy Trail of Charlie and the Family"; Amok Books.

Grossman, Dave; "On Killing: The Psychological Cost of Learning to Kill in War and Society"; 1995; Little, Brown; Boston.

Guinn, Jeff; "Manson: The Life and Times of Charles Manson"; Simon & Schuster; New York.

Hare, Robert D.; "Without Conscience: The Disturbing World of the Psychopaths Among Us"; 1999; The Guilford Press.

Haycock, Dean A., PhD; "Murderous Minds: Exploring the Criminal Psychopathic Brain: Neurological Imaging and the Manifestation of Evil"; Pegasus Books; New York, London.

Hill, Frances; "A Delusion of Satan: The Full Story of the Salem Witch Trials"; 1995; Tantor Media, Inc.; Old Saybrook, CN.

Hutton, Ronald; "The Triumph of the Moon: A History of Modern Pagan Witchcraft"; 1999; Oxford University Press; New York.

James, Geoffrey, ed. and trans.; "The Enochian Evocation of Dr. John Dee"; 2009; Red Wheel/Weiser, LLC; San Francisco.

Jared, George; "Witches in West Memphis: The West Memphis Three and another tale of false confession"; 2016; Groves-Holliman Publishers.

Kahaner, Larry; "Cults that Kill: Probing the Underworld of Occult Crime"; 1988; Warner Books, New York.

Kelly, Aidan A.; "Crafting the Art of Magic"; 1991; Llewellyn; St. Paul, MN.

Keppel, Robert D., Phd, with William J. Birnes; "The Riverman: Ted Bundy and I Hunt for the Green River Killer"; 2005, revised edition; Pocket Books; New York.

Kupelian, David: "How Evil Works: Understanding and Overcoming the Destructive Forces that are Threatening America"; 2010; Threshold Editions, a division of Simon & Schuster, Inc; New York.

Lachman, Gary; "Aleister Crowley: Magick, Rock and Roll, and the Wickedest Man in the World:' 2014; Jeremy P. Tarcher/Penguin; New York.

———; "Turn Off Your Mind: The Mystic Sixties and the Dark Side of the Age of Aquarius"; 2001; The Disinformation Company Ltd.; New York.

Lanning, Kenneth; "Investigator's Guide to Allegations of 'Ritual' Child Abuse"; 1992; National Center for the Analysis of Violent Crime; Quantico, Va.

———; "Satanic, Occult, Ritualistic Crime: A Law Enforcement Perspective"; 1989; National Center for the Analysis of Violent Crime; Quantico, Va.

LaVey, Anton; "The Satanic Bible"; 1969; Avon Books; New York.

———; "The Satanic Rituals"; 1972; Avon Books; New York.

Leake, John; "Entering Hades: The Double Life of a Serial Killer"; 2007; Sarah Crichton Books Farrar, Straus and Giroux; New York.

Leland, Charles G.: "Aradia or the Gospel of the Witches"; 1899; David Nutt; London.

Leveritt, Mara; "Devil's Knot: The True Story of the West Memphis Three"; 2002; Atria, a division of Simon & Schuster Inc.; New York.

Leveritt, Mara, with Jason Baldwin; "Dark Spell: Surviving the Sentence"; 2014; Bird Call Press; Little Rock.

Levi, Eliphas, translated and with a preface and notes by Arthur Edward Waite; "The History of Magic, Including a Clear and Precise Exposition of its Procedures, its Rites and its Mysteries"; 1922; William Rider & Son, Limited; London.

London, Sondra; "True Vampires"; 2004; Feral House; Los Angeles.

Louv, Jason; "The Angelic Reformation: John Dee, Enochian Magick & the Occult Roots of Empire"; 2015; Ultraculture Incorporated.

Lykken, David T.; "The Antisocial Personalities"; 1995; Lawrence Erlbaum Associates, Inc., Publishers; Hillsdale, NJ.

Lyons, Arthur; "Satan Wants You: The Cult of Devil Worship in America"; Mysterious Press, 1988.

———: "The Second Coming: Satanism in America"; 1970; Award Books; New York.

McDonough, Sam Dennis; "The West Memphis Boogieman, Condensed Version"; 2014

Medway, Gareth J.; "Lure of the Sinister: The Unnatural History of Satanism"; 2001; New York University Press.

Metzger, Richard, ed.; "The Book of Lies: The Disinformation Guide to Magick and the Occult (Being an alchemical formula to rip a hole in the fabric of reality)"; 2015; Disinformation Books; San Francisco.

Michaelsen, Scott, ed.; "Portable Darkness: An Aleister Crowley Reader"; 2007; Solar Books;

Michaud, Stephen G. and Hugh Aynesworth; "The Only Living Witness: The True Story of Serial Sex Killer Ted Bundy"; 1999; Authorlink Press; Irving, TX.

Millon, Theodore with Roger D. Davis; "Disorders of Personality; DSM-IV and Beyond, Second Edition"; 1996; John Wiley & Sons, Inc.; New York.

Millon, Theodore, Erik Simonson, Morton Birket-Smith and Roger D. Davis, eds.; "Psychopathy: Antisocial, Criminal, and Violent Behavior"; 1998; Guilford Press; New York.

Monaco, Richard and Bill Burt; "The Dracula Syndrome"; 1993; Avon Books; New York.

Moorhouse, Frank; "Satanic Killings"; 2006; Allison & Busby Limited; London.

Mount, Michelle Echols; "Love Forever and After"; 2012.

Moynihan, Michael and Didrik Soderlind; "Lords of Chaos; The Bloody Rise of the Satanic Metal Underground," Revised and Expanded Edition; 2003; Feral House; Los Angeles.

Murray, Margaret Alice; "God of the Witches"; 1933; Sampson Low, Marston & Co.; London.

— "The Witch Cult in Western Europe"; 1921; Oxford University Press; London.

Nathan, Debbie and Michael Snedeker; "Satan's Silence: Ritual Abuse the Making of a Modern American Witch Hunt"; 2001; Authors Choice Press; Lincoln, NE.

Oakley, Barbara and David Sloan Wilson; "Evil Genes: Why Rome Fell, Hitler Rose, Enron Failed, and My Sister Stole My Mother's Boyfriend"; 2008; Prometheus.

Olsen, Jack; "I: The Creation of a Serial Killer"; 2002, St. Martin's Paperbacks; New York.

———; "The Misbegotten Son: A Serial Killer and His Victims"; 2000-2014; Crime Rant Classics.

———; "Son: A Psychopath and His Victims"; 2015; Crime Rant Books.

Pettrey, Amanda and David Pietras; "Hunting the West Memphis Boogeyman"; 2014.

Pietras, David; "Evil in a Small Town: The Evidence that the Documentaries Refused to Show You"; 2015.

Provost, Gary; "Across the Border: The True Story of the Satanic Cult Killings in Matamoros, Mexico"; 1989; Pocket Books; New

York.

Ramsland, Katherine; "The Human Predator: A Historical Chronicle of Serial Murder and Forensic Investigation"; 2005; The Berkley Publishing Group; New York.

Ramsey, William; "Abomination: Devil Worship and Deception in the West Memphis Three Murders"; 2012.

Reel, Guy, Mark Perresquia and Bartholomew Sullivan; "Blood of Innocents: The True Story of the Multiple Murders in West Memphis, Arkansas"; 1995; Pinnacle; New York.

Ressler, Robert K., Ann W. Burgess, John E. Douglas; "Sexual Homicide: Patterns and Motives"; 1992; The Free Press; New York.

Rhodes, Richard; "Why They Kill: The Discoveries of a Maverick Criminologist"; 1999; Vintage Books; New York.

Rose, Elliot; "A Razor for a Goat: A Discussion of Certain Problems in the History of Witchcraft and Diabolism"; 1989; University of Toronto Press.

Ross, Anne and Don Robins: "The Life and Death of a Druid Prince: The Story of Lindow Man, an Archeological Sensation"; 1989; Summit Books; New York.

Samenow, Dr. Stanton E.; "Inside the Criminal Mind, Revised and Expanded Edition"; 1984, 2004, 2014; Broadway Books; New York.

———; "The Myth of the Out of Character Crime"; 2007; Praeger; Westport, Conn.

Sanders, Ed; "The Family: The Story of Charles Manson's Dune Buggy Attack Battalion"; 1971; E.P. Dutton; New York.

Schultze, Jim; "Cauldron of Blood: The Matamoros Cult Killings"; 1989; Avon Books; New York.

Seabrook, William; "Witchcraft: Its Power in the World Today"; 1968; Lancer; New York.

Simon, George K., PhD; "Character Disturbance: The Phenomenon of Our Age"; 2011; Parkhurst Brothers, Inc., Publishers; Little Rock.

————; "In Sheep's Clothing: Understanding and Dealing with Manipulative People"; 1996, 2010; Parkhurst Brothers, Inc.; Little Rock.

Simpson, Teresa R.: "Memphis Murder & Mayhem"; 2008; The History Press; Charleston, SC.

Stone, Michael H., PhD; "The Anatomy of Evil"; 2009; Prometheus Books.

Stout, Martha; "The Sociopath Next Door"; 2006, Three Rivers Press.

Sullivan, Kevin M.; "The Bundy Murders: A Comprehensive History"; 2009; McFarland & Company, Inc.; Jefferson, NC.

Summers, Montague; "The History of Witchcraft and Demonology"; 2007; Dover.

———; "The Werewolf in Lore and Legend": 2003; Dover.

———; "Witch Covens and Grand Masters;The Witches Journey to the Sabbat, and of the Sabbat Orgy"; 2011; Read Books Inc.

Sutin, Lawrence; "Do What Thou Wilt: A Life of Aleister Crowley"; 2000; St. Martin's Press; New York.

Symonds, John; "The Great Beast: The Life and Magick of Aleister Crowley"; 1973; Mayflower Books.

Testa, Anthony; "The Key of the Abyss: Jack Parsons, the Babylon Working and the Witchcraft Decoded Updated and Revised," second edition; 2013.

Terry, Maury; "The Ultimate Evil"; 1987; Doubleday; New York.

Valiente, Doreen; "The Rebirth of Witchcraft"; 1989; Phoenix; Custer, Wa.

———; "Where Witchcraft Lives" 4th Edition; 2014, The Doreen Valiente Foundation.

Victor, Jeffrey S.; "Satanic Panic: The Creation of a Contemporary Legend"; 1993; Open Court; Peru, IL.

Vorpagel, Russell; "Profiles in Murder: An FBI Legend Dissects Killers and Their Crimes"; 1998; Dell; New York.

Vronsky, Peter; "Serial Killers: The Method and Madness of Monsters"; 2004; The Berkley Publishing Group/ Penguin Group; New York.

Wakefield, Stephen James; "Black Arts: Journeys on the Left-Hand Path"; 2014.

Wedge, Tom with Robert L. Powers; "The Satan Hunter"; 1988; Daring Books; Canton, Ohio.

Weishaupt, Isaac; "Johnny Depp: Vampire, Satanist, or Illuminati? ..." 2015.

Wiederhorn, Jon and Katherine Turman; "Louder than Hell: The Definite Oral History of Metal"; 2013; HarperCollins Publishers Inc.; New York.

Williams, Rev. John; "An Essay on the Question, 'Whether the

British Druids Offered Human Sacrifices"; 2013; AlbaCraft Publishing.

Wilson, Colin; "The Occult: A History"; 1971; Random House; New York.

Wilson, Colin and Donald Seaman; "The Serial Killers: A Study in the Psychology of Violence"; 2007; Virgin Books.

Wyllie, Timothy, and Adam Parfrey, eds.; "Love, Sex, Fear and Death: The Inside Story of the Process Church of the Final Judgement; 2009; Feral House; Port Townsend, WA.

Webb, Don; "Overthrowing the Old Gods: Aleister Crowley and The Book of the Law"; 2013; Inner Traditions; Rochester, VT.

Wickwar, John William; "Witchcraft and the Black Art"; 2012; Fonthill Media.

PHOTOS

ROBIN HOOD HILLS

DEANNA HOLCOMB

Gary Meece

DOMINI TEER

AARON HUTCHESON AT THE CRIME SCENE

VICTORIA HUTCHESON

JASON BALDWIN

L.G. HOLLINGSWORTH JR.

BUDDY LUCAS

Gary Meece

MICHELLE ECHOLS AND PAMELA HUTCHISON

JOE HUTCHISON

THE AUTHOR

Gary Meece is a longtime newspaperman who worked at the Commercial Appeal from 1980 to 2008 and as managing editor at the West Memphis Evening Times from 2010 to 2014.

CPSIA information can be obtained
at www.ICGtesting.com
Printed in the USA
BVOW07s1320011217
R8318500001B/R83185PG501560BVX3B/3/P